NOURISHING YOUR UNBORN CHILD

Other Avon Books by
Phyllis S. Williams

THE NATURAL BABY FOOD COOKBOOK,
with Margaret Elizabeth Kenda

REVISED EDITION

NOURISHING YOUR UNBORN CHILD

PHYLLIS S. WILLIAMS, R.N.

AVON
PUBLISHERS OF BARD, CAMELOT, DISCUS AND FLARE BOOKS

AVON BOOKS
A division of
The Hearst Corporation
1790 Broadway
New York, New York 10019

Book design by Joyce Kubat

Library of Congress Cataloging in Publication Data

Williams, Phyllis.
  Nourishing your unborn child.

  Bibliography
  Includes index.
    1. Pregnancy—Nutritional aspects. 2. Mothers—
Nutrition. 3. Food, Natural. 4. Cookery (Natural
foods) I. Title.
RG559.W54 1982   618.2'4   73-92973
ISBN 0-380-60657-7   AACR2

First Avon Printing, September, 1975
First Avon Trade Printing, September, 1982 (revised edition)

To Brenda Reynolds,
the "mother" of Parent-to-Parent,
and to Janet Danforth and Karol Hagberg, R.N.,
who gave new life
to the Maternal and Child Health Council
of Greater Bangor.

PREFACE

Over many years, we, in the health professions, were taught that the fetus was a parasite, taking what it needed from the mother's body regardless of what she ate. I learned that the size of the baby was in no way dependent on how much or how well the mother ate or on how much she gained.

The amazing thing is that I believed it. I accepted all of that information on authority, barely doubting what my intuition and Yankee horse sense tried to tell me was incoherent.

Perhaps we all believed subconsciously that those in the health professions had found a philosopher's stone that, by some alchemy, could change the basic quality of what went into the body, just as the ancients believed lead could be turned to gold.

We certainly expounded the idea that something could come from nothing. Even if the nutrients were not there, the fetus could get them. From where? How, if the mother didn't take in enough iron, would the fetus be able to fulfill its needs? How, if she failed to take in enough protein, could the fetus build healthy tissue? How, if she had to use body fat for calories, could the fetus have a healthy nervous system?

We need only to look around us to see the people—adults and children—who have been deprived of the foods they needed to insure quality of life. The cycle, set in motion, assures that the poor will always be with us, deprived of the brain cells and energy needed for success—deprived mainly by poor maternal nutrition followed by a deprived childhood and life for most of those who survive.

But the poor are not the only ones affected. Every woman who has dieted at the expense of nutrients during pregnancy may have seen the effects in her child of such folly, usually inspired by the health professions. It may be only poorer teeth or a little less intelligence—there is no real way to know. But these methods have produced their toll in higher mortality rates, more low-birth-weight babies, toxemia, learning disabilities and other problems.

In 1968, Dr. William Shubert, Chief of Obstetrics at Eastern Maine Medical Center, opened a Pandora's box by inviting me to a conference on maternal nutrition at the hospital. I wish to thank him for the inspiration the conference provided, his encouragement of parent education, and his tolerance of our errors and thanks for our successes.

My thanks also to the obstetric staff at EMMC; to Mabel Wadsworth, R.N., director of Family Planning, and her associate, Nancy Page, R.N., coordinator for the Prenatal Care Project, along with the other nurses and outreach workers for showing the way; to Barbara Smith, R.N., director of Public Health Nursing, Bangor, Maine, for her encouragement and searching questions; to all the members of the Maternal and Child Health Council of Greater Bangor, Inc., and to the members of the parent classes; to Cindy Blease, a leader of the La Leche League; and to Cindy Hopper and Margaret Kenda, for encouragement.

I would also like to thank my good friend at the University of Maine, who has provided me with information and inspiration; the librarians of Hampden Regional Library and the Bangor Public Library; the members of the nursing and administrative staffs at EMMC for providing me access to their libraries; to the Society for the Protection of the Unborn Through Nutrition, and to Dr. Tom Brewer, for their information and encouragement and for their selfless crusade on behalf of women and present and future generations.

CONTENTS

NOURISHING YOUR UNBORN CHILD

CHAPTER ONE
THE CHICKEN OR THE EGG

If you don't eat right during pregnancy, you will deprive your baby and yourself of the nutrients needed for health. Indeed, good nutrition is the most important ingredient in producing healthy, quality people. Yet, the dogs at the local kennel or the cows of a nearby dairy farmer are probably better nourished during their pregnancies than you will be if you follow the classical medical regimen of a low calorie, low salt diet with diuretics.

Ideally, preparation for your pregnancy should have begun before *you* were conceived. While you cannot change the past, you can start now to provide the building blocks (the protein, nutrients, calories) to produce a healthy baby. You can improve your own health and assure the future health of your family.

A minister I once knew included a special ring ceremony in the weddings he performed. It was prefaced with: "From ancient times, the circle has been the symbol of eternity. The circle of the wedding ring becomes a symbol of eternal love which two people pledge to hold for each other." One couple whose wedding he performed sent him a birth announcement two years later with a note penned on it, "The circle is now complete."

That baby who completes the circle must have the best possible start in life. He must have all of his needs provided for while he is developing from a fertilized egg to a full-term baby. He should then have the right to the love and continued care and nourishment from healthy parents.

Within this century, doctors have taken over obstetric practice. They have done a good job saving the lives of mothers who used to

1

die from infection and hemorrhage. They have saved babies who formerly died of birth injuries, prematurity, and other causes. However, they have not been as successful in improving the overall well-being of mothers and babies.

Many doctors have been concerned mainly with the abnormal. They have developed methods to deal with abnormalities in pregnant women, in unborn babies, and during labor and delivery. It is not difficult to determine why doctors dealt with the abnormal when we realize that between 1846 and 1942 in the United States, more women died in childbirth than soldiers died in wars. Of every ten babies born alive in 1915, one died before its first birthday. The same year, three out of every five hundred women who became pregnant died.

Through prenatal care and new and safer methods of treating complications of labor and delivery, these statistics have changed. It is now *safe* for a woman to give birth, and only one baby in fifty dies in the first year of life.

But these statistics don't tell the whole story. There are still infant deaths. In fact the United States has a higher infant mortality rate than many of the other developed countries. There are still far too many low-birth-weight babies born—babies who are liable to develop mental and physical defects. And, sadly, methods employed to deal with abnormalities have been increasingly used in normal births.

Toxemia, otherwise known as eclampsia or metabolic toxemia of late pregnancy (MTLP), has long presented an enigma to physicians. They didn't know what caused it or what to do about it, so they treated the symptoms. The edema, or swelling—which accompanies the high blood pressure, protein in the urine, and convulsions—was the easiest symptom to deal with. They told women to cut down their salt intake and gave diuretics (water pills) to get rid of fluid. Since excess fluid resulted in a large weight gain, the doctors limited calories to control weight.

According to a study undertaken by the Committee on Maternal Nutrition of the National Research Council,[1] "The idea that limitation of weight gain by calorie restriction protects against toxemia goes back to the observed reduction in the incidence of eclampsia

[1] *Maternal Nutrition and the Course of Pregnancy* (Washington, D.C.: National Academy of Sciences, 1970), p. 176.

in Germany and Austria-Hungary during World War I. Because of a war-imposed scarcity of meat and fats, pregnant women gained less, and it was concluded without further study that a restricted diet was protective. Caloric restriction to limit gain in weight during pregnancy became widely advocated as a means for preventing toxemia and many other complications. The idea found its way into textbooks of obstetrics and was widely adopted by the medical profession. Seldom has a medical idea with such a base (hearsay evidence) been applied so widely and subjected to so little scientific study."

This plan of limiting weight gain and even limiting salt began to be used with normal women in the hope of preventing toxemia.

Some physicians carried this regimen to extremes. They told pregnant women to gain only ten to fifteen pounds at the most or even to lose weight while pregnant. With women who were well nourished and healthy and who had good eating habits, these admonitions did not spell disaster. But who knows what problems might have been caused for their infants?

According to the study, ". . . there is no advantage to be gained by prescribing weight reduction regimens for obese patients during pregnancy either for improving the course of the pregnancy or for contributing to the woman's general health. The possible danger of inducing ketosis,[2] with accompanying hazards for the neurological development of the fetus [possible brain and nerve damage], must be borne in mind." For those women who were malnourished, suffering from the lack of proper nutrients, the regimen was a disaster.

Dr. Tom Brewer, formerly an obstetrician in the Contra Costa Health Services at Richmond, California, has been fighting for the elimination of MTLP through good nutrition for over a decade. A tireless crusader, Dr. Brewer is president of SPUN (the Society for the Protection of the Unborn Through Nutrition), a nonprofit corporation with headquarters in Chicago. In a letter dated May 8, 1973, Dr. Brewer stated:

---

[2] A condition in which the body uses fat for energy because glucose is either not available, as in starvation, or is not able to be utilized, as in uncontrolled diabetes, causing acidosis, an acid-base imbalance in the blood.

... "High risk" mothers are no longer high risk when they can escape the low calorie, low salt diet—diuretic—blind weight control regimen! "High risk" mothers are no longer high risks when they have enough decent foods to eat all through gestation and are protected from harmful, too often M.D.-prescribed, drugs ... When they (the doctors) try our methods with pregnant women, when they go down into the clinics and work with pregnant human beings and insure their optimal nutrition—then they will see for themselves the protective role of adequate balanced nutrition in the outcome of human pregnancy, then they will begin to catch up with our good farmers, sheep and goat herders, and veterinarians.

In December 1972, the periodical *Obstetrics and Gynecology* carried a review of the role of nutrition in pregnancy, the result of a study by an ad hoc committee of the American College of Obstetrics and Gynecology. The ACOG executive board approved a policy statement on nutrition and pregnancy. The committee noted that "the future health of mankind depends, to a very large degree, on nutritional foundations laid down during prenatal life." They admitted that physicians have too little working knowledge of nutrition and may have absorbed some dogmatic ideas of dietary management that are now being questioned.

They also questioned severe sodium restriction both because of the possibility of electrolyte imbalance[3] and the lack of palatability of food without added salt. They pointed out that fluid retention may be physiological, or normal. They questioned the value of the use of diuretics either for the prevention or treatment of toxemia. Moreover, they questioned the routine restriction of weight gain and recommended as optimal a gain of twenty-two to twenty-seven pounds.

While Dr. Brewer was encouraged by this report, he believed it was conservative and failed to recognize the role of protein deprivation as a cause of toxemia. He knows, as do most women, that as

[3] A situation whereby the blood contains abnormal concentrations of certain elements, or electrolytes, such as sodium, potassium, chlorides, etc. The concentration may be either too high or too low. The imbalances can be brought about in various ways—use of diuretics, lack of these minerals in the diet, severe loss of body fluids as in prolonged vomiting, diarrhea, etc.

long as there is a limit set on weight gain, malnutrition in pregnancy will continue to exist. Human nature being what it is, some who desperately need to nourish themselves and their babies may attempt to limit weight gain and/or eat imbalanced diets in their attempts to maintain Twiggy-like figures. Those who are overweight at the start of pregnancy are liable to eat the foods they like at the expense of good nutrition and then starve themselves for a couple of days prior to their next visit to the doctor. Or, worse, they may resort to dangerous crash diets which could further rob them of good nutrition.

It is doubtful that excess weight gain in pregnancy is a real cause of obesity. Most women know, though they may hate to admit it, that their excess pounds have been gained when they were not pregnant—that within a few months of their baby's birth they have returned to their normal weight before pregnancy.

Unless the *positive* is stressed throughout pregnancy—the foods that *must* be eaten to insure an adequate diet—nutritional deficiencies will continue. Perhaps we will find that when the nagging changes from "Mrs. Doe, you've gained eight pounds this month—you've got to cut down," to "Mrs. Doe, have you been eating the way you are supposed to eat? Have you been eating plenty of milk, meat and fish, eggs and cheese, green and yellow vegetables, citrus fruits and whole grains every day?" then and only then will the problem be solved.

A prescription for nutrition and nutrition training should be issued to every woman at the start of her pregnancy. Until the nation is retrained, the importance of following that prescription should be stressed and restressed at each visit. Each aspect of diet should be dealt with specifically. In the clinics, dietary evaluations should be carried out and foods which are needed *must* be made available to *every* poor pregnant woman along with training for their preparation and use. Only in this way will we be able to eliminate an important cause of learning problems, retardation, stunted growth, and poverty.

A program of nutrition education and food supplementation has been undertaken at the Montreal Diet Dispensary by the director, Mrs. Agnes C. Higgins, and her staff. Though the mothers have been poor, have had little education, and nearly one-third have been unmarried, the results have been astounding. They have gained more weight without complications and have had bigger babies than the average clinic patient. Their babies have been as large as those born to private patients in the same hospital; their new-born health records have been better than the Canadian average. And Mrs. Higgins' program is cost-effective. In the early seventies, the cost of food supplements for one mother came to about $125. At that time, the cost to the Canadian public for maintaining one defective child in an institution was estimated at more than $100,000. With the current rate of inflation, that cost has easily doubled. One can see that good nutrition in pregnancy pays off in dollars and cents as well as in quality of life.

In the United States, the WIC program (Special Supplemental Feeding Program for Women, Infants, and Children) has been one of the most effective preventive programs ever instituted. In those programs which have been well-administered, the nutritionists have observed a reduction in low-birth-weight baby rates. The drop in neonatal death rates in Maine (one of the poorest states) to the lowest in the nation coincided with the spread of the WIC program in that state. Unfortunately, the program, an unwanted stepchild of the USDA, has been threatened each time Congress deals with the budget.

A study entitled *Women and Their Pregnancies: A Collaborative Perinatal Study of the National Institute of Neurological Diseases and Stroke*[4] states: "... for whites and negroes of all pre-pregnant weights, the optimum maternal gains (in terms of highest birth weights) are 30–34 pounds or more.... There is a reasonably clear diminution in the abnormality rate with increased maternal weight gain for both whites and negroes." This is additional evidence of the protectiveness of good nutrition and the importance of adequate weight gain in pregnancy.

For too long, we have sat by and let the food and drug industries have their way. The enticing ads for carbonated drinks, fruit punches, whipped toppings, ice cream, gelatin desserts, pies, cakes, cookies, and pastries undermine good nutrition. These ads constitute a threat to every pregnant woman and developing embryo. They make these nonfoods, these synthetic concoctions important, sought-after fun foods. It's all for their profit at your expense. You are enticed to substitute these inferior products for

[4] National Institutes of Health (Washington, D.C.: Superintendent of Documents, 1972).

6

the high protein, mineral- and vitamin-carrying foods you need to have a healthy baby.

Nutritionist Dr. John Mayer, president of Tufts University, has said there is nothing good about sugar. Dr. John Yudkin of the University of London points out the relationship between sugar and disease. He ties excess sugar (sucrose) intake in with the epidemiology of a host of diseases—eschemic heart disease, obesity, dental caries, gout and diabetes, among others.

Read the lists of ingredients of a whole host of convenience foods from cereals to spaghetti sauce, and you'll find sugar included. Is it any wonder that the refined sugar intake of Americans is up to 115 pounds per person per year? This represents the equivalent of five ounces of sugar per day for every man, woman, child and infant. To put it another way, refined sugar provides a total of 600 calories per day or about one-quarter of the day's caloric intake as naked or empty calories.

While glucose is a normal and necessary constituent of the blood and an important part of metabolism, providing fuel for energy, it should not be abundantly provided in the form of the empty calories of refined sugar (sucrose). A sucrose-laden sweet as an occasional treat is one thing. As a continual diet in the form of sodas, candy, cakes, and pastries plus its addition to other foods, it is a menace.

Statistically, the increased incidence in heart attacks seems to parallel the rise in refined sugar consumption. Among the people of St. Helena, an island in the South Atlantic, who eat very little saturated fat, the rate of heart attack has paralleled ours. The reason may be because their sugar intake has increased in the same way ours has.

Research has shown that decreased sugar intake results in decreased fat levels in the blood. What is the meaning of this to you? Whatever you do to improve your dietary habits now will have far-reaching consequences for your whole family. You can set in motion a cycle to help protect you, your husband, and your children from the degenerative diseases caused in part by poor diet and poor eating habits. You can start now to build your family's future health.

Unfortunately, we do not know all there is to know about nutrition. New information is being turned up constantly. While animal nutrition is reasonably well established, experimentation with human beings has been, of course, far more limited. Perhaps one of the biggest obstacles to overcome in our search for nutrition answers is that of built-in prejudice. We may fail to turn up important information because we don't look for it. We may have a previous bias, or we may reject information without testing it thoroughly. Unfortunately, vested interests also may play a part in the choice and manipulation of scientific studies and findings.

There have been a number of controversies which illustrate some of these factors. Dr. Linus Pauling was soundly denounced and criticized for his publication of *Vitamin C and the Common Cold* (San Francisco: W. H. Freeman and Company, 1970). Yet some studies indicate that Dr. Pauling may, in fact, have a point. One such study was among Navajo boarding-school children in Arizona. Doses of from one to two grams of vitamin C per day cut the number of sick days by about one third. Though the vitamin did not actually prevent colds, the children recovered more rapidly and had fewer days of sickness from respiratory illnesses. The results of this study were reported at a Stanford University symposium on vitamin C by the investigators, Drs. J. L. Colehan, R. S. Reisingers, and K. D. Rogers. Other studies have shown varying results, both positive and negative.

There are a great many people who take additional vitamin C and believe it helps. As long as they don't take ludicrously large amounts, it is undoubtedly safer than most of the over-the-counter palliatives sold to treat colds. A word of caution to pregnant women, however. There have been reports of babies, whose mothers have been taking large doses of vitamin C daily during pregnancy, developing scurvy (vitamin C deficiency) after birth. If you have been dosing with large amounts of vitamin C during your pregnancy, be sure your doctor knows, so the baby can be observed for signs of scurvy and supplemented if necessary.

Vitamin E has been the subject of a great deal of controversy. It has been touted as the panacea of ailments from sexual frustration to coronary heart disease. Some authorities have flatly stated that vitamin E deficiency is almost nonexistent. In the past, there has been little indication of vitamin E deficiency in our diet. The only documented case was among premature infants fed a brand formula containing cottonseed oil as the fat but with no added vitamin E. Cottonseed oil, being polyunsaturated fat, tends to bind vitamin E and render it unavailable to the body. It is possible that with the manipulation of diet for the treatment or prevention of heart disease we may eventually see more vitamin E deficiencies.

Dietary manipulation either by the food and drug industries, by health fadists, or by the medical fraternity for treatment or prevention of disease is not without hazard—especially considering the limitations of our present knowledge and the lack of availability and, indeed, the inadvisability of experimentations with human beings.

What can we do? Eat the best and most varied diet we possibly can—a diet based on nutritious, nonrefined fresh or carefully canned and frozen foods. As much as possible, we must avoid the empty calories of refined sweets and those additives which are either known to be harmful or are of dubious value. We must eat a diet containing ample protein, plenty of highly colored fruits and vegetables, grains, and some fat. You and your baby will benefit from your prudence. In fact, such a diet will enhance the health of your whole family.

CHAPTER TWO

SAFE AND HEALTHY CHILDBEARING

Before you are aware that you are pregnant, your baby is developing at a dizzying rate. By the time your menstrual period is two weeks overdue, the tiny embryo you nurture is seven millimeters in length, three and one-half times larger than the ovum from which it grew.

To become an embryo, the ovum had to mature within the ovary, be released into the fallopian tube, and be fertilized by a sperm. Half of your baby's forty-six chromosomes, the hereditary elements, are provided by the ovum and half by the sperm. These chromosomes are made up of genes, arranged somewhat like beads on a string, each containing the potential for a specific trait. Eye color, hair color, disposition—in fact, all of the various physical characteristics, talents, and potentialities of each one of us—are contained within our genes. These hereditary materials are subject to environment. The health, genetic background, nutritional status of you and your baby's father at the time of conception; the nourishment of the baby while it is developing; diseases, chemicals, drugs, pollutants—each can exert an influence for better or worse on the vital and sensitive heritage of your unborn child.

Throughout your pregnancy, your baby will continue to grow faster than at any other time in his lifetime. The child who began as a speck barely discernible to the human eye will, by birth, have attained a weight of over seven pounds and a length of twenty inches or more.

If you consider your baby like a seed growing in the earth, you can understand how important the nutritional management of

11

your pregnancy is. If the earth is rich, containing the needed nutrients, if the right amounts of water and sun are available, the seed will grow abundantly. If the ground is well prepared, supplied with ample organic matter and minerals, the plants can survive limited drought. Even insects and diseases will affect them less severely. So it is with your baby. If you can provide a rich, healthy environment with the requirements necessary for the baby's development, a slight setback—a little exposure to hostility in that environment—will be far less damaging than if the environment is poor to begin with.

The fertilized ovum divides rapidly as it travels from the fallopian tube where it was fertilized to the uterus where it will embed itself. The nutrition for this early growth is provided by secretions of the endometrium (the soft, spongy blood-filled lining of the uterus). These secretions are referred to as "uterine milk."

The mass of cells formed is called a trophoblast. The trophoblast liquefies and digests the endometrium as it embeds itself, sending out villi (little fingerlike projections which hold the fetal blood vessels in the placenta) into blood-filled spaces within the uterine lining. By the third month, from this union of the villi and the uterine lining, the placenta is formed. The placenta is the unique disc-shaped organ through which you supply food to your developing baby. The umbilical cord vein carries the nutrients and oxygen to the baby. These substances have passed from your blood through the membranes into the villi. The cord also contains two arteries which carry the waste products, including carbon dioxide, formed within the baby's cells back to the villi. There, they are transferred back through the membranes to your blood for disposal.

It is important to remember that just as the simplest food substances and oxygen pass through the tissues of the villi to nourish the baby, so can chemicals, drugs, viruses, antibodies, hormones, and other substances. In fact, to quote Dr. Virginia Apgar, Clinical Professor of Pediatrics at Cornell University Medical School, as a barrier, the placenta is more like "a bloody sieve."

If you eat well, the placenta will grow large and healthy, capable of nourishing a large, healthy baby. The healthy placenta pours out hormones which help to maintain the pregnancy and bring about changes in the mother's body, enlarging the breasts and uterus and increasing the blood volume.

Until recently, little has been known about the life of the baby within the uterus. It was more or less assumed that the baby existed within a dark fluid-filled void. We now know that this is not so. Fluid is an excellent sound carrier. The baby is surrounded by the sound of his mother's heartbeat, the soft blowing sounds produced by the blood current in the placenta and the umbilical cord, and the sounds that reach him from outside his mother's body.

Nor is the uterus necessarily dark. Human tissue is not impervious to light. You can prove that by holding your hand over a lighted flashlight. There is no doubt, however, that the baby carried through a northern winter lives in a darker environment than one carried during the summer or in more tropical areas, thanks to the differences in layers of clothing needed for warmth as well as the length of the days. What effect, if any, this difference has on the developing baby's health and personality is unknown. But it does offer fascinating speculation for future research. Differences have been found in the well-being of babies born in certain months. Much of this difference has been attributed to seasonal variations in diet and appetite.

As any mother knows, her baby moves around and kicks within the uterus. We also know that a baby may have already learned to suck his thumb, stretch, urinate, swallow, and carry on a number of activities prior to birth. While the old wives' tale of marking a baby has little basis in fact, like so many old wives' tales it may contain an element of truth. There is growing evidence that prenatal influences do, indeed, have an effect on the baby. Who knows? Perhaps the woman who listens to good music throughout her pregnancy may contribute toward the development of music appreciation in her offspring.

When your baby has been living in your uterus for three months, he will be over three inches long and actually look like a human being. By now the buds for the baby teeth are present; tiny kidneys have developed; sex can be distinguished; membranes which will become fingernails and toenails are apparent.

Your baby continues to grow and become more active. The first movement you feel may be a slight fluttering in your lower abdomen. This is called quickening, because the ancients believed it was then that life was established. About this time, the examiner will be able to hear your baby's heartbeat with a head-type fetal stethoscope. The baby's body is now covered with a fine growth of downy hair called lanugo.

In the sixth month, the baby is about twelve inches long and weighs approximately one and one-half pounds. His skin has begun to develop a protective cheeselike coating called vernix caseosa. Your baby continues to grow and his organs continue to mature in the succeeding months. It is not until the last two months in the uterus that he begins to develop protective fat reserves to round him out and prepare him to greet the hostile, cold, noisy environment of the outside world.

The time it takes from conception to the development of a full-term baby is thirty-eight weeks or 266 days (280 days from the first day of the last menstrual period). It may take as long as 300 days or as little as 240 days. The important thing is that he have the time and the available nutrients and calories to develop the size and maturity that will help him thrive while he is adapting to the outside world.

CHANGES IN THE MOTHER'S BODY

Pregnancy is a normal condition, not a disease. But it's a normal condition which puts the body under stress. That is another reason your nutrition is so important. You must maintain your own health and bodily functions while you are adapting to changes in the physiology of your body. You also must provide the building material (basic nutrients) for your baby's development—the proteins, carbohydrates, essential fatty acids, vitamins and minerals. In addition, you pick up the waste products from the baby's cell metabolism and excrete them through your kidneys.

It's easy to see that the additional work your body has to do, combined with the extra space and weight taken up by the growing baby, puts stress on you. While the baby is increasing in size and pushing up toward your rib cage, you need to supply more oxygen to meet his needs. While the baby is pressing against your digestive tract, you must digest good wholesome food to provide you both with nutrients for life and health. While your blood is carrying oxygen, protein, and other nutrients to nourish you and your baby, it must also carry the additional waste products from the baby for you to excrete.

YOUR CIRCULATORY SYSTEM

While you are pregnant, the total amount of blood plasma in your circulatory system increases. This increase insures the proper functioning of the placenta, maintaining a fountainlike spurting of maternal blood against the fetal capillaries in the placenta. This fountain effect promotes optimal exchange of nutrients and waste products. The added plasma gives your heart more work to do. Your heart gets a little larger and pumps a little faster in response to this added work load.

The number of red cells circulating within the plasma is increased. Since the red cell increase is proportionately lower than the plasma increase, you will have a lower hemoglobin concentration than when you are not pregnant. Hemoglobin is the oxygen-carrying compound found in the red blood cells. Iron is a necessary element in hemoglobin formation. You can readily see why, with the need to increase your blood's oxygen-carrying ability, you must have ample iron available. You also provide iron for your baby. In fact, toward the end of your pregnancy, the baby will store iron in his liver, enough to provide him with adequate iron during his first four to six months of independent life, until he is able to eat iron-containing foods.

You may also find that if you have a tendency to varicose veins, the combination of pressure on the veins in your legs from your enlarging uterus, along with the increased fluid in your circulatory system will cause your veins to enlarge. Be sure not to wear stockings with elastic tops or girdles with elastic bands on the legs. Support hose may be helpful. Elastic stockings may be necessary if varicose veins develop. It is especially important during pregnancy that you walk and exercise regularly. When you sit down, elevate your legs. Try not to stand in one spot or sit constantly with your legs down. If you work at a sit-down job, get a stool for your feet and get up and move around frequently to promote circulation.

YOUR DIGESTIVE TRACT

Not only is your digestive tract, the stomach and small and large intestines, displaced and compressed during pregnancy due to the space taken up by the growing baby, but the muscular movements also are slowed. The stomach secretes less hydrochloric acid and pepsin, the substances which start the breakdown of the proteins we eat. As a result, food remains in the stomach longer than usual and the muscle between the esophagus and stomach is more relaxed. While the food nutrients seem to be absorbed far more efficiently as a result of the slowing, this is a mixed blessing. This slowing is one cause of the nausea (morning sickness), heartburn, and constipation which frequently plague pregnant women.

Probably one of the best remedies for morning sickness is to keep your stomach from becoming empty by eating six small meals a day rather than three large ones. Eating a dry carbohydrate food prior to getting up in the morning may help. Crackers are the traditional aid, but you could try dry popcorn, dry toast, or, if you're really lucky, breakfast in bed. It helps to set your alarm to go off a bit early so you can move more slowly and deliberately rather than rushing. Eat fruit or drink juice at the end of breakfast rather than before, and go easy on fats. If you work, carry a mid-morning snack with you.

I was teaching school during my first and second pregnancies and found that a banana placed in my desk drawer solved my mid-morning wave of nausea. Obviously I couldn't leave my class for a meal, and the banana was easy to eat while the students were changing classes.

Heartburn is a miserable problem which, contrary to the old wives, has nothing to do with the hairiness of the baby. Antacids suggested by your doctor may help, but I found them to be of dubious value. My own ideal remedy was old-fashioned buttermilk. The store-bought cultured buttermilk was not quite as effective but helped some. Yoghurt is also helpful, especially that which contains active culture such as Dannon, Breyer, or Breakstone. Whatever you do, don't rely on baking soda. Too much, too often, can upset the delicate acid-base balance of your blood.

Constipation may or may not bother you. In any event, it is relatively easy to deal with. Drink plenty of water and juices. A cup of hot water three times a day is helpful. Exercise cannot be overemphasized. Eat fresh fruits and high-bulk raw and cooked vegetables. If constipation persists, try some prune or fig juice. Just be careful in the use of laxatives, even the natural ones. They should be avoided unless advised by your doctor. You should also remember that being normal does not necessarily mean having bowel movements every day. For you, every second or third day may be sufficient. In any event, persistent constipation or diarrhea should be reported to your doctor or midwife.

YOUR RESPIRATORY SYSTEM

As your baby grows, your lungs have less space. This is compensated for, in part, by an increase in the size of your rib cage. Since this increase is permanent, even though you lose every pound you gained in pregnancy, you may find you need a larger bra or blouse after your baby is born.

While you are pregnant, you may sometimes be conscious of the need to breathe. It is a common experience of pregnant women. Moving about, taking a walk or some other exercise will probably alleviate the feeling. While your total lung capacity does not increase—it actually decreases in late pregnancy—the *vital* capacity remains the same. Of this vital capacity, the actual amount of air breathed in and out is greater. Because there is less residual air in the lungs, oxygen can move through the alveoli into the blood far more efficiently, insuring the oxygen supply for both you and your baby.

YOUR EXCRETION OF WASTES

Your kidneys work more effectively during pregnancy, clearing waste products from your body more rapidly. Along with this increase in waste excretion, some nutrients are also wasted. Sugar, simple protein (amino acids), iodine and others may be found in the urine.

In the first three or four months of pregnancy, the amount of urine excreted is increased, which helps to account for your frequent need to urinate. As pregnancy advances, the excretion of urine diminishes to below the normal for a nonpregnant woman. In addition, the water retained in your legs (which may cause swollen ankles) moves to the kidneys at night when the pressure is off the legs. This is one of the reasons why many of us, when we are pregnant, have to get up at night to urinate.

The glands in your skin work harder too. Since you manufacture more heat, you pour out more sweat in order to maintain your body temperature and dispose of additional waste material. The oil glands become more active, increasing their output, so your skin becomes oilier. You may find your hair less manageable due to the increased oiliness. Because of the increased excretion of sweat and oil, you will probably need to bathe and shampoo more frequently.

FLUID, FOOD, MEDICINE, APPETITE, AND WEIGHT

Your body retains additional fluid during pregnancy. Besides the extra fluid which is circulating in your bloodstream, there is also an increase of fluid in all of the body cells. In fact, in women who show no sign of edema, the total amount of water weight gained amounts to nearly fifteen pounds. Research in England has shown that about 40 percent of "normal" pregnant women show signs of edema with about one-third of them having generalized edema (swelling of the hands and face as well as the legs). This represents water weight gains of up to twenty-one pounds or more.

These researchers further note that women with edema had slightly larger babies than those without edema, and they had fewer premature babies. If we look at the patterns of weight gain, we find that women who are heavier tend to gain more water weight while those who are thinner gain more fat. Thus, if you are overweight at the start of pregnancy, even though you gain as much as your thin sister, a larger proportion of your weight gain will be water, while more of hers will be fat.

It stands to reason that to maintain the normality (salt concentration) of all the additional fluid in your body during pregnancy, you should need more, not less, salt. Research with rats has shown that *they* do, indeed, need more salt. Dr. Tom Brewer and others have found that restriction of salt and the use of diuretics (water pills) does *not* decrease the incidence of toxemia. Diuretics should not be taken unless they are required for a medical problem. The American College of Obstetrics and Gynecology has affirmed this fact.

As a matter of fact, during your pregnancy, the more you can avoid stimulants, depressants, pain pills—in fact, drugs or medications of any kind—the better your chances of having a healthy baby. Do understand that I am not referring to lifesaving or maintenance measures—insulin for a diabetic, heart medication for heart disease, a specific antibiotic for acute infection, or drugs for

18

particular medical problems. But while you are capable of conceiving or pregnant, keep away from optional drugs and medications such as diet pills, cold tablets, and tranquilizers.

You will probably find that by the fourth month your appetite has substantially increased. This is a normal response to the increase in your metabolism. It's nature's way of stimulating you to provide adequate nourishment to assure the proper growth of your unborn baby and to maintain your own health and well-being.

How much should you eat? Research indicates you should eat until your appetite has been satisfied. This does not mean eating potato chips, cakes, candies, cokes, and other empty calorie non-foods. It does mean eating dairy products, meat and fish, vegetables, fruits and whole grains. If you eat according to your appetite, a well-balanced protein-rich diet, you may find your total gain to be about thirty to thirty-five pounds. It will be less or more, however, according to your age, initial weight, the number pregnancy this is for you, and many other factors.

After you have carefully guarded your baby's health and development throughout your pregnancy, you will want to assure his health through his birth and developing years.

You can prepare by reading and attending parents' classes if they are available in your area. You will want to have as normal a birth as you possibly can in order to give your baby the best launching into his new environment. You will want to continue to nourish your baby, hopefully by nursing him to give him the added protection breast milk can offer. Breast feeding helps to strengthen the bond between you and your child. It is also a plus for you, helping your organs return to normal more quickly.

You will want him close to you in those crucial days after birth so you can continue to develop the relationship which has been growing throughout the previous nine months. In this connection, Dr. Lee Salk observed an interesting phenomenon first in monkeys and then in humans. Most mothers hold their babies on the left. This remarkable fact caused him to carry out research which showed this preference did not develop in women who had been deprived of their babies for twenty-four hours after birth. This may be an instinctive behavior which assures the baby the soothing sound of his mother's heartbeat (heart sounds are louder on the left). Babies in a nursery where recorded heart sounds were played were quieter and gained better than those in a nursery without the heart sounds.[1]

Drs. Marshall Klaus and John H. Kennell have described their research as well as that of others in this crucial field in their book *Maternal-Infant Bonding* (St. Louis: C. V. Mosby, 1976). These studies provide evidence that immediate contact between you and your baby is desirable. They are a convincing argument for rooming-in, a system whereby the baby is kept in his mother's hospital room.

In any case, rooming-in is desirable for a number of reasons. It gives you and your baby and his father a chance to get acquainted while help and support are available and without the interference of other family members. It gives you and your baby a chance to be together alone without any intervening household responsibilities. It gives you a better chance to initiate breast feeding. It's a more natural, healthier situation. If this is your firstborn, you will have an opportunity to care for your baby while expert help is available. You will not spend all of your time waiting for baby's next visit, which may come just when you are ready to nap.

When you get home from the hospital, it's best if you have some help available. Let your helper (be it husband, mother, mother-in-law, or hired assistant) take care of the house while you take care of your baby.

You may find it helpful to have the public health nurse or visiting nurse make one or two visits during your first weeks at home. You can ask your doctor or the hospital personnel to make a referral. Or you can call directly and request her assistance. She will be able to answer questions, make suggestions, and be generally helpful with the many little problems that you didn't anticipate concerning yourself or your baby. For help with breast feeding, contact La Leche League in your area. The members are mothers who have had breastfeeding experience and are well qualified to provide you with the support you need.

It takes about six weeks for your uterus to shrink to normal size. By then, both you and your baby are due for medical checkups to be sure everything is as it should be. While you are breast feeding,

[1] Reported by Dr. Lee Salk, "The Role of the Heartbeat in the Relations Between Mother and Infant," *Scientific American*, Vol. 228: No. 5, May 1973, pp. 24-29.

continue to eat as you did while you were pregnant, adding extra calories as noted in Chapter Four. Sit down, put your feet up, and relax while you are nursing. Drink plenty of fluids. Your baby is portable, you should have little trouble in managing him. You can take him with you without the fuss and bother of bottles, cans, and other paraphernalia. Just tuck a few diapers into his pack and take that hike, or attend that meeting.

TIMELINE FOR
GOOD PERINATAL NUTRITION

Baby

Cell differentiation

Cartilage → bone

Heart-circulation begins

Skin and organ development

Egg fertilized → embryo

fetus →

Nutritional Support Systems | **CONCEPTION**

| Endometrium "uterine milk" nourishes developing egg | Developing placenta begins function at 8 weeks. Fully functioning at 12 weeks. | Growing placenta serving as fetal liver. Healthy placenta functions well. Stores nutrients. Maintains ↗ hormone levels. |

Mother

First trimester

Second Trimester

May have nausea

Increasing appetite

↓ metabolic rate

Growth of uterus, breasts ↗ blood volume

↗ Chest expansion

↓ GI motility

↗ urine flow up to 30 ml/min. with wastage of nutrients. Renal blood flow is 1200 ml/min. up from non-pregnant 900 ml/min.

Brain cells developing and
myelinization taking place.
Fetus growing.
Bones developing.
Subcutaneous tissue and fat
for insulation and health,
iron storage.
Fetal liver functioning.

Well-developed baby able to withstand
stress of labor and extra uterine adjustments

Large healthy baby, alert, active,
responsive, hungry, well-
developed nervous system.
Resistance to infection.

————— Baby —————

Nutrients and O_2
passed through placenta.
Waste cleared.
Healthy placenta
✦ hormones to maintain
effective function.

BIRTH

Breasts deliver proper milk
for infant. Antibodies and nutrients
for health maintenance and growth.
Hormone production
facilitates involution
and promotes "mothering."

Third trimester

Continued appetite

Maintenance of tissue
health—1st line of
defense against disease
and infection

Promote healing

Deep fat storage for
breast feeding

Maintenance of ✦ blood
volume for placental
function and health.
Sufficient calories and carbohydrates
leads to normal glucose
levels, baby lays down
glycogen → normal glucose
levels after birth

35,000 cal. stored as energy to meet labor requirements. Muscles and tissues healthy and elastic for easier birth. Stretch more readily.

Post natal period

Tissue repair hastened

Involution rapid

Controlled bleeding

✦ Resistance to
infection

Easier initiation of
breast feeding

Energy reserves for
mothering and for
relations with partner

Healthy nervous tissue

CHAPTER THREE
AVOIDING HAZARDS

Because you and your baby are so vulnerable to the external and internal environment, it is important that you try to make your environment as safe as you can.

Hazards are legion and a part of life. If we spend all our time worrying about every little danger, we might as well give up living. Prudence, however, demands that we give concern to what we can reasonably avoid, change or lessen.

ENVIRONMENTAL HAZARDS

If you live in one of our large cities, the very air you breathe may be hazardous. Obviously you can't leave the cities, nor can you stop breathing. But you can minimize the hazard in certain ways. When smog levels are high, stay in air-conditioned atmospheres as much as possible. Don't unnecessarily expose yourself to smoke. Keep out of smoke-filled rooms, parties where people are smoking, small intimate smoky nightclubs, and theater loges where smoking is allowed.

You would be wise to avoid the use of aerosols. On most of them you will find the notation—"Intentional misuse by deliberately concentrating and inhaling aerosol products can be fatal." Unintentional misuse can also be fatal. Toxic fumes inhaled, however deliberately or accidentally, by a woman whose baby is a developing embryo could have a harmful effect. It is better not to take the chance.

There are any number of other products which should not be inhaled. Some of the most toxic include cleaning fluids, contact cements, volatile paints, lacquer thinners, some glues, and various household cleaning agents such as oven cleaners. While you are pregnant, be sure to read the labels of any material you use to look for warnings.

Heavy-traffic car and truck fumes are hazards to be avoided. Carbon monoxide, a poison gas, can rise to high levels in heavy traffic, closed garages, and even within closed cars with defective mufflers or worn-out floorboards. An open tailgate window in a station wagon may contribute to a buildup of exhaust fumes within the car. Another toxic component of engine fumes is the lead—an additional reason not to breathe exhaust fumes while you are pregnant or could be pregnant.

Unvented heaters, stoves, and barbecues used indoors can be hazardous to anyone if the house is closed tightly. To you and your growing baby the danger is even greater.

If you plan on flying anywhere, be sure you go in a pressurized plane. If you contemplate taking a job in a high-altitude community, wait until after the baby is born or be sure you are there well in advance of pregnancy to get acclimated to the lowered amount of oxygen.

Lead has been mentioned as a component of gasoline. There are other ways this highly toxic metal can enter your body. Many paints have, until recently, contained lead. Some years ago, legislation was passed banning the use of lead in interior paints. It was still allowed in paints destined for exterior use. Unfortunately, the fact of labeling paint "Exterior" did not prevent its being used inside. Worse, however, is the fact that, in the past, interior paints contained lead. If you are in the process of restoring an old house, as so many people are, do not sand or strip the old paint yourself. In fact, since sanding sends paint dust into the air, you should not be around while the old paint is being sanded. This admonition applies to old plaster and putty and the refinishing of old painted furniture too. If you want to paint, be sure the paint you use contains no lead or toxic vapors. Most latex paints are safe. Read the labels and check with your local health department for further information or lead testing.

Another source of lead poisoning is improperly glazed pottery. The danger is increased by using the pottery for acidic beverages such as orange juice. In one instance a family got lead poisoning by keeping their apple juice in a pottery pitcher. In another, a doctor was poisoned by drinking cola from a cup made by his son.

According to Dr. J. Julian Chisolm, Jr.,[1] the government has instituted testing procedures to prevent pottery which gives off lead from being imported. Unfortunately, the standards are still inadequate because of failure to take into account the "quantity of the food or beverage consumed, its acidity, the length of time stored and whether or not it is cooked in the pottery." Dr. Chisolm also points out that "In the young children of urban slums lead poisoning is a major source of brain damage, mental deficiency and serious behavior problems."

Mercury and other heavy metals can also cause problems by their presence in the environment. Swordfish has been banned for interstate sale because of high mercury levels. Tuna is tested and not allowed on the market if the mercury levels are high. Certain game birds have been found to contain mercury. Seeds intended for planting are often mercury-treated so be sure any seeds you buy for eating, including peas and beans, are intended for food and not for planting.

X rays are another potential hazard. Physicians usually do not order abdominal X rays on any woman of childbearing age unless absolutely necessary. If other X rays are unavoidable, be sure your abdomen is shielded with a lead apron. In late pregnancy, X rays are occasionally ordered to aid obstetrical diagnosis of certain problems that might affect delivery, such as twins, abnormal position, a placenta implanted by or over the cervix, or a contracted pelvis.

Sonography is a more recent procedure to be routinely employed in prenatal diagnosis. Though many authorities attest to the safety of this technique, others hesitate to give it unqualified endorsement. Sonography uses ultrasound waves to form an image of the underlying tissues. Thus the fetus and placenta are visualized by this technique. The ultrasonic fetoscope uses ultrasound to detect and amplify fetal heart sounds. The hand-held electronic fetoscope and the external fetal monitor are examples of this use of ultrasound.

Pesticides, herbicides, and fertilizers, if misused, can constitute a

---

[1] "Lead Poisoning," *Scientific American* 224:2, February 1971, pp. 15-23.

hazard to women in childbearing years and their unborn babies. Some pesticides can be absorbed through the skin in toxic doses. All fruits and vegetables bought from commercial growers should be washed before eating. Root vegetables such as carrots have a tendency to absorb excess pesticide from the soil. Since pesticides are seldom used on carrots, the problem is unlikely unless they are being grown in soil containing persistent pesticides (DDT, aldrin, and dieldrin) used in past years.

Our current problems with pesticides just point out the haste with which new products are embraced and the resistance to abandon them. Any of you who are old enough to recall the end of World War II might remember seeing newsreels showing health officials dusting the heads of thousands of refugees and displaced persons with DDT to get rid of lice. Incredible as it seems, this method was being employed among the poor in some areas as recently as 1971.

Herbicides are used by nearly every commercial farmer and by increasing numbers of homeowners for everything from growing "no-till" corn to getting rid of crabgrass. Perhaps those used in agriculture today are completely safe. However, one widely used herbicide—2,4,5-T—was found to cause a breakdown in chromosomes and is now banned for agricultural use. Unfortunately, this potentially dangerous chemical was used in Vietnam as a defoliant. Who knows what the results will be for future generations of Vietnamese?

Here in the United States at least one state continues to use 2,4,5-T for spraying roadsides. Although it would be less of a threat to people, it is still conceivable that it could get into wells and springs near the roads. Worse, however, was its use in the summer of 1973 in Baxter's State Park, a beautiful wilderness park surrounding Mount Katahdin, the northern peak of the Appalachian Trail. Again, who knows how it will affect the wildlife in the area? The spraying programs were carried out despite campaigns by the citizenry against them. Hopefully the protests have been at least partially effective. There has been a diminishing of roadside spraying, particularly in areas where there are farms. Also the extent of the spraying at Baxter's Park was cut back from the original plan.

Since the DDT ban has been in effect, there have been attempts to get it cleared for use again. In fact, on October 25, 1973, the

Bangor Daily News in Maine published a quotation from an official of the International Paper Company that studies of DDT by the Department of Inland Fisheries and Game "showed little harmful effect" on the forest environment. The Maine Commissioner of Inland Fisheries and Game, in a letter to the editors, rebutted the statement, noting a study published in the January 1962 issue of *Journal of Wildlife Management.* He wrote:

. . . the study revealed convincing evidence that brook trout and other fishes were reduced considerably as a result of DDT spraying for spruce budworm control . . . Further, this department (Inland Fisheries and Game) investigated three reported fish kills . . . of these, DDT was implicated in mortality of fish in fourteen streams and seven lakes. The decline of salmon fisheries in Sebago Lake was directly associated with shoreline spraying of DDT for black-fly control.

Our concern is . . . also for its long-term persistence in the environment. In Maine, for example, research by Dr. John Dimond of the University of Maine has shown that this chemical persists in the mud of lakes and streams and in the bodies of fish, birds and a variety of animals for at least a decade after spraying. It is almost certain that the long-term decline of several species of wildlife, like the eagle, is at least in part due to the past use of persistent pesticides such as DDT.

We believe that our forest resources must be protected from the ravage of nature for the best use of man. We also believe that such protection should not be to the detriment of another important natural resource, our fish and wildlife. Other alternatives to the use of persistent and lethal chemicals such as DDT must be found.[2]

With more responsible and responsive public officials such as this, perhaps future generations of people as well as wildlife will be safeguarded. And yet as recently as the summer of 1980, St. Regis Paper Company employed airplanes to spray hundreds of acres of land in Washington County, Maine, to the horror of many farmers in the area who feared for the safety of their families and their

[2] *Bangor Daily News*, November 6, 1973.

crops. Again, the summer of 1981 was disturbed by the Mediterranean fruit fly spraying program authorized by Governor Brown in California.

Disposal of hazardous wastes continues to pose problems across the nation. We are all familiar with the horror of Love Canal, and yet far more hazardous dumping sites exist across the nation. Nuclear reactors have also been cited for their potential to harm. Areas adjacent to these reactors may be hazardous to the unborn even without a reactor "accident."

Fertilizers which contain nitrates pose a problem if they get into the drinking water. In addition, there are some vegetables which tend to absorb too much nitrate if available through excessive use of fertilizer. If you live on a farm, have your water tested to be sure the nitrate content is within safe limits. Guard against nitrate getting into the water by plowing in fertilizers immediately after spreading, and by not spreading manure on snow in the winter, thus allowing it to run off in spring thaws. Gardens and livestock should be located well away from your source of water.

FOOD ADDITIVES

Nitrates and nitrites are deliberately added to cured meats, frankfurters, bologna, luncheon meats, and some smoked fish. In many instances, they are used to impart a red color to the meats. In some cases, they may also help to kill the botulinum organism which is responsible for the deadly botulism toxin that develops in an oxygen-free environment if botulines are present.

Nitrite is highly toxic, being able to combine with the hemoglobin in the red blood cells to form methemoglobin, a compound that will not carry oxygen. The amounts of nitrite contained in meats should not be enough to threaten adults. The greatest danger is to infants whose digestive tracts convert nitrates to nitrites.

For adults, the greatest dangers of nitrites are from accidental ingestion due to human carelessness or the possible reaction of nitrites with amines to form nitrosamines. These can cause cancer. Of special concern to women in childbearing years is that the nitrosamines are teratogens (capable of causing birth defects). Nitrosamines can be formed in plants, food, or in your stomach.

According to Dr. Michael F. Jacobson, nitrosamines have been found in cooked sausage, cured pork, dried beef, bacon, and fish.[3]

While you are pregnant or capable of becoming pregnant, try to limit your intake of frankfurters, ham, luncheon meats, commercially corned beef and other processed meats. While an occasional slice of ham or a frankfurter may do no harm, everyday use could create problems. The laws of Canada and Minnesota prohibit the use of nitrites in smoked fish, so check your fish source and labels if available. Even if the individual packages of fish do not bear a label, ask the dealer. The box it was packed in probably does.

BHA (butylated hydroxyanisol) and BHT (butylated hydroxytoluene) are antioxidants which are added to many foods. While they have not been found to be dangerous, Dr. Jacobson feels the testing has been inadequate. They are put into so many different foods that you could conceivably get these chemicals in just about everything you eat if you're not careful. Some oils and shortenings contain them; some don't. Most cold cereals contain them (exceptions are Grape Nuts, puffed wheat and puffed rice). They are added to some potato chips but not to others. They are contained in nearly all the snack chips, twists, curls, etc. They are found in sausage meat, in various cake mixes, and even in some canned foods. That they are not in *all* of these products is an indication that their use is not required. Read the labels and, whenever possible, purchase those products which do not contain BHA and BHT, since they accumulate in body fat and the safety of their long-term use is not adequately proven.

Caffeine is a common component of soft drinks (Coke, Pepsi, Dr. Pepper, etc.), coffee, tea, and a number of analgesics (APC, Anacin, aspirin compound). Even though caffeine has been used for years, there is recent evidence that it may be a cause of birth defects. Dr. Jacobson states: "As a reasonable precaution, women in the first three months of pregnancy should reduce or totally eliminate their consumption of caffeine-containing beverages, foods, and drugs."[4] Try using decaffeinated coffee. If you are a tea drinker, do not let the tea steep too long or boil. Although tea leaves contain more caffeine than coffee, if served as it should be,

[3] *Eater's Digest* (New York: Doubleday and Company, 1972).
[4] *Eater's Digest*, p. 92.

fresh and steeped only three to five minutes, not as much caffeine will be leached from the leaves.

There are a number of other additives which, according to Dr. Jacobson and/or the FAO/WHO Expert Committee on Food Additives, have not been adequately tested. Among them are stearyl citrate, isopropyl citrate, tannin, tannic acid, theodipropionic acid, dilauryl theodipropionate, ethyl vanillin (not vanillin). The food additive problem is one which should be of concern to us all. Additives are not all bad. Some are very necessary for preservation and safety. It is when their safety is questionable or when they are substitutes for more nutritious products or designed to make inferior foods more palatable and appealing that their use should be condemned.

MEDICATIONS AND DRUGS

Since alcohol and tobacco are two of the most widely used drugs, they should be considered first in their effects on pregnancy. Alcohol provides calories without nutritional value. Since alcohol cannot be changed to a storable form, it must be metabolized—used by the body when ingested. Alcohol interferes with the absorption and utilization of other nutrients. In fact, it actually wastes nutrients by using them for its metabolism. Even worse, it is a poison which may damage the nerve cells of the brain. The alcohol you drink reaches the baby through the placenta. This is not a substance you want his brain cells exposed to during the critical development period.

Fetal alcohol syndrome affects up to 6,000 of the infants born each year. Babies with this condition have small heads, receding chins, lowered intelligence, and other defects. Consumption of as little as two ounces of alcohol per day by the pregnant woman may result in fetal alcohol syndrome (FAS).

Tobacco is also a drug. Nicotine has been found to inhibit the transport of oxygen across the placenta to the fetus. The babies of women who smoke are smaller than those of women who don't smoke. Statistics compiled both here and in England bear that out. We know that premature and low-birth-weight babies are weaker and run greater risks than larger, normal full-term babies. This may be one factor that accounts for a recent report from England that there is a higher death rate among babies of smokers. The more a woman smokes, the higher her chances of having a small baby, and the smaller her baby is liable to be.

LSD is reported to cause chromosome breakdown in those who take it. This could be responsible for birth defects. Use by the mother of such narcotics as heroin and morphine are known to cause addiction in an unborn baby. They may cause the death of the baby. In any event, an addicted baby needs to be treated as soon as it is born.

In a study carried out by the American College of Physicians and Surgeons through a research group headed by Dr. Gabriel Nahas, new information on the effects of marijuana has been uncovered.

It was found that marijuana may interfere with the ability of some white blood cells to fight viruses. This effect may cause one to be more susceptible to viral infections, at least one of which has been known to cause birth defects (rubella). In addition, with extended use, it is known that the products of marijuana build up within the germ cells of the ovaries and testes. It is thus wise to avoid the use of marijuana during the childbearing years.

We are all aware of the thalidomide tragedy, but there are other drugs which may be responsible for malformed babies or spontaneous abortion. Many new drugs come on the market yearly, some lacking adequate testing; and, of course, the testing for capability of producing birth defects is, of necessity, done on animals rather than human beings. Some of these drugs bear warnings in their literature that they should not be given to pregnant women. If they should not be given to pregnant women then they should not be given to women capable of becoming pregnant, since the most crucial period of fetal formation takes place before a woman even knows she is pregnant.

Sex hormones of various types can cause difficulties in the infant by advancing bone development and possibly having a masculinizing effect. Diethylstilbestrol (DES), which in the past was used to try to prevent miscarriage, has been implicated in the sudden increase of a rare form of vaginal cancer in girls whose mothers were given the drug.

In 1973, as the first edition of this book was being written, the FDA's ban on the use of DES in animal feed and as pellet implants had been ruled illegal by court order. Six years passed before that ruling was overturned. As of November 1, 1979, the use of DES in animal feed has been banned.

One grower stated that the retail prices of meat would drop 5 to 10 percent with the use of DES. Since the use of the drug results in fatter, more marbled meat, the saving is mostly an illusion. It's somewhat akin to saying that cutting fish filets thinner before breading them, thus selling them at a slightly lower price per pound, saves money, when one is actually getting less fish and more breading. Why pay five or ten cents less per pound for meat which probably contains more fat (and less protein) and which could possibly create a health hazard? It is known that DES shows up in the livers of the animals fed it. Though growers are warned not to use DES feed for two weeks prior to slaughter, there is little to prevent them from doing so. The meat is only spot-checked.

Aspirin (acetylsalicylic acid) and other salicylates have been found to interfere with blood clotting. In most adults, this is relatively innocuous, but in the newborn it can result in bleeding. Aspirin also interferes with the utilization of vitamin C. Vitamin K, the anticlotting vitamin, is not produced within the baby's intestines until sometime after birth (see Chapter Four).

Some of the antibiotics are known to affect the baby. Examples of these are the tetracyclines which may have an effect on bone growth and the development of tooth enamel; some which may cause jaundice; and chloramphenicol (Chloromycetin) which may even cause death. Because chloramphenicol is particularly toxic to certain susceptible people and should only be used for treating diseases like typhoid fever, typhus, and Rocky Mountain spotted fever, most people will *never* require it and a woman is not likely to need it during pregnancy.

There are a number of over-the-counter drugs which have not been subjected to exhaustive screening. Consequently, when a woman is capable of childbearing, she should avoid drugs and medications unless specifically ordered for a particular disease. She should also be sure to tell the physician treating her if she has any reason to suspect that she might be pregnant.

ILLNESS AND DISEASE

Illness and disease may affect your infant. One of the best-known diseases affecting the unborn baby is rubella or German measles. Over 25 percent of the babies born to women who have had rubella in the first three months of pregnancy will have birth defects. The rubella vaccine should eliminate this problem in the future. However, if you have not been vaccinated against rubella, you should *not* be while you are capable of becoming pregnant and sexually active. Be sure you avoid exposure to German measles. If you are exposed in early pregnancy, see your doctor. He can perform a test to determine how well you are protected against rubella and, if necessary, give you an immune serum for more protection.

Other viral infections have been reported to cause various fetal problems. Your best defense is to avoid exposure and maintain a high level of protection through a nutritious diet.

A most dangerous bacterial infection is syphilis, which is caused by a spirochete known as the *Treponema pallidum*. A pregnant woman with infectious syphilis can miscarry at any time after the fourth month, or give birth to a stillborn child. Babies born with congenital syphilis (contracted before birth from an infected mother) may be afflicted with such abnormalities as saddle nose (a flat nose lacking a bridge), blindness due to opaque cornea, deafness due to syphilis of the auditory nerve, and abnormal pegged teeth—the last three symptoms known as Hutchinson's triad—baldness, rashes and lesions, and any of a great number of internal problems. About one-fourth of syphilis-infected babies die before birth and nearly a third more die after birth. Early diagnosis and treatment of syphilis in the mother will cure infection in the unborn baby.

Toxoplasmosis, a relatively mild disease caused by a protozoa, is another source of birth defects. Cats are carriers of this organism, which is also found in raw meat. Consequently, if you are pregnant you should not eat undercooked meat or decide to get a cat. If you have always had cats and/or eaten raw meat, chances are you have had toxoplasmosis. A blood test can be done to find out if you are immune. If you are not or are not sure of immunity, be sure all your meat is cooked to at least 140° (the temperature at which the organism is killed). Do not handle strange cats or take care of a cat's litter box. It is even advisable that you not hand-dig in areas where cats have buried their feces, since one form of the organism can live in soil for as long as a year. The greatest danger from toxoplasmosis is in the latter months of pregnancy rather than in the early months, as in the case of German measles. Infection can cause retardation and other neurological disorders.

One other disease warrants mention, if only because it is on the increase and because some couples have been undertaking the risk of delivering their own baby. If a pregnant woman is infected with the gonococcus organism which causes gonorrhea, the baby can contract the germ as it passes through the birth canal. In the past, gonorrhea was the leading cause of blindness. It has now been virtually eliminated by using silver nitrate in infants' eyes at birth.

Aside from malnutrition, diabetes is undoubtedly the maternal illness most responsible for problems. For this reason, women who are diabetic should seek expert medical advice as soon as they know they are pregnant. Medical checkups prior to pregnancy are also advisable for all women. Babies of diabetics tend to be large, but only part of that largeness is due to fat. Some of it is due to retention of extra fluid in their body tissues. It is through careful medical supervision of diabetic women throughout pregnancy that their babies are born healthy. I have a few friends who are diabetics and they have had beautiful, healthy children delivered normally. I know many others who have had to be delivered by Cesarean section to insure a healthy baby. All of these women have had their pregnancies carefully monitored by medical specialists.

Other maternal illnesses which require expert medical care include kidney disease with high blood pressure, heart disease, tuberculosis, mental illness, and anemias.

Even though there are multiple hazards created by this modern, technological world which can affect your unborn baby, many of them are avoidable. Some hazards are natural ones—sun radiation, food toxins, chemicals, poisonous plants and animals—which humans have been subjected to since before the dawn of civilization. Uncounted hazards have been lessened through modern technology—the development of vaccines, safer methods of food preparation and preservation, new methods of diagnosis and treatment of disease, and modern biochemical techniques. The first line of defense against any of the hazards is a healthy body. With good nutrition you can help build health and provide extra protection against the unavoidable hazards of modern life.

CHAPTER FOUR

BASIC NUTRITION

In order to nourish yourself and your developing baby in the best way, you must have some knowledge of basic nutrition. You need to know what nutrients are, what they do, how they are used in your body, and what foods contain them if you want to provide a good diet for yourself and your family.

The three basic components of food are carbohydrates, fats, and proteins. In addition, foods contain vitamins and minerals which are vital to the maintaining of our bodies' functions.

CARBOHYDRATES

Carbohydrates in the form of starches and sugars are probably the most abundant and cheapest of the world's available food supply. The grains and a number of fruits and vegetables can be stored for considerable periods—either by drying or in their fresh form like root vegetables, winter squashes, and cabbages. Carbohydrates are important because they provide fuel and energy. The natural carbohydrates are major sources of vitamins and minerals. This is another reason why carbohydrates form a vital part of our diet.

Sugars are one common form of carbohydrates. Glucose or dextrose is a simple sugar less sweet than sucrose (table sugar). It is metabolized in our bodies to form energy. All carbohydrates used by our bodies are eventually converted to glucose. Fructose, or levulose, is another simple sugar, the mirror-image of glucose, found in honey and fruits. It is very sweet, up to one and three-quarters times sweeter than sucrose. The other important simple sugar is galactose. It is not very sweet and is never found free in foods, being converted from lactose (milk sugar) by enzymes in the digestive tract.

The double sugars are composed of two simple sugars. The most common is sucrose, which is found in a number of natural sources: sugar cane, beets, maple syrup, pineapple, and carrots.

Lactose, the sugar of milk, is the other important double sugar. Your body manufactures lactose during lactation and late pregnancy. Since a majority of the people of the world, after about the age of two, and most animals after babyhood, do not have the enzyme lactase which breaks the lactose of milk into glucose and galactose, they cannot tolerate large amounts of sweet milk. You are more liable to be lactose intolerant if you are black, Israeli, Oriental, Eskimo, or South American Indian. You can use acidophilus milk, yoghurt, buttermilk, or cheese as your primary source of milk. In these forms, most of the lactose has been changed to lactic acid and is not liable to cause the pain and diarrhea that large amounts of sweet milk may.[1]

Many of the recipes in this book call for buttermilk (yoghurt or sour milk can be substituted). Milk is such an important and inexpensive source of calcium, riboflavin, and protein, that you should drink it in pregnancy. See the section on beverages for recipes to make buttermilk and yoghurt, as well as other drinks using buttermilk as a base.

Foods containing simple and double sugars are important to your diet—fruits, many vegetables, and milk. But pure refined sugars add nothing but calories and energy which are just as available in the vitamin- and mineral-containing foods supplying sugar. Keep your intake of refined sugar to a minimum. There is no need for any of us to eat more than 100 pounds of sugar each year. Contrary to the ads, refined sugar is not a good food.

Dr. John Yudkin puts it this way: "There is no physiological requirement for sugar; all human nutritional needs can be met in full without having to take a single spoon of white or brown or raw sugar, on its own or in any food or drink."[2]

In this book you will find the sweetener used in most of the

[1] Kretchmer, Norman, "Lactose and Lactase," *Scientific American*, Vol. 227: No. 4, October 1972, pp. 70-78.
[2] *Sweet and Dangerous* (New York: Peter H. Wyden, 1972).

recipes to be either honey or molasses. Molasses is less refined than sugar and contains some nutrients, especially iron and some B vitamins. Blackstrap molasses is the most nutritious while light molasses (golden syrup) is just molasses-flavored sugar syrup.

Honey contains traces of nutrients, especially B vitamins. It has three other advantages. Being sweeter than sucrose, only about two-thirds as much is needed to provide the sweetening power of sugar. While it is immediately absorbed, it does not trigger the cycle—insulin, low blood sugar, more sugar, insulin—in the way sucrose does. That explains the third advantage which is that honey satisfies and one is less likely to eat it to excess. With sucrose, the more you eat, the more you want.

Brown sugar is refined sugar with just small amounts of molasses added for flavor and color. So-called raw sugar is also refined, due to FDA regulations. For this reason it makes little difference whether you use white or brown sugar.

Complex carbohydrates are composed of many simple sugars. The most important one nutritionally is starch. Many of our grains and vegetables are composed principally of starches. Cooking renders starch more digestible by breaking down the cell walls. Ptyalin, an enzyme in saliva, starts breaking down starch into its component sugars. Chewing food thoroughly helps the ptyalin work by mixing it into the food. Refined starches such as bleached white flour have been stripped of many of their nutrients. Only three are replaced through enrichment.

One complex carbohydrate which is not digestible by man (though cows do a great job on it) is cellulose. Cellulose is supportive tissue in plants. In the human it contributes bulk to our diet and is important for promoting regular bowel habits.

Each gram of carbohydrate you eat provides you with four calories. During pregnancy, if you are an adult woman of average size and moderately active, you will need to eat approximately 2,400 calories. You may need up to 3,000 if you are very active or underweight or pregnant with twins. Mrs. Agnes Higgins of the Montreal Diet Dispensary says that 400 of these calories (100 grams) should be provided by protein. The National Research Council recommends 74 grams of protein. About 700 calories (nearly 80 grams) will be provided by fat, and 1,300 calories (325 grams) by carbohydrates. While nursing your baby, you will need 200 additional calories.

If you are in your teens and still growing, you will need more calories and protein than an adult woman does. You can get them by drinking an extra glass of milk and eating some fruit or a slice of bread.

Carbohydrate forms an important part of your diet. For example, 1 banana provides 23 grams (92 calories) of carbohydrate, a baked potato, 21 grams (84 calories), 1 cup cooked carrots, 10 grams (40 calories), or a 1-pound loaf of enriched white bread, 229 grams (916 calories) of carbohydrate.

PROTEINS

Proteins are the building blocks—the basic material from which most cells are formed. Proteins are composed of amino acids, eight of which are essential; another two are essential during the growing period, and the remainder our bodies manufacture.

Both animal and plant foods contain protein, but whereas animal proteins are complete—that is, contain enough of all the essential amino acids in a proper ratio to meet the body's needs—plants contain incomplete proteins which are lacking in one or more of the essential amino acids. Incomplete plant proteins can be supplemented by adding animal protein (for example, use milk in making pea soup or add bits of ham to it; egg and milk powder used in making bread enhances the grain protein). Plant proteins also can be mixed so as to balance the ratio of amino acids.

If you are a vegetarian or are living on a limited income, I recommend that you purchase a copy of *Diet for a Small Planet* by Frances Moore Lappé.[3] Also of interest is *Recipes for a Small Planet* by Ellen Ewald.[4] The recipes have been carefully balanced to assure an intake of complete protein. They also give the number of grams of protein provided per serving. The percentage of the daily allowance noted on the recipes does not apply to pregnant or lactating women. Those recipes I have tried have been quite acceptable. You can create your own recipes and menus using Ms. Lappé's instructions for balancing protein. Though it may take a bit

[3] New York: A Friends of the Earth/Ballantine Book, 1971. Spiral-bound, $3.95; paperback, $1.25.
[4] Ballantine, $1.50.

of ingenuity on your part, your health and that of your unborn baby are worth it.

The most common complete protein foods are meat, fish, milk, eggs, and cheese. Incomplete proteins include legumes (dried beans and peas), grains, seeds, and nuts. Most vegetables contain small amounts of protein. Fruits, however, generally have negligible amounts.

Since protein provides for the growth and maintenance of body tissues, it is vital during pregnancy that you eat good amounts of protein. As previously noted, you need at least 74 grams of protein per day, and probably closer to 100 grams, to promote the normal growth of your baby and maintain your own health.

FATS

Fats are used as food in varying amounts depending on the culture—from the exceedingly high fat intake of the Eskimo to the low fat intake of some Oriental cultures. In the United States, our fat intake approaches 40 percent of total calories. The National Research Council's Food and Nutrition Board believes that an intake of fat representing 25 percent of our total calories should be adequate. In pregnancy and lactation, in order to get adequate calories, your fat intake will probably be closer to 30 percent of your total calories.

There has been a great deal of controversy recently on the role of fats in the development of atherosclerosis and coronary heart disease. Some physicians have been recommending lowering fat intake, using polyunsaturated fats, and limiting cholesterol-containing foods as a means of preventing these diseases.

In fact, as Dr. John Yudkin has pointed out, there is a far clearer relationship between sugar consumption and coronary heart disease. Also, our bodies manufacture cholesterol from any food source, so limiting the intake of cholesterol-containing foods is not necessarily the answer. Cholesterol is necessary to the functioning of our bodies, being used in the manufacture of sex hormones, vitamin D, and bile.

Recent research by Drs. Joseph L. Goldstein and Michael S. Brown of the Southwestern Medical School at the University of Texas indicates that high cholesterol levels may stem from overproduction by the body. This tendency to over-synthesize and accumulate cholesterol is inherited—if from both parents, progressive heart disease can start in childhood; if from one parent the problem is manifest later. They are continuing their research into this genetic problem to find effective ways of treating it.

In any event, to promote health it is wise to limit sugar consumption, eat a varied well-balanced diet, maintain as much as possible a normal weight, exercise daily, and eat a balance of polyunsaturated and saturated fats in moderation. Dr. Roger J. Williams in his book *Nutrition Against Disease*[5] notes that if fat is accompanied by a nutritious diet, it should not cause heart disease. He also cites research indicating that heating polyunsaturated fats interferes with their ability to eliminate excess cholesterol from the blood. Fats are found in animal protein foods such as meat, milk, and eggs (yolks). They are found in nuts, grains, and seeds. They are also found in certain fruits such as the avocado and the olive.

Generally speaking, animal fats are more saturated and vegetable fats less saturated. The least saturated animal fat is lard, which may be less saturated than some hydrogenated vegetable shortenings. By far, the most saturated fat available is coconut oil. Palm oil and cocoa butter, the fat of chocolate, are also highly saturated. Because nondairy creamers may contain coconut oil, they can actually be higher in saturated fats than cream.

There is one essential fatty acid which the body is unable to synthesize. It is the polyunsaturated linoleic acid which is found in most vegetable, nut, cereal, and grain fats.

Fat does have certain functions in addition to providing the essential linoleic acid. Fat provides a high ratio of energy calories (9 calories per gram compared to 4 calories per gram of protein and carbohydrate) which is helpful in maintaining body heat in cold climates. It slows the emptying time of the stomach. It aids in the absorption and utilization of carotene—the vegetable form of vitamin A. Limited amounts of fat aid in the absorption of calcium.

The recipes in this book call for either solid or liquid fats in the foods to be cooked or for cooking purposes. The effectiveness of polyunsaturates is diminished by heating, so there appears to be little advantage to using them in foods cooked at high heats. To gain the greatest benefits from polyunsaturated fats, use cold-

[5] New York: Pitman Publishing Corporation, 1971.

pressed oils for preparing salad dressings and in uncooked foods or those to be warmed only slightly.

VITAMINS

Vitamins may be classified according to their solubility. This will be helpful in cooking since one group, which includes the C and B-complex vitamins, is soluble in water and can easily be discarded in cooking water. The other group is the fat-soluble vitamins: A, D, E, and K.

Vitamins are neither carbohydrates, fats, proteins, nor minerals, but are compounds which are vital to life. There are undoubtedly many vitamins as yet undiscovered or whose role in human nutrition has not been recognized. It is only since the late nineteenth century that vitamins have been isolated and synthesized although the need for vitamin C, for example, has been recognized for centuries.

FAT-SOLUBLE VITAMINS

Vitamin A

Vitamin A is needed to enable the eyes to adapt to light changes. Lack of this vitamin causes "night blindness." It is also necessary in forming healthy skin, mucous membranes, tooth enamel, hair, and fingernails. It is necessary for the growth and proper functioning of the thyroid gland.

Vitamin A can be toxic if taken in very large amounts. It can cause joint pain, yellowing of the skin, and thinning of the hair. Large overdoses have been associated with birth defects in animals. The recommended intake of vitamin A during pregnancy is 5,000 units (6,000 units during lactation), but considerably more than that may be safely absorbed. In fact, it is unlikely you will take in too much through food sources unless you go on an Arctic expedition and partake of polar-bear liver, which contains phenomenally high amounts of vitamin A. Research does indicate, however, that consuming large doses of vitamin A in early pregnancy may cause birth defects. Pregnant women should avoid taking vitamin supplements containing over 10,000 I.U. of vitamin A.

Vitamin A-rich foods include fish liver oils, liver, kidney, butter, fortified margarine, egg yolk, and deep green and yellow vegetables. Cooking vegetables breaks down the cell walls and releases the vitamin A for absorption. Hence, cooked carrots will supply you with vitamin A more readily than raw carrots.

Bile salts and dietary fats aid in the absorption of vitamin A. The vitamin is stored in the liver. During illness and disease, these stores may be diminished. Also, mineral oil will interfere with absorption of this fat-soluble vitamin. The oil, being undigested and unabsorbed, will absorb vitamin A or carotene causing it to pass out through the digestive tract. Vitamin A can be destroyed by long exposure to heat, drying, or rancidity of oil.

Vitamin D

Vitamin D is known as the sunshine vitamin. It is absolutely essential for absorption and use of calcium and phosphorus in forming strong teeth and bones. It is not easy to determine the requirement for vitamin D intake since it depends upon how much exposure one has to the sun, what one's complexion is (whether light or dark) and, of course, one's stage of growth. The National Research Council recommends an intake of 400 International Units for pregnant and lactating women and for children. Since dark-complexioned people have more melanin in their skin, their skin is better shielded from the sun. Consequently, they need more exposure to sun in order to manufacture vitamin D.

The sources of vitamin D include yeast, fish liver oils, mackerel, salmon, tuna, sardines, and herring. Milk is irradiated to provide 400 I.U. per quart. If you rely on milk as your source of vitamin D, be sure it is listed on the label. Many brands of nonfat dry milk and margarines contain added vitamins A and D. D-fortified margarines which provide 2,000 I.U. of vitamin D per pound will give you a little less than one-sixth of your recommended daily allowance per tablespoon.

Lack of vitamin D causes rickets in children, resulting in poor growth, bone deformities, poor teeth, and loss of tone in muscles; it causes osteomalacia in adults with a softening or decalcification of the bone.

Excessive doses of vitamin D can cause toxicity with a reversal of the effect of normal doses. The natural forms of vitamin D are unlikely to cause toxicity. The vitamin D of a daily prenatal vitamin supplement along with that in fortified milk and margarine and sunshine conversion will be easily tolerated. If you overdo the supplementation with large doses combined with large amounts of the sugar-coated "vitamin" cereals, pastries, and so forth, you might get into trouble.

Vitamin E

Vitamin E has been known as the antisterility vitamin. It is a potent antioxidant and as such helps to preserve vitamins and unsaturated fatty acids both in our bodies and in our foods. The function of vitamin E within the human body has yet to be clearly established. There is evidence that it protects against certain toxic chemicals such as carbon tetrachloride; that it may be necessary for the development of healthy red blood cells; that a high intake of polyunsaturated fats leads to an increased need for vitamin E because of the tendency of these fats to bind the vitamin.

In pregnancy, your baby will absorb vitamin E supplied by you. It is important to note that in female rats, vitamin E deficiency causes faulty placenta implantation with resorption of the fetal rats. After the baby's birth, if you breast-feed, he will get far more vitamin E from your milk than from cow's milk formula, and his vitamin E level will rise far faster than in the bottle-fed infant. This tends to indicate that vitamin E is important to both the unborn and the newborn baby.

The recommended daily allowance for vitamin E in pregnancy is 10 milligrams of alpha tocopherol equivalents; in lactation, 11 milligrams of alpha tocopherol equivalents. The estimated average daily dietary intake of vitamin E is about 14 milligrams. Foods rich in vitamin E include corn oil, cottonseed oil, margarine, peanut oil, soybean oil, eggs, liver, brown rice, wheat germ, other whole grains, and leafy green vegetables such as turnip greens.

Vitamin K

Vitamin K is the antihemorrhagic vitamin. Since this vitamin is manufactured by bacteria in the intestines, deficiencies are rare. However, under certain conditions, vitamin K may not be synthesized or absorbed. Continued use of antibiotics may upset the normal bacterial environment of the intestines. In this case, the synthesis of vitamin K would be diminished or cease. Bile acids are necessary for vitamin K absorption, so gall bladder disease or other liver ailments may result in a deficiency of K.

Babies' intestines do not contain the K-producing bacteria at birth. It, therefore, takes a few days before the bacteria are available to manufacture vitamin K. To prevent hemorrhage, vitamin K may be given to the newborn baby. For some years, the vitamin K injection was given to the mother prior to delivery in hopes that enough would be transferred through the placenta to the baby. This was not very effective, however, due to the problem of timing.

Vitamin K is found in such foods as alfalfa, spinach, cabbage, cauliflower, liver, oats, and tomatoes.

THE WATER-SOLUBLE VITAMINS

The family of vitamins known as B complex serve many important functions. This discovery was stimulated by a need to find a cure for beriberi, a paralyzing disease rampant in the Orient and other areas where refined grains formed the basic diet. While the original researchers believed they had discovered a single vitamin, it was later found that they had actually found a number of vitamins and related substances. These are all water-soluble and, with vitamin C, constitute the group of water-soluble vitamins.

Thiamine or Vitamin B$_1$

Thiamine was eventually found to be the anti-beriberi substance. Thiamine is essential for appetite, digestion, and muscular tone in the gastrointestinal tract. It is needed for fertility, growth, lactation, and during illness and infection.

Insufficient thiamine may result in loss of appetite, indigestion, constipation, loss of alertness and reflexes. Pain, numbness or prickly feelings, paralysis, weakening of the heart, and edema are also signs of thiamine deficiency. Since thiamine is not stored in the body, the supply can be used up in just a few days. Ample thiamine must be consumed each day.

In pregnancy, the recommended thiamine intake is 1.5 milligrams; in lactation, 1.6 milligrams. The best sources are pork and pork products, liver, heart, kidneys, peas and beans, whole and enriched grains, and brewer's yeast. It is relatively stable in dry heat and in acid solutions but is destroyed by alkalis—a good reason to avoid adding baking soda to food to preserve color.

Riboflavin or Vitamin B$_2$

Riboflavin is a yellowish-green fluorescent material which is stable in dry heat and in acid solutions. It is very sensitive to light, hence food sources should not be stored in clear glass containers or cooked in clear glass cooking utensils. Use a minimum of water and be sure the container is covered. It is not well stored by the body so must be supplied daily.

Lack of riboflavin results in eye problems such as burning, itching, dimness of vision, light sensitivity, and even cataracts. Skin difficulties include impairment of wound healing, cracking of the lips, and lesions at the corners of the mouth, dermatitis and inflammation of the tongue tip and edges.

Riboflavin is necessary for the normal growth and development of the baby from conception.

The best food source of riboflavin is milk, each quart containing 2 milligrams or approximately the amount needed per day in pregnancy and lactation. Other sources are organ meats and some vegetables, fruits, and nuts.

Niacin or Nicotinic Acid

Niacin is the anti-pellagra vitamin. Pellagra is a disease characterized by diarrhea, dermatitis, dementia, and death. It is prevalent among people who exist on low-quality protein combined with an inadequate niacin intake. People who eat high-quality protein which contains adequate amounts of the amino acid tryptophan may never have pellagra even if their diet is relatively low in niacin.

Signs of niacin deficiency include loss of appetite, nausea, vomiting, abdominal pain, headache, dizziness, burning hands and feet, numbness and weakness. In pregnancy, the recommended intake is 16 milligram equivalents of niacin; in lactation, 19 milligram equivalents.

The best sources of niacin are organ meats, meat and fish, and legumes (peanuts, peas, and beans).

Pyridoxine or Vitamin B$_6$

Pyridoxine is essential for the metabolism of fats and fatty acids as well as in the production of antibodies (which help fight disease).

Some pyridoxine is manufactured in the intestines by bacteria. However, some must be provided by diet. Lack of pyridoxine results in dermatitis around the eyes, eyebrows, and mouth. As with other B-complex vitamins, deficiency causes sensory disturbances—numbness, tingling, and loss of the sense of position. It may also cause anemia and a decrease in the number of lymphocytes. It has been used to treat the severe vomiting of pregnancy, but there is no scientific evidence of success. The recommended daily allowance is 2.6 milligrams per day.

The best sources of pyridoxine are brewer's yeast, wheat bran, wheat germ, soybeans, brown rice, and blackstrap molasses. Good to fair sources include bananas, barley, beef, corn, liver, heart, kidney, lamb, peanuts, dry peas, pork, rye, salmon, sardines, tomatoes, tuna, veal, white flour, rice, yams, potatoes, carrots, and cabbage.

Pantothenic Acid

Pantothenic acid is found in all living organisms. This ubiquitous substance is vital to the proper functioning of the adrenal glands as well as for carbohydrate and fat metabolism. It helps to maintain normal skin, normal growth, and normal development of the central nervous system.

Dr. Roger Williams, who first isolated and synthesized pantothenic acid, reports, in his book *Nutrition Against Disease*, on research in France in which female rats were fed a diet deficient in this vitamin. Those receiving very little were not able to deliver any baby rats. As the deficiency was diminished, the reproductive success increased. He further notes that a good number of defects such as prematurity, stillborns, mental retardation and malformation may be the result of a lack of pantothenic acid.

Although most sources state that a pantothenic acid deficiency in the human diet is unlikely, prudence dictates that while pregnant you make a special effort to eat more foods containing large amounts of pantothenic acid. Although the average daily intake is 10 to 20 milligrams and the excretion rates range from 2.5 to 9.5

milligrams, Dr. Williams wagers that providing women in the childbearing years with up to 50 milligrams per day would decrease reproductive failures.

The best sources of pantothenic acid are organ meats, eggs, peanuts and wheat bran—which contain anywhere from 2.1 to 8.9 milligrams per 100-gram portion; liver, beef, broccoli, mushrooms, oats, dried peas, fresh pork, whole wheat, wheat germ, containing from 1 to 2 milligrams per 100 grams; and dried lima beans, cauliflower, cheese, chicken, lamb, oysters, peas, bacon, ham, white potato, sweet potato, salmon, whole wheat bread, containing from 0.5 to 1 milligram per 100 grams.

Biotin

Biotin was first synthesized from egg yolk. Among its functions is to aid in the synthesis of some fatty acids and amino acids. The amount of biotin needed has not been established, but deficiencies (skin lesions, lack of appetite, insomnia, muscle pain, and changes in the electrical activity of the heart) have been seen. The usual intake of biotin from American diets is 150 to 300 milligrams, which is considered to be sufficient.

Raw egg white contains a substance known as avidin which combines with biotin to render it useless to the body. Cooking egg white destroys the avidin. It is unlikely anyone would eat enough raw egg to cause biotin deficiency, but it has happened.

The best sources of biotin are cooked eggs, liver, peanuts, chocolate, dried peas and beans, nuts, cauliflower, and mushrooms.

Folic Acid

Folic acid got its name from Latin: *folium*, leaf, since it was first discovered in spinach leaves. This vitamin is extremely important in pregnancy because it is essential for normal growth of cells. The need for folic acid increases greatly during pregnancy, the pregnant woman requiring as much as 800 micrograms (0.8 milligrams). Some medical experts have pointed to an increase in premature separation of the placenta, toxemia, premature birth, hemorrhage, and even infant birth defects when the mother receives too little folic acid. Be sure your prenatal vitamin contains folic acid. For some years, nonprescription prenatal vitamins contained insufficient folic acid to meet pregnancy requirements. That they are now adequate is due to the efforts of physicians who pointed out the relationship between lack of folic acid and problems in pregnancy. In addition, the use of alcohol, and certain other drugs such as Dilantin sodium (diphenylhydantoin—used in its salt form to treat grand mal epilepsy) interfere with the body's ability to use folic acid.

There are two forms of folic acid in foods. The free acid is only slightly soluble in water. The salt is much more soluble and may be poured down the drain if you discard cooking water. Long storage of food and overcooking destroy folic acid. Liver, including chicken liver, is a good source. Asparagus, broccoli, cauliflower, beet greens, endive, kale, spinach and turnip greens are all good sources. Vegetables like cabbage and white potato are variable sources depending on the length and method of storage.

Cobalamin or Vitamin B_{12}

Vitamin B_{12} is essential for the development of red blood cells and for proper growth in children. Its deficiency results in macrocytic anemia. It is available in animal protein and highest in organ meats. Muscle meats and fish are medium sources. Other sources include corn, wheat, soybeans, yeast and milk. There is a real danger of deficiency in true vegetarians—those who eat no animal products. According to an animal nutritionist friend, one excellent source of B_{12}, though hardly of interest in the human diet, is the manure of herbivorous mammals like the cow. The microorganisms of their digestive tract manufacture B_{12}. Humans, however, must provide theirs through diet or supplements—the amount recommended in pregnancy being 4 micrograms.

Lipoic Acid

Lipoic acid is a sulfur-containing fatty acid which, while not a true vitamin, is closely related in function to thiamine. It is necessary in carbohydrate metabolism. The amount needed is not known yet. Among the best sources are liver and yeast.

Para-aminobenzoic Acid (PABA)

PABA is a component in the formation of folic acid. It is used as a drug in fighting rickettsial diseases such as typhus and Rocky Mountain spotted fever. The food sources are the same as for folic acid.

Inositol

Inositol is a substance found in muscle tissue and closely related to glucose. It is also found in brain and eye tissue and in red blood cells. The function is uncertain. Although intestinal bacteria may manufacture it, it is also widespread in nature, being found in meat, milk, fruits, grains, nuts and legumes.

Choline

Choline is undoubtedly manufactured by the body. It is allied to protein metabolism. It forms an important part of the phospholipids, lecithin used in fat metabolism, and sphingomyelin in the brain and nerves. Choline is also a component of acetylcholine, which is necessary for the transmission of impulses from nerve to nerve. Protein foods such as meats, eggs, grains, and legumes contain choline.

Vitamin C or Ascorbic Acid

Vitamin C is undoubtedly the first vitamin actually recognized by man. Descriptions of scurvy, the deficiency disease, date back to ancient Egypt. The prevalence of scurvy aboard ships during the period of exploration following Columbus's voyage led to various "cures" ranging from pine needles to lemon juice. Eventually an English surgeon decided that a substance in citrus fruits must be the answer, thus making limes and lemons a daily part of the English sailors' diet. This decision undoubtedly helped insure Britain's supremacy at sea and gained for the sailors the epithet "Limeys."

It was not until 1932 that the substance was finally isolated and positively identified. One of the fascinating facts about vitamin C is that, though we usually think of it as being a component of citrus fruits, it is available in the basic foods in each climate. For example, the potato and cabbage, which are staples for those of us in the northern reaches of the temperate zone, are good sources of vitamin C.

Other than man, the guinea pig and primates are the only common mammals who are not able to manufacture the vitamin within their bodies.

Vitamin C might be said to supply the cement that holds the cells together. It is important in bone and tooth formation, repair of fractures, wound healing, and maintenance of the strength of blood vessels. It helps with the utilization of iron and the maturing of red blood cells. Ascorbic acid is important for the use of folic acid, and a relationship may exist between it and vitamin A. In rats, there have been indications that vitamin C can reverse the toxicity of overdoses of vitamin A and can also alleviate some symptoms of vitamin A deficiency in these same animals.

Vitamin C helps the body to resist infection. Consequently, infection, fever, and other bodily stress factors deplete the body of vitamin C. Other factors which interfere with absorption and/or levels of ascorbic acid in the body include smoking, alcohol, the "pill," and aspirin.

While 20 to 30 milligrams of C daily is enough to prevent clinical signs of scurvy, you can readily see why that is not the optimum amount to carry on the functions of this important vitamin. In the 1979 revision of the Recommended Daily Allowances (RDA), the National Research Council increased the RDA for pregnancy to 80 milligrams and in lactation to 100 milligrams. Obviously individual needs may differ depending on the various factors that inhibit vitamin C absorption and metabolism (smoking, for example) and the biochemical individuality of each person.

You can be aware of some of the signs that your intake of vitamin C is lower than optimal. Swollen reddened gums, susceptibility to infection, and easy bruising all may be indicators that you need more of this fragile vitamin. Increase your intake of C-rich foods. The best sources of vitamin C include citrus fruits, cantaloupe, strawberries, sweet red and green pepper, broccoli, kale, tomatoes, potatoes, cauliflower and parsley.

Overcooking, cooking in too much water, and careless storage destroy C. It is stable in acid media. Cooking tomatoes, for example, destroys relatively little of their C.

Bioflavonoids

Bioflavonoids and ascorbic acid are associated in nature. Some studies have indicated that flavonoids may be useful in treating thromboembolism and in reducing blood cholesterol levels in rats. They have, however, been deprived of the name vitamin and are not officially considered essential nutrients.

THE MINERALS

The last group of nutrients which are essential to man are the minerals. These are distributed in nature in many forms and are constituents of numerous vital body materials. Some of them, such as calcium, we need in large amounts. Others are only present in tiny traces and may be lacking in certain soils or eliminated in foods through the refining process.

Calcium

Calcium is one mineral with which we are all familiar. It is an important part of bone and teeth. The body uses it in many other ways—for normal clotting of the blood, to promote muscle tone, and for regulation of the heartbeat.

Absorption of calcium is aided by vitamins C and D. A certain amount of fat is needed, but too much may hinder absorption. Calcium occurs in milk with fat in a ratio which seems to enhance absorption. Lactose, the sugar of milk, also aids in the absorption of calcium.

There are other factors that negatively influence calcium absorption. Among these are oxalic and phytic acids and an alkaline rather than acidic intestinal environment. Oxalic acid is found in certain leafy green vegetables such as spinach and beet greens and in rhubarb. Fortunately, all contain some calcium since the oxalic acid combines with calcium to form highly insoluble calcium oxalate. As such, it is no longer available to the body. These vegetables are valuable for the other nutrients they contain and should not be avoided because of their tendency to bind calcium. Phytic acid is present in whole grains, especially wheat. A diet very high in whole wheat and low in calcium-containing foods could cause losses of calcium greater than intake. This is another good reason for eating a widely varied diet and not depending on any one food.

Adequate calcium intake in pregnancy is crucial to both your baby and you. Calcium is necessary to build strong teeth and bones. "For every child a tooth" need not apply to you in your pregnancy if you get enough calcium and other nutrients.

The recommended daily allowance of calcium in pregnancy and lactation is 1.2 grams (1.6 grams if you are under age eighteen). Lack of calcium during lactation will decrease your milk supply, so if you have trouble producing enough milk for your baby, increase your intake of calcium foods. One quart of milk contains about 1 gram of calcium. Cheese is another excellent source. Other sources include egg yolk, leafy green vegetables (other than those cited containing oxalic acid), nuts, whole grains (again phytic acid may bind the calcium), peas, beans, and some fish, especially canned sardines and oysters.

Phosphorus

Phosphorus is allied to calcium in the body. It is used in the development and growth of bone and teeth and in the metabolism of muscle, brain and nerve tissue. It is necessary for the maintenance of acid-base balance in the blood and for the activity of vitamins and enzymes. Phosphorus occurs with calcium in milk and other foods. It is also present in meat and fish. If you have an adequate intake of calcium your intake of phosphorus should be ample—a fortunate circumstance since they are interrelated in bone-building and in their definite ratio within the blood serum. The recommended allowances are the same as for calcium.

Magnesium

Magnesium is reasonably abundant in the human body. Much of it is combined in the bone with calcium and phosphorus; the remainder is distributed throughout other tissues of the body.

Deficiency of magnesium can cause dilation of blood vessels, spasm, twitching of muscles, jumpiness, and in severe cases convulsions. Magnesium is needed for the formation of protein from amino acids.

The recommended daily intake is 450 milligrams for women. The major sources of magnesium are nuts, cocoa, peas and beans, oatmeal, brown rice, peanuts, whole wheat, corn, barley, and seafood. It is possible that slight deficiencies of magnesium may be more common than has been recognized. There is no doubt that diets relying heavily on refined grains, meat, and few vegetables could easily be lacking adequate magnesium.

Sodium

Sodium is a crucial component of the body fluids. It is necessary to maintain fluid balance and acid-base balances, thus helping to maintain the normal pH of the blood. Your health depends on these functions. The extent to which fluid balance and pH are important can be recognized by witnessing the havoc raised when they are out of kilter. Consider, for example, the devastating results of heat prostration, burns, and prolonged diarrhea.

Sodium has an effect on the function of muscles including the heart muscle. There is a high loss of salt (sodium) when a person sweats profusely or has prolonged vomiting or diarrhea. In animals, low salt intake results in less efficient digestion of protein and inhibits reproduction. Authorities now believe that pregnancy is one time when sodium should not be limited—in spite of past and present practices.

Common table salt is the major source of sodium in our diets. Those of us who are *not* pregnant may take in considerably more than we need, but the pregnant woman should salt her food to taste unless she has congestive heart failure or kidney disease. There are a number of foods which contain good amounts of sodium, such as milk, eggs, meat, and leafy vegetables.

Potassium

Potassium, like sodium, is important in maintaining fluid balance. It is amply supplied by our normal diet, though in some situations the delicate balance can become disturbed with serious consequences to the heart muscle and to brain function. Certain metabolic diseases such as diabetes and adrenal dysfunction can, if not controlled, result in an upset in potassium metabolism. Certain diuretics (for example, Diuril and Diamox) will cause a loss of potassium. Anyone taking these types of diuretics needs additional potassium in his diet. Excessive cortisone is another cause of potassium deficiency and sodium retention. Severe malnutrition, prolonged vomiting, and diarrhea can result in loss of potassium.

I have observed the effects of potassium deficiency on the elderly, especially following surgery. The confusion and disorientation in a bright, intelligent, usually witty person are disheartening. With administration of potassium, the change is dramatic.

Remember, potassium is supplied in ample amounts by diet. It is only under conditions noted above that more is needed. This is another indication of the body balance and the intricate relationship of nutrients which can be interrupted by interference or illness. It is an excellent reason why in pregnancy, except for such medical problems as congestive heart failure or kidney disease, diuretics should not be prescribed.

Foods containing potassium include bananas, legumes, whole grains, leafy vegetables, meats, and citrus fruits.

Chlorine

Chlorine is another important element in maintaining fluid balance and acid-base balance. It is also contained in hydrochloric acid in the stomach. Just about all of the chlorine in our diet comes from table salt.

Sulfur

As a component of amino acids, sulfur is an essential element in the body. While cud-chewing animals can convert inorganic sulfur to an organic form, humans must get theirs from diet. The major food sources are the amino acids methionine and cystine. If you are a vegetarian, the best vegetable sources are millet, wheat bran, mushrooms, sesame seeds, and brazil nuts. Other vegetable sources are wheat, rye, barley, oatmeal, rice, buckwheat, cornmeal, corn, spinach, sunflower seeds, cashews, pistachio nuts and black walnuts. Eggs, milk, cheese, most fish, and meat are, of course, all good animal sources of the sulfur-containing amino acids. Excessive intake of inorganic sulfur can be toxic. If your diet is adequate in protein (contained in all the essential amino acids), it will be adequate in sulfur.

Iron

Iron is one mineral about which we hear a great deal. It is an essential constituent of hemoglobin, the oxygen-carrying compound in the red blood cells. We must take in a great deal more iron than we absorb. Less than 30 percent (probably close to 10 percent) of the iron we ingest is actually absorbed from the stomach and the first part of the small intestine. Iron is absorbed better in an acid medium, the hydrochloric acid of the stomach being ideal for the absorption of iron. As you know from Chapter Two, hydrochloric acid production is reduced in pregnancy. This is compensated for by a protein-iron compound contained in the cells of the mucosa of the intestines. When the supply of this compound (ferritin) is low, as it is in pregnancy, more iron is absorbed.

Vitamin C also enhances iron absorption and utilization. Yet another important factor is high calcium intake. Phosphates, phytates, and oxalates interfere with iron-absorption-forming insoluble iron salts. If calcium intake is high, it will help to bind these agents, making more iron available for absorption.

It is important to note that some of the forms of iron enrichment of foods may be of little use in the body. Often, phosphate compounds of iron are used to enrich refined cereals and flours. We know phosphates are insoluble in the human digestive tract. There is a possibility that in processing and cooking, iron phosphates may be changed to a point where at least some of it is absorbable. The problem is, how much?

I have corresponded with the manager of nutritional services for a food corporation regarding the following statement on their cans of instant cocoa mix: "Each serving of 2 heaping teaspoonfuls . . . supplies 50 percent of the minimum daily requirements of . . . iron. . . . " The opposite side of the can gives the iron source as ferric orthophosphate. First, ferric forms of iron are less efficiently absorbed than ferrous forms. Second, phosphates are highly insoluble.

He admitted that this was so but pointed out that processing may render it more available, citing references which report a higher availability after processing of sodium iron pyrophosphate. The problem is, what processing of what foods? He pointed out that in 1971 the company began a research project "aimed at determining the true availability of iron from [their product], as well as our other iron-fortified products. In the very near future, we will have a much better understanding of iron availability as it relates to our products."

In the meantime, a person buying the cocoa mix would have believed that two glasses of milk with the mix added would provide the whole day's quota of iron. It is possible their research project has been completed with negative results, since on a trip to the supermarket, I picked up a new can of their product to find that the claim as well as the enrichment had been eliminated.

Cooking in cast-iron cookware is one way of adding iron to your diet. Used for sautéing, heavy cast-iron skillets can appreciably increase the iron content of foods cooked in them. Spaghetti sauce cooked in a cast-iron dutch oven contains immense amounts of iron at the expense of vitamin C. Be discriminating about what you cook in your cast-iron pots. Do not heat or cook high vitamin C vegetables in them since the iron causes destruction of the vitamin C. The iron content of the American diet has dropped with the lessened use of cast-iron cookware.

The Food and Drug Administration's recent order to double the iron content of white bread because of the decline in the use of cast-iron utensils has set up a reaction from a number of physicians. They are afraid of an iron overload as a result. Perhaps people who live on white bread will be at some risk. Perhaps a wiser course on the part of the FDA would be to carry out an educational campaign to promote judicious use of cast-iron cookware.

Your iron requirements in pregnancy are greatly increased, due not only to your own increased need, but also because you must provide enough iron to last your infant through his first four to six months of independent life. The recommended daily allowance for a woman throughout adolescence and childbearing years is 18 milligrams with up to a 60-milligram supplement in pregnancy. A 4-ounce serving of liver provides 10 milligrams; a 3-ounce lean hamburger patty (about 5 patties per pound) provides 3 milligrams; 2 boiled eggs will give you 2.3 milligrams; 3 ounces of clams, 5.2 milligrams; 1 cup of cooked dried beans or peas, over 4 milligrams; and 1 tablespoon blackstrap molasses, 3.2 milligrams. Other foods which provide reasonable amounts of iron include meats, fish, whole wheat, leafy green vegetables, prunes and raisins.

Copper

Copper works with iron in the formation of hemoglobin. While deficiencies are unusual, about 2.5 milligrams are required daily. Copper deficiency results in an iron-deficiency anemia and a whitening of hair. The best sources are liver, oysters, wheat, rye, oats, avocado, dry peas and beans, corn, eggs, prunes, and dark green leafy vegetables.

Iodine

Iodine is needed by the body in only very tiny amounts (100 to 200 micrograms or 0.1 to 0.2 milligrams daily). But even that tiny amount is crucial to our health and well-being. Without iodine, we can develop goiter and enlargement of the thyroid gland in its attempt to produce more thyroxine. Thyroxine is the hormone which regulates metabolism. With an insufficient supply, one becomes intolerant to cold; his appetite declines though he may become heavy; his skin thickens; his hair becomes coarse, dry, and thin; his voice gets husky; he may become dull, irritable, and disagreeable, and he will probably find it difficult or impossible to reproduce.

If during pregnancy you fail to take in enough iodine, your baby could be born with a thyroid deficiency. A child born with this condition is known as a cretin. He must take thyroid extract all of his life, yet he still may be limited intellectually if the deficiency developed early in his prenatal life.

Because soils may be deficient in iodine, iodine deficiencies were once widespread in mountainous areas and those removed from the sea. The addition of iodine to table salts has nearly eliminated the problem. It is wise to use iodized salt in order to prevent iodine deficiency. Seafoods are the only other guaranteed source of iodine since vegetables will not contain the element unless it is available in the soil in which they are grown.

Manganese

Manganese is found in the pancreas, kidneys, sex organs, skin, muscle and bones. The role of manganese in human nutrition is not clear. It may play a role in cell enzymes for protein, carbohydrate, fat metabolism and urea formation. The requirement is unknown. Best food sources are dried peas and beans, oatmeal, wheat, rice, lettuce, bananas, corn, spinach, sweet potatoes, kale, beets, and prunes.

Cobalt

Cobalt is present in traces. Being a component of vitamin B_{12}, it is important for the prevention of pernicious anemia. The amount necessary is unknown, but good sources grown on soils containing cobalt (and most do except in some circumscribed regions of the world) are onions, pears, potatoes, spinach, turnip greens, beans, peas, cabbage, walnuts, Swiss chard, buckwheat, and apricots.

Zinc

Zinc is relatively abundant in many tissues of the body. It is a component of enzymes used in carbohydrate and protein metabolism. It is tied in with pancreatic function, particularly insulin storage. It is also present in white blood cells. Just recently, researchers at the National Heart and Lung Institute reported that undersized children who ate poorly had low levels of zinc in their bodies. When fed foods rich in zinc, their appetites improved, probably because the zinc improved their senses of taste and smell. Dr. Robert I. Henkin, one of the researchers, reported that he believed copper and nickel deficiencies may also be responsible for poor appetite.

Foods rich in zinc include organ meats, lean meat and poultry, fish and seafood, eggs, dried peas and beans, brussels sprouts, cocoa, oatmeal, and peanuts.

Molybdenum

Molybdenum is found in the body in minute amounts. It is a component of various enzymes. The sources include legumes, whole grains, dark green leafy vegetables, liver, kidney, spleen, fruits, berries, root or stem vegetables, and brewer's yeast.

Fluorine

Fluorine in tiny amounts helps to protect the teeth from decay. It can be detrimental to adults who habitually take in too much, causing abnormal density of the bone. The greatest danger from fluoridated water supplies exists if the water is used for kidney dialysis which can result in a huge intake for the person being treated. There have also been a few reports of reactions to fluorides causing severe behavior problems. Perhaps the ideal answer to the fluoride problem would be fluoride supplements and/or dental treatment with fluoride, since its benefits are confined to babies and children. There appears to be little value to supplementing the pregnant woman's diet with fluoride, since the element does not cross the placental barrier in significant amounts.[6] Food sources of fluoride are eggs, fish (especially mackerel), chocolate, chicken, cheese, parsley, and tea.

Other Elements

Chromium has been found to effect sugar metabolism. It is needed only in tiny amounts. Selenium has a probable role in fat metabolism. Aluminum's function is not known. Boron's role is still a mystery, though there are tiny traces found in the body. The function of cadmium still is not defined.

You can see there is still much to be learned in human nutrition. If one thing can be driven home through this nutritional information, it is the intricate interrelationship of all the nutrients, and the fact that a widely varied diet of relatively unrefined and less-processed foods should be consumed.

Nutritional Supplements

Should one take vitamin-mineral supplements during pregnancy? Since we still do not know all there is to know about human nutrition, no supplement can possibly be considered complete. Only a widely varied diet can provide all of the nutrients we need. There is also a certain danger inherent in relying on food supplements for our nutrients. We may easily fall into bad habits.

[6]De Paola, D. P. and M. M. Kuftinec, "Nutrition in Growth and Development of Oral Tissues," *Dental Clinics of North America*, 20 (1976):441.

Believing our needs are met, we might avoid important foods that provide trace minerals, unknown vitamins, and other vital dietary factors whose deficiencies—while not causing a dramatically fatal disease like scurvy or beriberi—might, nevertheless, deplete our resources and leave us more susceptible to degenerative diseases.

Each person is an individual and has an individual body chemistry. The amounts of nutrients actually needed vary from person to person according to size, metabolic rates, and the influence of many internal and external factors. Much depends on your nutritional status at the start of pregnancy, too. Research on reproductive success in World War II has shown that some women had good babies in spite of famine and starvation, while others aborted, had stillborns, or produced babies that could not survive. Much of the difference in outcome was attributed to their prior nutritional status.

When I was pregnant with my first child, the doctor did not want me to take supplements. He told me to eat a good diet and prescribed no supplements at all. In early pregnancy, I was teaching high school English and physical education, requiring a great deal of stamina and energy. The latter five months of that pregnancy, I taught maternal and infant health in a hospital school of nursing. That job also required a great deal of exercise and walking.

Because I recognized the value of good nutrition, I was careful to prepare well-balanced, nourishing meals. To my doctor's horror, I gained thirty pounds which, incidentally, I lost within days of delivery. My baby weighed over nine pounds.

He was the most active, vigorous baby I have ever seen. He turned over by himself at ten days, stood up in his crib at five and one-half months, and was walking by himself at eight and one-half months. To top it off, now at age twenty-three, he has yet to have a filling in his teeth, though in his early years, our water supplies were not fluoridated. In addition, he has missed only two days of school in four years.

With my other children I did take supplements, and with the second and third tried unsuccessfully to limit weight gain. While both were large and vigorous, their teeth are not nearly as good as those of their older brother—in spite of fluoridated water supplies. The youngest had the benefit of both supplements and a nutritious diet. She is a lovely, healthy little girl.

First, when your doctor prescribes a supplement, check to see that it contains adequate folic acid (0.8 milligrams or more). Second, do not rely on the supplement to provide your nutrients. Think of it only as a supplement. If supplements are taken as a means of meeting requirements in spite of diet, then the purpose is defeated. They should be considered as an addition to a nutritionally sound diet. Third, make every calorie you consume a nutritional plus, not an empty filler.

CHAPTER FIVE

CONSERVING NUTRIENTS

Even though you know what foods to eat, it will do little good if you do not choose them carefully, store them properly, and prepare them so they retain their nutrients. When you shop in the supermarket, make it a habit to pick and choose—carefully, wisely reading labels. Get the best value for your food dollar.

BREAD

If you do not make it yourself, one item you will buy most frequently is bread. Witness the blown-up, soft, squishy wind pudding being sold as bread. Enriched? Yes, with three of the B vitamins, an iron preparation which may or may not be well utilized by your body, and in some cases calcium—also of dubious value depending upon its source. The loaves usually have some type of mold inhibitor added so they will last longer on the shelf and in your bread box.

Choose a bread with a high proportion of whole grains. Some companies such as Arnold and Pepperidge Farm put out bread which is entirely whole grain. The reason for preferring whole grains is that they contain various trace minerals as well as additional B vitamins and vitamin E which are lost from white flour in the milling and bleaching processes. It is the *germ* of the grain which contains the bulk of the nutrients. It is the *germ* of the grain which is removed in the refining process.

Ingredients are listed according to amounts, starting from the major ingredients down to the least important. Wheat flour refers to the usual refined white flour, so don't be misled. French and Italian breads are not nutritionally superior to the soft American variety. In fact, they probably contain fewer nutrients even if they are enriched, since they are usually made with water rather than milk. They may be fun on special occasions, but because they provide mostly empty calories, they should not be considered the staff of life. Look for whole wheat, rye, oatmeal, and various combinations of grains. Check the weight. The large blown-up loaves may be lighter than the more compact loaves. By letting the yeast work overtime and using inferior ingredients (water instead of milk) and adding artificial coloring, the baker can conjure you into buying an inferior, profit-laden product if you are not an inveterate label reader.

The cakes, cookies, and coffee rolls are of no use. Most of them are not even made with enriched flour. Some sugary sweets are "fortified" with innumerable vitamins. This fact does not make them good food. They still contain little or no protein which you so desperately need in pregnancy, nor do they contain the trace minerals or other possibly vital nutrients whose "minimum daily requirements" have still to be established. Worse, they are usually laden with sucrose and myriad chemicals which may or may not be safe. Why use these wholly artificial, high-caloric, sham substitutes for good nutrition? They are a very expensive way to buy vitamins.

With bread and pastry items so high in price today, you will be fortunate to locate a commercial outlet where you can buy at reduced prices (better yet would be to bake your own bread). Commercial bread which contains preservatives will keep in your bread box for days. If you buy several loaves at once, keep the extras frozen or refrigerated. Unpreserved bread, either purchased or homemade, should be refrigerated or frozen if you intend to keep it for more than a couple of days.

DRINKS

What are your choices in drinks? It is not possible to find a soda pop that is really good for anyone. Most of them are merely concoctions of chemicals and sugar, some even with possibly harmful additives. They will do nothing for you except ruin your teeth, add useless calories, and take up room in your stomach which should be used by natural fruit juices, milk, and pure cleansing water. And they are expensive! They cost as much as fresh milk and considerably more than nonfat dry milk. They are far more expensive than pure natural fruit juices.

Beer, wines, and liquor should be avoided during pregnancy even though the former two do contain some nutrients. The possibility of subjecting your baby to fetal alcohol syndrome is not worth the risk. Ideally, abstinence is the goal to strive for. Remember, each time you drink, your baby drinks. Think of the effect alcohol has on your ability to function and just imagine the effect that same concentration of alcohol has on the tiny fetus.

DAIRY PRODUCTS

The dairy case deserves your consideration. Fresh milk, buttermilk, yoghurt, cottage cheese and a whole host of natural cheeses await your pleasure. Buy plain yoghurt and use it to make your own from nonfat milk at far less expense. The flavored yoghurts are spiked with unnecessary sugar. Flavor your own with fresh fruit and a little honey, if necessary. Remember, if you have an intolerance to the lactose of sweet milk, buttermilk, yoghurt, and cheeses should be your choice. The lactose has been converted to lactic acid and should not cause you difficulty.

Natural cheeses are usually your best buy. They provide more flavor per pound than do the pasteurized process cheeses, which are a blend of aged and fresh cheeses. Process cheeses tend to be more bland and less tasty than the natural cheeses. Pasteurization stops the aging process, so process cheeses do not continue ripening and aging as the natural ones do. Cheese foods and cheese spreads are truly inferior, gum-laden, watery concoctions. They are bland and pallid, containing a number of chemicals, coloring agents, fillers, and artificial and natural flavors. Considering their contents, they are a poor value for their cost, providing far too little good nutrition. It is important to point out that it is only by careful search and label reading that you can avoid the cheese foods. They come packaged in an excellent imitation of the process cheeses. It is only through searching that you can sometimes locate the cheese-food label. The fact that the companies go to such great lengths to disguise the product to make you think you are buying the higher quality cheese is a good proof of profit incentive.

Dairy products should be kept refrigerated until ready to use.

Pick the freshest milk or milk product you can find. Bacteria multiply rapidly in milk left at room temperature. Nonfat dry milk should be stored in a cool dry place, and evaporated milk should also be kept cool and dry.

Eggs cannot be overemphasized. Even at current high prices, they are an excellent bargain, being a good source of protein, iron, vitamin A, and other nutrients. The color of the egg shell in no way changes the quality of the egg, even though northern New Englanders are willing to pay more for brown eggs, while white eggs command a higher price on the New York market. Being from brown-egg country, I prefer them, but I buy whatever is less expensive rather than indulge an idiosyncrasy.

Eggs need to be handled and stored properly. They absorb odors easily, which may affect the flavor of the egg. Fresh grade A eggs have a high yolk. The whites may be cloudy, stick to the shell, and remain close to the yolk and thick when dropped into the pan. The yolk does not break easily. Eggs are excellent for poaching, frying, coddling, and baking. When boiled, they may be hard to peel.

Grade B eggs may have a wider, flatter yolk. The white is transparent and spreads out more. The eggs graded C spread out with wide, flat yolks that are easily broken. They are best used for adding to dishes for boiling or scrambling.

The quality of eggs deteriorates rapidly by improper storage at room temperature. Cracked eggs may harbor salmonella, the organism often responsible for food poisoning, and should be used only for dishes that are thoroughly cooked. In fact, it is wise to use only cooked eggs, in any event, for an unbroken egg may contain salmonella and uncooked egg white interferes with the absorption of biotin (a B vitamin).

Cooked egg products should be refrigerated immediately to prevent the buildup of bacteria. Do not buy cooked egg products (custards, cheese cakes, etc.) which have not been kept refrigerated. And be sure they are fresh.

FISH AND SEAFOOD

Fresh fish should be fresh! Preferably it should be kept on chipped ice—not wrapped in plastic and left on the meat cooler. Fresh fish does not smell bad. It has a relatively sweet bland smell. Fillets should be firm and properly colored for the type of fish—halibut, flounder, turbot, sole, cod, and haddock—clean and white. Hake is white with pinkish areas; salmon, pale pink to red with brownish fatty areas near the backbone. Fresh herring is cream colored with brownish fatty areas. Pollock is white, but tends more toward a gray than do the other white fish. It's a relatively inexpensive fish, perfectly tasty, often salted and dried. Unscrupulous dealers occasionally try to substitute it for the expensive haddock. Ocean perch fillets are also white, but are small and have a pink color on the side where the skin has been removed.

Whole fish should be firm with bright eyes. The flesh should be pleasant smelling. Be sure to watch for any abundant local fish specialties of your area. Examples are smelts, alewives and others which have seasonal runs. Shark is often available in some markets and is a remarkably tasty fish, broiled and seasoned with lemon.

Smoked fish can be fresh smoked with little salt as are: finnan haddie (smoked haddock), smoked whole bloaters (alewives), or smoked fillets (cod or other white fish). These smell quite pleasant, like well-smoked bacon with fish overtones, and may be delicate and tasty. They spoil readily and must be used right away.

Salt-smoked fish—herring and alewife fillets—keep longer, are stronger in smell, and very salty. See Chapter Three for information on the use of nitrates and nitrites in smoked fish.

There is no waste to fish fillets, so they may provide more high quality protein per pound than do the leanest of meats. They have somewhat less iron but are still very good sources. Fish must be refrigerated and used up rapidly. Fresh fillets and whole fish freeze very successfully.

Shellfish are an excellent source of trace minerals as well as protein. Mollusks, like clams, oysters, and scallops, must come from uncontaminated water. If you dig clams yourself, be sure you do not take them from polluted flats. Commercial dealers are able to retain mollusks in unpolluted areas long enough to cleanse them of contaminants. Mollusks are high in nutrients and when purchased shelled have no waste. Even at relatively high prices, you will find they are far less costly than steak and many other meats when you consider the number of servings per pound. Incidentally, when buying meat and fish, choose in terms of cost per serving rather than cost per pound.

Shrimp may be used fresh, frozen or canned. Lobster, however, deteriorates in flavor and tends to toughen if frozen. Crab can be used in many of the same dishes as lobster. It does freeze more successfully than lobster. The price of lobster is usually so high that it is a luxury food. However, if you live in a lobster-producing area, buy some cooked bodies, pick out the meat and use it for a tasty lobster stew.

MEATS

You will be better off buying a lower grade of meat and using a tenderizer or cooking it long and slowly. The lower grades contain less fat, hence more protein, so they not only give you better yield for your money, but are more nutritious. If you have a butcher, you can probably buy better beef (more nutritious, that is) more cheaply than you can get it in supermarkets where they frequently sell only USDA "choice" cuts. It may be that local or native beef will be your best buy. The animals usually have not been force-fed with doctored grain since they are often culls from local dairy farms. Use tenderizer and the native beef will probably have more flavor than the overfed, doctored, stockyard variety. Be sure you don't pay a premium price for pretenderized beef. You can do it yourself far more cheaply.

When buying meats, keep away from the fatty cuts having a large percentage of bone. Note the amount of waste in the cut you buy to determine the cost per serving. When buying hamburger, be sure you note the fat content. Some dealers are labeling their ground beef by the percentage of fat contained in it. Do some quick calculations to determine just how much you are paying for the lean meat.

Chicken continues to be one of the best meat values available, even though with inflation, the price per pound has nearly doubled. Turkey prices have not kept pace with inflation. In fact, one can still buy turkeys for little more than they cost in 1965.

Variety meats provide good quality for the money. Liver, particularly pork liver, is always an excellent buy. Lamb liver is delicate and tasty and usually costs about the same as pork liver. Beef liver may run about ten cents more a pound than the others. Calves liver is very expensive and no more nutritious. Often baby beef liver is available. I buy a whole one at a local meat packinghouse, cut it exactly as I want it, and freeze it in family-size amounts. If you plan on freezing the liver you buy at a store, be sure it has not been previously frozen. Chicken livers are also reasonable in price when chicken is available on special.

One of the liver's functions is to detoxify, or purify, the blood. You may hear that it contains a higher concentration of pesticides, antibiotics, etc., if these have been fed to the livestock. The nutritious value of liver is such, however, that one should eat it once a week without fail. Since hydrocarbon pesticides like DDT are stored in fat and liver is low in fat, it is probably as free of these pesticides as meat. If you are really concerned, try to buy liver from native animals if you can. Lambs are unlikely to have been fed undesirable products. We need to keep things in perspective and decide which is more important. Remember, a nutritious diet is protective.

Heart is an excellent muscle meat and contains very little waste. It is tasty when used in stews or stuffed and braised. Tongue is another relatively inexpensive variety meat. Kidneys are high in nutrients and very tasty, either by themselves or combined with beef. There is practically no waste. Brains and sweetbreads are delicate and nutritious but must be used when fresh.

Veal is usually prohibitive in cost, but lamb may be available at reasonable prices. Kid is lamblike and, with the current trend toward goat-raising, should be available in some areas. Lamb and veal recipes can be used for cooking kid. Some of you may have wild game as a seasonal source of protein.

Buying variety luncheon meats such as bologna and salami is expensive compared to deli-sliced turkey breast, boiled ham, and roast beef. The fillers and extenders as well as the various additives used in variety luncheon meats contribute to a high cost per gram of protein. All beef bologna contains 3.4 grams protein per ounce, with 8.1 grams fat and 88 calories. Contrast that with one ounce of each of the following: turkey breast, 7.7 grams protein, 2 grams fat, 59 calories; baked ham, 7.5 grams protein, 6.5 grams fat, 123 calories; boiled ham, 5.3 grams protein, 4.8 grams fat, 66 calories. The latter represent good value even when they cost one and one-half or more times as much per pound as luncheon meat.

Meat packers sometimes sell to retail customers in large amounts. If you have a freezer, try to avail yourself of this less expensive way of buying meats. Even if you don't have a freezer, get together with a few friends and plan your meat purchases to take advantage of the lower prices of quantity purchases.

Meat should be stored in a cold area of your refrigerator. Ground meats, unless heavily spiced like sausage, spoil very quickly. If for some reason you misjudge and can't cook a roast when you planned on having it, corn it and treat yourself to a nutritious New England boiled dinner. The recipes are in this book. To freeze meats, wrap them in airtight, moisture-proof wrappings and fast-freeze. Meat which is plain-cooked (without fancy sauces) keeps well. In fact, if you have been involved with civil defense, you know that whole meat roasts can, in a pinch, be used after considerable lengths of time.

Chicken and other poultry should be refrigerated immediately. If roasted with stuffing, the meat should first be removed from the bones, the stuffing removed, and the meat, stuffing and gravy chilled rapidly. The bones and skin can then be covered with water and simmered to produce a good chicken stock.

Cooked ground meats or those cooked with fancy sauces, should be used up as quickly as possible. They also should be chilled immediately. The importance of refrigeration and quick cooling for cooked foods cannot be overemphasized. Not only does it help to maintain the safety of the food, it also helps to protect the nutritive value. Try to keep an accurate inventory of the leftover foods in your refrigerator. Plan your menus around them. Small amounts can be served as appetizers; larger amounts prepared in any number of imaginative ways. Most leftovers can be easily converted to tasty soups; some can even be added to tossed green salads.

FRESH PRODUCE

The produce department of your supermarket may be the most frustrating. Although there are increasing varieties of fruits and vegetables available, many supermarkets package all produce in plastic. Thus, you cannot choose the particular fruits or vegetables you want. Often you will find spoiled fruit within the package you buy. Plastic packing may keep long-storing vegetables like carrots, cabbage, and turnips in good condition; but easily perishable fruits and vegetables quickly become overripe and spoil—i.e., pears, peaches, oranges, grapefruit, and others. In addition the use of excess packaging is ecologically unsound. It is with true horror that I confront such ridiculous situations as plastic-wrapped whole coconuts and bananas. You can help change these situations by calling them to the attention of the produce manager. He is likely to do what he thinks his customers want.

Occasionally insurance regulations may be a problem. The produce manager of a large supermarket where I shop was forced to wrap many of his items after a lady slipped on a grape. Through the requests of his many customers who appreciated his fine department, he was finally able to get the regulation changed.

Another source of fresh produce is the produce market that specializes in fruits and vegetables. If the proprietor is also a distributor in the area, you are likely to find his prices lower than those of most stores, and his produce fresher. If it is a fruit stand or small specialty market, you may pay a premium price. Farmers' markets are another good source of produce. Of course, you are limited to what they have available. If you go shortly before closing, you can often buy items more cheaply because they don't want them to spoil. Local farms may be willing to sell quantities for canning or freezing quite cheaply—and then there are always the pick-it-yourself farms. Just be sure you are getting a bargain. I can buy seconds and drops at a local orchard for less money than other nearby orchards charge for picking them yourself.

Don't neglect the produce that is free for the taking. I'm referring to those truly nutritious and delicious vegetables scorned as weeds by those people who spend their lives chasing crabgrass. The dandelion and peppercress grow wild in most parts of the United States and are there for the taking—be sure you ask permission if they are on property other than your own. For other sources of wild foods, see Euell Gibbons' *Stalking the Wild Asparagus.*[1]

What do you choose for fresh produce? First, look for the specials. The fruits and vegetables that are on sale that week should give you good value for your money. Consider the cost per serving and the nutritive value. For example, lettuce is not particularly high in nutrients. Thus, when the price is high, pass it up for the more nutritious cabbage and endive. Be sure you can use up the produce you buy while it is still fresh. Check to be sure it is a better value than canned or frozen would be. With modern canning methods, the canned goods may be higher in nutrients than so-called fresh produce, depending on how it has been handled and shipped.

[1] David McKay Company, New York, 1962.

The cellophane-packaged tomatoes are not good buys. Better to buy vine-ripened Mexican tomatoes. If you figure out the price per pound, the latter may be cheaper as well as more nutritious. Most of the cellophane-packed tomatoes are picked when immature and then artificially ripened with a resulting lack of flavor and nutrients. The Mexican tomatoes are picked at maturity (though not fully ripe) so are far tastier as well as demonstrably higher in nutritive value. Perhaps if more of us ignore the inferior, tasteless U.S. winter tomatoes, farmers might start growing and harvesting them properly with a better product resulting.[2]

If you have a sunny windowsill, try growing some Tiny Tom or Patio tomatoes in a large plant pot. The vines are attractive and the tomatoes are tasty and high in vitamin C. While you are at it, plant a pot of parsley. It's also high in C and makes a welcome addition to your winter's salads, besides producing a beautiful edible garnish for your cooked dishes.

Potatoes are a staple food in this country. For some people no meal is complete without potatoes. Unfortunately, in this diet-conscious land potatoes have been condemned by many as high in calories. Actually, potatoes are only a little higher in calories than apples, yet each potato contains three grams of protein compared to a trace in an apple; more calcium than an apple; twice as much iron, thiamine, and riboflavin; vastly more niacin; and seven times as much vitamin C. Potatoes also contain varying amounts of folic acid and a number of trace elements. Use solid smooth potatoes with no green on their skins. Store them in a *dark*, cool, dry place. Potatoes should not be exposed to the sun because they will produce the toxic green color which must be cut off. Since more nutrients are concentrated just under the skin, you lose much of the value of the potato. If you get green potatoes from your store, return them for a refund.

CEREALS AND GRAINS

You may find that the natural food store has a better choice of whole grain cereals at a lower price than does your supermarket. In any event, if a natural (or "health") food store is not available in your area, you can do very well in your supermarket.

[2] See *Consumer Reports*, Vol. 38: No. 1, January 1973, p. 68.

Oatmeal or rolled oats is always available. Buy the largest bags they carry for the best value for your money (it is usually cheaper in bags than in the round boxes). Regular oatmeal is tastier and less processed than the quick cooking and takes little more time to prepare. Whole wheat cereals are also readily available. Undegerminated cornmeal is very difficult to find in a supermarket. The degerminated cornmeal, which of course keeps longer, is bereft of the corn germ and just enriched with the usual niacin, thiamine, riboflavin, and iron.

Cold cereals are mostly inferior, sugar-laden products preserved with BHA and/or BHT. There are exceptions. Grape Nuts are without added sugar and preservatives and are enriched. Unfortunately, shredded wheat has either BHA or BHT added. Otherwise, it is a reasonable choice since it loses but little of its food value in the processing. Puffed wheat, while less nutritious, does not contain additives. Be sure to get the enriched variety. Do note the price per pound of various cereals. You will find the whole grains far better value than the empty calorie or sugar-laden, vitamin-dry cereals with their preservatives. Granola, even though it appears expensive, when considered by weight may actually be cheaper than corn flakes. Many of the new commercial brands are high in sugar, containing only a little oil in addition to the oatmeal and sugar. At over $1.00 per pound for oatmeal granola, you pay a premium price for a sugar-laden product. Even at today's high prices, you can make your own for about 60 cents per pound, using expensive honey instead of sugar.

At the natural food store you will find many other types of cereals—rye, rolled wheat, millet, cracked wheat (Bulgur), buckwheat, barley, and others. Experiment with any or all.

Whole grains should be stored in airtight containers in a cool, dry place. If they are finely ground, it would be better to refrigerate them. This applies especially to flours. The more broken down they are, the more they are subject to spoilage—rancidity of the germ oil. Whole-grain flours can be frozen if necessary.

FRUIT JUICES

You will find, if you do some quick arithmetic in your head, that pure fruit juice is invariably cheaper than either fruit drinks or carbonated drinks, "soda pop." Sixteen ounces of pure frozen-orange-juice concentrate, which will make one-half gallon, costs less than $1.25, while soda pop costs from $1.00 to $1.50 for one-half gallon. Tomato juice and unsweetened pineapple juice also represent good value at less than $1.00 for a 46-ounce can. Apple juice and apple cider are both available for approximately the same price as soda pop. Pure unsweetened grape juice is another possibility. It can be used to concoct a fruit cocktail extraordinaire.

Other possibilities are unsweetened grapefruit juice, prune and fig juice, cranberry juice, and apricot nectar. The latter, though sweetened, is far superior to drinks having nothing but sweetness to offer. Be sure you read the labels carefully so you know what you are buying. Look for the word "drink" on the label. If the name is followed by "drink," it is not pure fruit juice but just an inferior concoction. You are paying extra for a less nutritious product. Don't be misled by the powdered "breakfast drinks" that are high in vitamin C. They are just concoctions of chemicals combined with sugar. You might as well buy vitamin C tablets since they are far cheaper. Another product which is inferior to the real thing is the one which is advertised as better than plain orange juice. It has a higher price, but if one can call additions of corn syrup, citric acid, etc., as producing a better product than pure orange juice, then it is a shock to me. If you must add them do it yourself—it's cheaper.

For those of you who are "hooked" on soda pop, you might try making your own from pure concentrated juices. Buy plain seltzer water or soda water and dilute frozen concentrated juices with it. That way you can continue to indulge your taste for the "fizzy" drinks but without sacrificing good nutrition.

CANNED AND FROZEN FRUITS

Many fruits are available without added sugar. Whole strawberries, raspberries, and blueberries are often frozen with no sugar added. Pineapple and blueberries are frequently canned without sugar. Pineapple in all forms is available unsweetened, canned in its own juice, and no more costly than that packed in sugar syrup. Other fruits may be found water-packed or juice-packed, such as apples, apricots, pears and peaches. Unsweetened canned orange and grapefruit sections are always available. The diet food section may yield water-packed fruits, though they sometimes have extraneous substances added. Also because of the word "dietetic" on the can, the cost may be higher.

RICE, DRIED PEAS AND BEANS

Brown rice is available at supermarkets. You may, however, find it is cheaper at the natural food store. If for some reason you want white rice, get the "converted" white rice which retains more of its nutrients than ordinary white rice.

Dried peas, beans, and lentils provide incomplete protein and represent a relatively inexpensive protein addition to your diet if accompanied by a complete protein or another complementary protein. Soybeans are among the most nutritious but are often unavailable at the supermarket. Incidentally, you can find soybeans toasted for a nutritious snack food.

The legumes are good sources of B vitamins, iron, and numerous other nutrients. Consequently they should have a prominent role in your food planning, especially in this inflationary time.

CRACKERS AND SNACKS

Many crackers are made of unenriched refined bleached flours. A number of snack crackers and crisps contain additives including BHA and BHT. Hardtack is a whole rye cracker without additives. Graham crackers, while made partly of white flour and sugar, are reasonably good. Read ingredients and compare the contents.

FLOURS

Buy whole grain flours—rye, whole wheat, graham. Many flours are bromated to make them less palatable to weevils. If you are not one of the unfortunate few who are sensitive to bromides, this shouldn't cause you any problems. Robin Hood graham and whole-wheat flours are not bromated at this writing. If you use white flour, try to buy unbleached, enriched white flour. King Arthur is a brand available in the East. Bleaching rapes the flour of most of the nutrients remaining after the germ and bran have been removed.

At your natural food store you will be able to find such flours as barley, buckwheat, and undegerminated cornmeal. Be sure to store them in airtight containers in a cold place.

OILS AND SHORTENING

Read oil and shortening labels carefully. Even though the label states boldly "100 percent pure corn oil," close inspection may show BHA and BHT added to protect flavor. All of the shortenings vary. Even some lard has numerous additives. The most important thing is to read the labels. As you know, not all preservatives are bad, nor are all those of unproven safety necessarily unsafe when taken in tiny amounts occasionally. However, those as ubiquitous as BHA and BHT which accumulate in the body should be avoided when possible.

At this time BHA and BHT are not ingredients in Planters Peanut Oil (strangely it is in Fleischmann's Oil put out by the same company), Wesson Oil, Ann Page Corn Oil (A & P Company), Crisco Shortening, Crisco Oil, or olive oil. Some liquid oils are also partially hydrogenated. Be sure to continue checking labels because what is pure today may not be tomorrow. Worse is the fact that these additives are usually found in tiny print, well hidden on an inconspicuous part of the label.

FOOD PREPARATION

After buying wisely and storing carefully, you must prepare foods so they retain their nutrients.

Vegetables should be cooked in as little water as possible. Some, such as summer squash and many greens, need no water added at all. Cook vegetables only until tender-crisp. The Chinese stir-fry method is an excellent one which insures a maximum retention of nutrients. Leftover vegetable water may be thickened and used as a sauce, added to soups and gravy, or used in baking as the water in bread.

When adding vegetables to soups, time their addition so they will be just cooked at serving time. Add any previously cooked vegetables just prior to serving to heat through.

Bake or boil potatoes in their skins in order to preserve their nutrients. The skins of the boiled potatoes are easily slipped off with no waste.

Vegetables to be frozen must be blanched first in order to prevent aging enzymes from causing them to deteriorate. Studies show that unblanched frozen vegetables deteriorate very rapidly with a resulting loss of vitamin content. I have found that many directions for freezing give too long a blanching time. From experience I have learned that the ideal length of time to blanch vegetables is until they change color, becoming much brighter. The greens get greener, the oranges and yellows brighten. This is a better guide than most of the timetables found in cookbooks since the time varies with the size, freshness, and variety of the vegetable.

It is well to remember in buying frozen vegetables (and other frozen foods) that the presence of ice crystals in the package indicates that the food may have been partially thawed or may have been stored at temperatures above 0° F., the ideal frozen food storage temperature.

If cooking fruits like apples, pears, and peaches, it is wise to cook them in their skins until just done. If the skins are too tough to eat, purée the fruits. The skins are easily removed. Actually this method assures a smooth, tasty, and colorful fruit sauce. A little ascorbic acid (vitamin C) added to the fruit will help to preserve color and prevent darkening. You can buy Ascorbic Acid Crystals, USP, in the drugstore. A pinch is sufficient to preserve the color in one pound of fruit.

One should eat some raw foods each day, but remember that many foods are rendered more digestible and nutritious through cooking. Examples of these are grains, certain vegetables such as potatoes, beans, peas, and others with a starch base. Cooking converts the starch to a more digestible form by softening and rupturing the cells.

Do not add soda to vegetables to preserve their colors as this will result in destruction of alkali-sensitive nutrients. If you must make brightly colored vegetable soups, try adding a little lemon or a pinch of ascorbic acid. They will help preserve color and add piquancy.

Be sure you cover pots when cooking foods to prevent destruction of light-sensitive nutrients.

Store fresh vegetables and fruits in a cool, dark place. Canned goods also should be kept where it is cool. Frozen foods should be maintained as close to 0° F. as possible to prevent deterioration. Handle foods carefully. Don't let them soak in water for any length of time. Wash them quickly and prepare them just prior to cooking or serving. Remember, frozen vegetables take less cooking time than fresh since they have already been blanched.

If you do your own canning and freezing, use only the freshest of produce. "From the garden into the jar or freezer" should be your motto. Be certain to store the jars in a cool, dark place to prevent loss of light-sensitive nutrients. One problem with home-canned vegetables is that nonacid ones should be boiled uncovered for ten to fifteen minutes with a resulting loss of some nutrients. For more information on home canning and freezing, contact your county extension service or the land-grant university in your state.

COOKING UTENSILS

There has been a great deal of controversy in recent years concerning types of cooking utensils, their safety and effectiveness. There is no question that clear glass utensils designed for use in stove-top cooking are not the best choice. They let light in and may cause loss of light-sensitive nutrients. Glass is also not a good heat conductor, thus hot spots may develop over the hotter sections of your burners causing thick or semi-solid foods to scorch. If you have clear glass utensils, use them for boiling water rather than cooking foods.

In using glass for baking, be sure to set your oven about twenty-five degrees cooler because the glass does not reflect the heat as a shinier metal pan does. This is also true of enamel, cast iron or blackened pans.

Cast-iron cookware is an excellent choice for sautéing, cooking meats, eggs, and so forth. One reason cast iron is good, aside from its durability, thickness, and even heat, is that it adds some iron to food. The trend away from the use of cast-iron cookware is believed to be partly responsible for the increase in iron-deficiency anemia in the United States. You can get too much of a good thing, however. Cast iron should not be used for cooking vitamin C–rich foods as it will destroy the vitamin C.

In order to get the best service, be sure you keep your cast-iron pot seasoned. After use, dry it thoroughly and rub the inside with a salt-free oil or fat. After a pot is well seasoned you will only need to oil it as necessary. In purchasing a cast-iron dutch oven, be sure you get one with a ceramic-lined lid, otherwise rust will form on the lid and run down into your food, giving it a red tinge and a slightly irony taste.

Stainless steel utensils which are kept in good condition work well, particularly if the bottom is copper-clad. Copper, being an excellent heat conductor, assures even heating without hot spots. There have been reports of chromium getting into food from stainless steel. The dangers are likely magnified, and pots which are unpitted or unscratched should not be a source of the problem.

Aluminum is another good conductor and is not liable to cause hot spots. It is not advisable to cook acid foods in aluminum since it will darken and pit. Aluminum is especially good for baking pans. You get even baking and predictable results.

It's a good idea to have an enamel pot or two for cooking acid foods like tomatoes or making cottage cheese from buttermilk. The cheap enamel on steel is short-lived and has hot spots. Far better is the heavy enamel on cast iron or aluminum.

The new Teflon is far tougher and stays on better than the early Teflon coatings did. Teflon is inert and does not enter your food. I find it good for heating foods, cooking rice, and helpful in baking pans, especially muffin tins. Brushing pans with lecithin prior to cooking can accomplish similar results. One thing Teflon pans are not good for is poaching eggs. It is nearly impossible to get the cooked egg albumin off the pan.

Pressure cookers are handy to use and conserve energy. Meat can be cooked in minutes rather than hours. Vegetables take very little time. Pressure cookers come in assorted sizes, from small ones for cooking vegetables to the large canners. If you contemplate canning vegetables or meats, then pressure canners are mandatory. Prices for the smaller cookers start at under ten dollars to well over fifty dollars for large pressure canners. Pressure cookers are simple to use if you follow directions. Be sure not to remove the pressure weight or cock until the pressure has lowered or you will have a stained ceiling. You can lower the pressure rapidly by running a little cold water over the pan. I find a pressure cooker especially valuable for preparing stews.

Steaming food is an excellent method of cooking. You can use a steamer, a blancher, or just a steaming rack to set in one of your regular pans. Most foods can be steamed, but it is an especially good way to cook whole fish and vegetables.

81

We all have certain favorite pots, ones we use for nearly everything. They get to be like old friends. You know their idiosyncrasies, what they can do and what they can't. The cookware you are happy cooking with and which gives you good results is, after all, best for you. Thin, poor conductors insure failure by burning foods and losing nutritive value. Know your pans, their good points and their failings. You will be rewarded with better cooking and better eating.

CHAPTER SIX
MENUS AND RECIPES

Basic Daily Menu for the Adult Pregnant Woman.

4 cups milk
2 or more servings meat, fish, poultry,
    cheese, or dried peas and beans
    (include at least 1 serving liver weekly)
2 eggs
1 or more servings dark green vegetables } some raw
1 or more servings deep yellow vegetables } every day
1 or more servings of a high vitamin C
    source—1 orange, ½ grapefruit,
    ½ cup orange juice, ½ cantaloupe,
    1 cup fresh strawberries, 1 fresh
    green or red sweet pepper, 1 cup papaya
1 or more servings of a second vitamin C
    source—1 potato, 1 tomato, glass
    tomato juice, cabbage, broccoli,
    kale, collard greens, turnip greens,
    mustard greens, Brussels sprouts,
    cauliflower, raspberries
2 servings of other vegetables and fruits
4 to 5 servings whole-grain cereal,
    bread, or rice; *enriched* white
    bread, noodles or other pasta may be used occasionally
Fats as needed for calories—butter,
    margarines, oils, shortenings

Basic Daily Menu for Pregnant Teenager.
To the Basic Menu for the Adult Pregnant Woman add:

> 2 cups milk
> 1 serving meat, fish, poultry,
>   cheese or legumes

Basic Daily Menu for Lactation.
To the Basic Menu for the Adult Pregnant Woman and Pregnant Teenager add:

> 1 cup milk
> 1 serving cereals or breads

Approximate Serving Sizes

Protein Foods:	lean meat or poultry	3 ounces
	cottage cheese	¾ cup
	tuna, crab, lobster	¾ cup
	shrimp, clams, oysters	8-10 medium or 15 small
	scallops	3 large
	peanut butter	6 tablespoons
	luncheon meats	3 slices, ⅛ inch
	eggs	3
	milk	8 ounces
	cheddar cheese	3 ounces
	fish fillets	3 ounces
	dried peas, beans, cooked	1 cup
Bread and Cereal:	bread	1 slice
	cornbread	1½ inch cube
	tortilla	1
	bagel	½
	cooked cereal	½ cup
	puffed cereal	¾ cup
	corn	⅓ cup

rice, noodles, pasta	½ cup
saltine crackers	5
graham crackers	2
corn, ears	1 small
popped corn	1 cup

Vegetables: ½ cup or more is one serving

Suggested Menus

Breakfast   2 eggs, scrambled
Whole-grain toast with butter or margarine
½ grapefruit
Sanka

Midmorning   1 glass milk
1 whole-grain muffin with butter or margarine

Lunch   Hearty vegetable soup with beef
1 slice whole-wheat Irish soda bread with butter
  or margarine
1 glass milk
1 banana

Afternoon   1 cup yoghurt with pineapple

Dinner   Braised liver with onions
Mashed potato—cooked in skins, then peeled
  and mashed with milk
Green peas
Apple, carrot, cabbage slaw
1 glass milk

Evening   1 dish bread pudding

*   *   *

Breakfast	Whole-grain cereal with milk and honey
	Whole-grain toast with butter or margarine
	1 glass orange juice
Midmorning	1 eggnog
Lunch	Broiled open-face sandwich with slice meat, slice cheese, slice tomato, lettuce
	1 glass milk
	1 apple
Afternoon	1 cup cream soup made with milk and a vegetable
Dinner	Oven-fried chicken
	Baked potato
	Baked acorn squash
	Tossed green salad
	1 glass milk
Evening	Whole-wheat biscuit (or rye crackers) with cheese

*　　*　　*

Breakfast	Granola with milk
	Whole-wheat toast with butter or margarine
	1 glass vegetable juice
	Sanka
Midmorning	2 hard-cooked eggs
	1 glass milk
Lunch	Cheese, rice, tomato casserole
	Spinach-mushroom salad
	1 glass milk
	1 cup fresh strawberries
Afternoon	Cottage cheese with whole-wheat crackers or hardtack
Dinner	Meat loaf with tomato sauce
	Baked potato
	Cooked carrots
	Cole slaw
	1 glass milk
Evening	Oatmeal-sesame cookie
	1 glass milk

*   *   *

Breakfast	2 poached eggs on whole-grain toast with butter or margarine ½ cantaloupe Sanka
Midmorning	1 enriched buttermilk doughnut 1 glass milk
Lunch	1¼ cups New England clam or fish chowder 1 whole-wheat biscuit with butter or margarine 1 peach
Afternoon	1 cup egg custard
Dinner	Baked stuffed fish Baked potato Green beans Carrot-raisin salad 1 glass milk
Evening	1 glass tomato juice Whole-wheat crackers with cheese

*   *   *

Breakfast	¾ cup cottage cheese with pineapple 2 slices whole-grain toast with butter or margarine Sanka
Midmorning	Apple 1 glass milk
Lunch	1 omelet made with 2 or 3 eggs Tomato sauce 1 orange 1 glass milk
Afternoon	1 glass milk Oatmeal cookie
Dinner	Hearty pea soup Spinach-endive salad Johnny cake with butter or margarine 1 glass milk
Evening	1 piece squash pie

*   *   *

Breakfast	Broiled kippered herring with poached egg
	Whole-grain toast with butter or margarine
	Sanka
Midmorning	1 glass orange juice
	1 hard-cooked egg
Lunch	Peanut butter-honey sandwich
	Carrot sticks
	1 glass milk
	Pear
Afternoon	1 glass milk
	1 hard-cooked egg (deviled)
Dinner	Baked beans with lean salt pork or bacon
	Brown bread with butter or margarine
	Cole slaw
	1 glass milk
Evening	1 glass milk
	1 piece cheesecake

*   *   *

Breakfast	Whole-wheat cereal with milk and honey
	Whole-grain toast with butter or margarine
	½ grapefruit
	Sanka
Midmorning	1 glass milk
	1 slice rye bread with butter or margarine
Lunch	2 to 3 eggs, scrambled
	Whole-grain bread
	Lettuce and tomato salad
	1 glass milk
Afternoon	1 apple
	1 piece Cheddar cheese
Dinner	New England Boiled Dinner (corned beef, cabbage, turnip, carrots, potatoes, optional beets, parsnips)
	1 glass milk
Evening	1 glass milk
	1 piece gingerbread

*   *   *

Breakfast	Corned beef hash with poached eggs 1 orange Sanka
Midmorning	1 glass milk Crunchy orange muffin with butter or margarine
Lunch	1 cup cream of vegetable soup Celery sticks stuffed with cottage cheese Whole-grain biscuit with butter or margarine
Afternoon	1 glass milk Carrot sticks
Dinner	Spaghetti with meat sauce and cheese Tossed green salad Enriched hard roll with butter or margarine Peach
Evening	1 glass milk Whole-grain crackers with cheese

* * *

The suggested menus can be augmented with additional vegetables. Use fats according to the amounts you need to insure adequate calories. Make use of additional protein foods, if desired. Servings of salads should be liberal.

Keep a snack tray in the refrigerator, tightly covered with plastic. Replenish it daily.

Suggested Foods for Snack Tray:

Carrot sticks
Celery sticks
Wedges of hard-boiled egg
Slivers of cabbage
Green-pepper slices
Cauliflower pieces
Cooked green beans
Radishes
Kohlrabi slices
Zucchini slices
Apple wedges
Olives
Cheese cubes
Tomato wedges
Turnip slices
Sardines
Chunks tuna
Fresh mushrooms
Fresh spinach leaves
Pineapple chunks
Cucumber sticks
Marinated artichokes
Orange sections

BEVERAGES

Beverages made with milk (whole, skim, or reconstituted nonfat dry).

EGGNOG

(1 serving)

1 cup milk
1 tablespoon honey
1 or 2 eggs

Heat milk and honey in a small saucepan over medium heat to simmering. Beat egg with a fork or whisk. Add a little of the hot milk to the egg, stirring. Slowly pour the egg mix into the milk, stirring constantly. Remove from heat immediately. Chill thoroughly. (This recipe can be easily multiplied.)

Variation: Use 1 tablespoon blackstrap molasses in place of honey.

MOLASSES SHAKE

(1 serving)

1 cup milk
1 tablespoon blackstrap molasses

Whirl the combined milk and molasses in blender or beat with an eggbeater until frothy.

COCOA

(2 servings)

1 tablespoon regular cocoa
1 tablespoon honey
2 cups milk
pinch salt

Combine honey and cocoa in small saucepan. Stir in a little of the milk, blending thoroughly. Stir in the remaining milk. Add salt. Bring to a simmer on medium heat, stirring occasionally. Serve.

Variation: Add 2 teaspoons Sanka instant coffee for a mocha drink.

HIGH PROTEIN MILK SHAKE

(1 serving)

1 cup milk
2 or more tablespoons nonfat dry milk

1 teaspoon brewer's yeast
1 tablespoon honey, molasses or maple syrup

Combine milk, yeast, nonfat dry milk, sweetener. Blend in blender or beat with an eggbeater until frothy.

Variations: To the above mixture add ½ banana, ½ cup orange juice, ½ cup pineapple juice, ½ cup apple juice, ½ cup prune or fig juice.

COFFEE MILK SHAKE

(1 serving)

1 teaspoon decaffeinated instant
  coffee
1 tablespoon hot water

1 cup milk
1 tablespoon honey
1 ice cube

Combine coffee with hot water to dissolve. Add with milk and honey to blender. Blend on high speed until frothy. Crush ice cube, add, and blend again to a creamy consistency.

BUTTERMILK

(1 quart)

Prepare one quart milk from nonfat dry milk according to package directions, using water at room temperature. You may add extra nonfat dry milk to increase the protein content if you wish. Add ¼ cup cultured buttermilk. Let set overnight at room temperature until clabbered. Refrigerate. It is far less expensive to make your own buttermilk than to buy it already made. You will need to purchase the first quart. From then on, you can continue to make your own, using some of the previous lot.

BUTTERMILK WITH YEAST

(1 serving)

1 cup buttermilk
1 tablespoon brewer's yeast
optional honey to taste

Combine buttermilk with yeast. Blend if you have a blender. If you have no blender, add a little buttermilk to the yeast, blending thoroughly. Add remaining buttermilk, stirring. If you must, add honey to taste.

BUTTERMILK-FRUIT SHAKE

(1 serving)

1 cup buttermilk
½ cup fresh or thawed frozen
  fruit

1 tablespoon honey if fruit not
  sweetened

Blend until thick and thoroughly combined.

YOGHURT

(1 quart)

1 quart milk (reconstituted nonfat
  dry milk, diluted evaporated
  milk, skim milk, or whole milk
  if desired)

3 tablespoons yoghurt

Combine the milk and yoghurt. It must be allowed to stand for 3 to 6 or more hours at a temperature of about 100° F. until thick and custardy. It is a good idea to warm the milk to about 100° F. initially. You can use a yoghurt maker or an electric fry pan set at an estimated 100° F. If using the latter, it is advisable to divide the milk among ½-pint containers. Place hot water in the fry pan. Put on the lid and leave undisturbed until custardy. Another method is to place a bowl of the milk mixture in a large pot, adding hot water around the bowl. Cover. Add more hot water to maintain temperature.

An additional method is to place hot water in an insulated picnic cooler. Set bowl of milk mix in it. Cover. Let set until thick. Yoghurt can be used in any recipe calling for buttermilk.

BUTTERMILK FREEZE

(2 servings)

1 cup buttermilk
1 cup frozen fruit

Put buttermilk into blender container. Break up frozen fruit but leave frozen. Add fruit and blend until smooth and frosty.

FRUIT AND VEGETABLE DRINKS

FRUIT PUNCH

(16 or more servings)

1 12-ounce can frozen orange juice
1 46-ounce can unsweetened pineapple juice
1 bottle unsweetened grape juice
1 quart sparkling water or ginger ale
1 ice cube tray of ice

Combine orange, pineapple and grape fruit juices. Add sparkling water or ginger ale and ice.

Variations: Add a 46-ounce can pure unsweetened apple juice.
Add reconstituted frozen lemonade.
Add juice of two limes or lemons.
Add reconstituted frozen limeade.
Add a 46-ounce can unsweetened grapefruit juice.

FRUIT SHAKE

(1 large serving)

1 cup milk
2 teaspoons honey
½ cup fresh or drained canned fruit

Combine milk, honey, and fruit in blender and blend until thick.

PIQUANT TOMATO JUICE COCKTAIL

(2 servings)

1½ cups tomato juice
1 teaspoon lemon juice
1 dash Worcestershire sauce

1 drop liquid pepper
celery salt to taste

Combine tomato juice, lemon juice, Worcestershire sauce, liquid pepper, and celery salt to taste. Stir thoroughly. Garnish with a sprig of parsley or a slice of lemon if desired.

VEGETABLE JUICE COCKTAIL

(2 servings)

1½ cups tomato juice
1 stalk celery
1 cabbage leaf
1 medium carrot
1 sprig parsley
1 slice sweet pepper

2 large lettuce leaves
½ clove garlic
1 green onion (scallion)
1 teaspoon lemon juice
2 drops liquid pepper

Put tomato juice in blender container. Cut up celery, cabbage, carrot, parsley, sweet pepper, lettuce, garlic and onion. Drop into blender a little at a time, running blender intermittently to liquify. Add remaining seasonings. Blend. Strain into glasses.

SUMMER VEGETABLE DRINK

(6 servings)

This is based on a Spanish soup called Gazpacho. It is refreshing and thirst-quenching on a hot summer's day.

3 large tomatoes	5 tablespoons olive oil
2 green peppers	2 tablespoons vinegar
1 clove garlic	4 cups ice water
½ small onion	salt and pepper to taste

Cut up tomatoes after removing stem end. Cut up peppers, removing seeds and core. Mince garlic. Cut up onion. Combine them with olive oil and vinegar. Blend well until liquified. Strain into ½-gallon container. Add ice water. Stir and season to taste.

Variations: For even more vitamin-rich drink, use tomato juice or vegetable juice in place of the ice water.

TOMATO JUICE

If you have a garden and surplus tomatoes or have some given to you, you can make a delicious thin tomato juice and a nice thick base for tomato soup and sauce.

Wash and quarter tomatoes and place in a heavy pot. Heat on medium heat, stirring and pressing until the juice runs. Cover and continue cooking on low heat until tender. Pour through strainer. Refrigerate the juice for a refreshing drink. Purée the pulp until only the skin remains. If you cannot use it immediately, store in the freezer in pint or quart containers until needed or process in canner according to the manufacturer's directions.

Soups may be used as a snack, as the appetizer for a meal, or as a meal in themselves, depending on how they are made and what is in them. They may be served hot or cold as jellied consommé, vichyssoise, or borsch.

As main dishes, soups and stews are admirable because they usually require only one cooking pot, thus using less energy for heat and cleanup.

CREAM SOUPS

Cream soups are amazingly easy to make. With their milk base, they contribute protein and calcium, providing an excellent mid-morning or afternoon pickup. They also provide a good basic luncheon dish.

CREAM OF MUSHROOM SOUP

(about 3 cups)

¼ pound mushrooms or 1 8-ounce can, drained
2 tablespoons chopped onions
2 tablespoons butter or margarine
2 tablespoons unbleached, enriched flour

1 cup hot water, broth, or mushroom liquor with 1 or 2 bouillon cubes
1½ cups hot milk
¼ teaspoon nutmeg
salt, pepper

Wipe mushrooms with a damp cloth to clean. Slice lengthwise. Sauté onions in butter in heavy saucepan over medium heat for 5 minutes. Add mushrooms, sautéing 5 more minutes. Remove from heat. Add flour and blend. Return to heat. Add stock and milk gradually, stirring constantly. Cook, stirring until slightly thickened. Add nutmeg. Salt and pepper to taste. Serve immediately.

WHITE SAUCE FOR CREAM SOUPS

(3 cups)

Make this white sauce ahead of time. Refrigerate with plastic wrap or wax paper laid over the surface to prevent skin from forming. When ready to use, remove and heat over low heat, stirring occasionally to keep from lumping or burning.

2 tablespoons butter or margarine
2 tablespoons unbleached, enriched
  flour

½ teaspoon salt
white pepper
3 cups milk

Melt butter or margarine in heavy saucepan over low heat. Remove from heat. Blend in flour, salt and pepper. Return to heat, stirring in milk. Heat, stirring constantly until thickened and bubbling.

CREAM OF ONION SOUP

(4 cups)

¼ cup butter
4 medium onions
¼ teaspoon salt
½ cup milk

3 cups white sauce for cream
  soups

Melt butter in skillet. Add thinly sliced onions and salt. Cover. Cook over medium heat until the onions are tender. Add the milk. Add the onion mixture to the hot white sauce. Heat through, season and serve.

CREAM OF CELERY SOUP

(4 cups)

2 cups chopped celery with leaves   3 cups white sauce for cream
½ cup chopped onion   soups
1 cup boiling, salted water

   Cook celery and onion in water until tender. Make or heat white sauce. Add vegetables and water to white sauce, stirring. Season. Serve.

CREAM OF POTATO SOUP

(about 5 cups)

2 cups diced, cooked potatoes   3 cups white sauce for cream
1 tablespoon chopped pimiento   soups
                                     salt, pepper

   Add potatoes and pimiento to white sauce and heat. Season to taste.

CREAM OF SPINACH SOUP

(about 5 cups)

2 cups chopped spinach leaves   3 cups white sauce for cream
¾ cups boiling water   soups
1 bouillon cube

   Cook spinach in water with bouillon cube just minutes until tender. Add to hot, white sauce, stirring. Serve. (*Note:* You may blend spinach mixture prior to adding to white sauce if desired.)

CREAM OF LETTUCE SOUP

(about 5 cups)

Lettuce soup, made fresh, is surprisingly good and a beautiful light green color. Proceed as for spinach soup (above), but cook only seconds. Serve immediately.

CREAM OF CABBAGE SOUP

(about 5 cups)

Proceed as for spinach soup, but the cabbage will require a little longer cooking. Serve.

CREAM OF GREENS SOUP

(about 5 cups)

Proceed as for spinach soup using any of the various greens—turnip, kale, endive, chicory, dandelion, beet, and chard—but vary the cooking time for the greens according to need—dandelion and kale requiring more time than spinach and chard, for example.

CREAM OF PEA SOUP

(about 5 cups)

2 cups fresh peas
½ cup boiling water
1 bouillon cube (optional)

3 cups white sauce for cream soups

Cook peas in boiling water until just done. Blend pea mixture in blender until smooth. Stir into hot white sauce. Serve.

CREAM OF BEAN SOUP

(about 5 cups)
   Proceed as for cream of pea soup (above), substituting beans for the peas.

CREAM OF ASPARAGUS SOUP

(about 5 cups)
   Use 2 cups washed, sliced asparagus in place of peas in the cream of pea soup recipe.

Variations: Any other fresh or frozen vegetable may be substituted in the above recipes.

CREAM OF TOMATO SOUP

(about 5 cups)

1 No. 2 can tomatoes or 4 large tomatoes, chopped	¼ teaspoon cinnamon
	dash cloves or allspice
2 slices onion	2 tablespoons butter
1 bay leaf	2 tablespoons enriched, unbleached
1 teaspoon salt	flour
¼ teaspoon pepper	2 cups milk

   Simmer tomatoes, onion, bay leaf, salt, pepper, cinnamon, and cloves or allspice for 10 minutes. Strain. While the tomatoes are simmering make the cream sauce. Melt butter in saucepan over medium heat. Remove from heat, stir in flour. Replace on heat. Stir in milk. Cook until thickened and bubbling, stirring constantly. Pour the tomato mixture into the cream sauce, stirring constantly. Serve.

CREAM SOUPS WITH
LEFTOVER VEGETABLES

Blend any leftover or canned vegetables in blender and add to basic white sauce, stirring constantly. Heat and serve.

CORN CHOWDER

(about 6 cups)

3 tablespoons diced, salt pork
1 onion, chopped
1 cup boiling water

3 cups corn, fresh or canned,
   cream style
3 cups rich, hot milk
salt and pepper

Fry out the salt pork in a large heavy saucepan. Add onion and cook until golden brown. Add boiling water and corn. If using fresh corn, cut it from the cob and scrape the cob into the corn. Cook until corn is done, about 5 minutes if fresh. Heat through if canned. Add milk, and salt and pepper. Serve.

Variations: Use 2 cups of diced potatoes in place of 2 cups of corn if desired. Cook potatoes until nearly tender and add corn, cooking until done.

CLAM CHOWDER

(serves 4)

1 pint chopped clams
1 onion, sliced
3 potatoes, cubed
4 tablespoons diced salt pork

1 quart of whole milk
2 tablespoons butter
salt and pepper

Cook onion and potatoes in enough water to keep them from scorching. You may use the clam liquid as part of the water. Cook until nearly tender. Add clams and continue cooking about 5 minutes—until clams are done, if fresh. Fry out the salt pork until brown and crisp. Drain on paper towel. Add pork scraps to clam mixture. Add heated milk to the chowder. Add butter and season with salt and pepper to taste.

Classic Downeast clam chowder is made with relatively large cubes of potatoes, thus the length of cooking time is longer than if the potatoes are finely cubed. Also, though white pepper is the more genteel in appearance, most Downeasters use black pepper which floats on the top with the butter and pork scraps.

FISH CHOWDER

(serves 4)

1 or more pounds fish
2 onions, sliced
3 large potatoes, sliced
¼ cup diced salt pork

1 quart rich, whole milk
1 tablespoon butter
salt and pepper
½ cup cream or evaporated milk

Cook fish in water to cover. Remove fish from stock. Cook potatoes and onions in fish stock until tender. Fry out salt pork until crisp. Add with fat to chowder. Remove skin and bones from fish. Add to chowder. Heat milk and add to chowder. Just before serving, add butter, salt and pepper, and cream.

Variations: Use 1 pound salt cod, soaking thoroughly to freshen. Use finnan haddie or other smoked fish.

OYSTER STEW

(about 5 cups)

1 pint of oysters
1½ pints milk
¼ cup pulverized oyster crackers

2 tablespoons butter
salt and pepper

Heat milk on low with cracker crumbs to simmering. Add oysters and seasonings. Cook just until oysters are puffed up—overcooking toughens them. Serve immediately with oyster crackers.

BOUILLABAISSE

(serves 4)

1 medium onion, chopped
1 minced clove garlic
¼ cup olive oil
2 tomatoes, peeled and chopped
1 bay leaf
⅛ teaspoon thyme
½ teaspoon saffron

3 tablespoons hot water
salt
5 peppercorns
¼ teaspoon fennel seeds
1 pound white fish
1 pound shellfish or any
  combination

Sauté onion and garlic in olive oil until golden. Add tomatoes, bay leaf, thyme. Soak saffron in 3 tablespoons hot water. Strain the saffron and add the water to tomato mixture. Add salt and peppercorns, and fennel seeds. Simmer about 8 minutes. Add fish—larger pieces first. Add water to nearly cover fish. Add smaller pieces of fish and any shellfish which require short cooking time when the other fish is nearly tender. Cook until tender. Serve the fish from a platter and pour the broth over toasted, buttered bread in a bowl. (*Note:* Shellfish can be added in the shell for additional flavor and a more interesting appearance.)

PEPPERPOT

(about 3 servings)

2 tablespoons chopped celery
¼ cup chopped, green pepper
2 tablespoons chopped onion
2 tablespoons butter
1½ tablespoons enriched,
    unbleached flour
¼ pound tripe

¾ cup diced potatoes
¼ teaspoon pepper
2 tablespoons celery salt
2½ cups hot water with 3 chicken
    bouillon cubes
¼ cup light cream or evaporated
    milk

Cook celery, green pepper, and onion in butter until tender but not brown. Remove from heat, add flour and blend. Add cooked tripe. (Soak pickled tripe to remove acid. Boil in two changes of water to further remove acid and cook until tender.) Add potatoes, pepper, celery salt, and stock. Cover and cook until potatoes are tender. Before serving, stir in cream.

BARLEY SOUP

(makes about 6 cups)

1¼ pounds lamb combination
6 cups water
1 cup pearl barley

1 cup diced turnip
1 cup diced potato
1 cup diced carrots

Cook the lamb in the water until nearly done. Add barley and cook until it is nearly tender, about 1¼ hours. Add turnip, potato, and carrots. Simmer until tender.

LIVER SOUP

(2 servings)

½ pound liver
2 cups water
1 medium onion
1 tomato
2 teaspoons chopped parsley

1 tablespoon rice
1 egg
2 tablespoons lemon juice
salt and pepper

Wash liver, slice thinly, and simmer in water until tender. Cool, remove gristle and membranes. Put through food chopper. Add liver, onion, tomato, chopped parsley, and rice to liver water. Simmer until rice and onions are cooked (about 15 minutes if converted rice is used, about 30 minutes for brown rice). Just before serving, beat the egg; add the lemon juice to the egg, beating until well mixed. Stir a little of the soup into the egg mixture. Gradually add the egg mixture to the soup, stirring constantly. Serve.

CHEESE SOUP

(about 4 cups)

4 tablespoons butter
4 tablespoons enriched, unbleached
  flour
1 teaspoon celery salt
¼ teaspoon pepper
2 cups milk
1 teaspoon dry mustard
2 teaspoons Worcestershire sauce

1½ cups grated, sharp Cheddar
½ cup minced onion
½ cup minced celery
¼ cup minced green pepper
4 tablespoons butter
1 cup chicken stock or 1 cup
  boiling water with 1 chicken
  bouillon cube

Melt butter. Add flour, stirring to blend. Add salt and pepper combined with the milk, pouring slowly and stirring constantly. Combine mustard, Worcestershire sauce, and grated cheese. Add to the milk mixture. Cook, stirring until cheese is melted. Keep warm. Sauté onion, celery, and green pepper in butter until soft. Add the chicken stock and add all to the cheese mixture. Heat to serving temperature.

OXTAIL SOUP

(8 servings)

1 oxtail
2 tablespoons butter
1 chopped onion
2 chopped carrots
3 stalks celery, chopped
1 tablespoon chopped parsley
3 whole cloves
1 tablespoon flour

6 cups bouillon or beef stock
1 No. 2 can tomatoes or 3 fresh
  tomatoes
1 tablespoon celery salt
⅛ teaspoon pepper
⅛ teaspoon cayenne pepper
dash of nutmeg

Wash the oxtail and cut up at joints. Sauté oxtail and onion in butter and when onion is transparent, add carrots, celery, and parsley. When brown, add cloves, flour and bouillon. Cover and simmer four hours. Add tomatoes (if fresh, chop first). Continue cooking 15 minutes. Add seasonings. Strain. Add meat bits to soup. Serve.

LENTIL AND SPINACH SOUP

(4 to 6 servings)

2 cups lentils
1 medium onion, sliced thin
3 tablespoons olive oil
½ pound spinach, coarsely
  chopped

salt
lemon juice
sour cream (optional)

Put lentils in saucepan, cover with water and cook until tender, about 1½ hours. Sauté the onion in the olive oil. Add to the lentils and cook about 30 minutes. Add the spinach and salt and cook another 7 minutes. Stir in lemon juice and serve. If you wish, add a little sour cream to each serving.

PEA SOUP

2 cups dried peas
1 quart boiling water
4 stalks celery, chopped
2 chopped onions
ham bone or piece of salt pork
   (optional)

salt and pepper
1 quart milk
⅓ cup butter

Soak peas in water overnight. Drain. Cover with boiling water. Add celery, onions, and ham bone or pork. Simmer until the peas are soft, about 1½ hours. Press through a sieve. Add salt and pepper. Heat milk. Reheat soup to boiling point and add hot milk and butter, stirring. Serve.

BEAN SOUP

(8 servings)

1½ pounds kidney beans
1 No. 2 can tomatoes
1½ cups chopped onions
1 teaspoon celery seeds
1 bay leaf
1 tablespoon chopped, dried
   parsley or 5 sprigs fresh parsley
1½ teaspoons dried thyme

4 whole cloves
1 teaspoon celery salt
dash black pepper
2 cups diced potatoes
1 chopped green pepper
1 tablespoon brewer's
   yeast
parsley for garnish

Wash and soak beans for about 12 hours. (Or add 6 cups of water to beans, bring to boil, turn off heat, let set 1 hour.) Add tomatoes, onions, celery seeds, bay leaf, parsley, thyme, cloves, salt, and pepper. Heat to boiling, lower heat and simmer for about 1½ hours until tender. Add potatoes, green pepper, and yeast. Cook for about 20 minutes or until potatoes are tender. Serve garnished with fresh parsley sprigs.

BAKED BEAN SOUP

(8 servings)

2 cups cold, baked beans
2 onions, chopped
4 cups cold water
2 cups canned tomatoes
2 tablespoons butter

2 tablespoons flour
1 tablespoon celery salt
½ cup uncooked, high protein,
   elbow macaroni

Simmer beans, onions, and water for ½ hour. Add tomatoes. Combine butter and flour. Add a little of the soup mix to form a thin paste. Stir into the soup. Add celery salt. Purée or push through a strainer. Return to heat. Add macaroni and cook about 8 minutes or until macaroni is tender.

LAMB STEW

(4 servings)

1½ pounds lamb combination
4 medium potatoes
1 large onion, sliced
½ teaspoon salt

⅛ teaspoon pepper
water
parsley

Cut meat off the bones and cut into small cubes. (Use bones to prepare a stock for barley or bean soup.) Pare potatoes thinly and slice. Form layers in casserole of lamb, potatoes, and slices of onion. Add seasonings. Pour water in so you can just see it. Cover the casserole and bake at 325° F. about 2 hours. Serve garnished with parsley.

MINESTRONE

(8 servings)

Minestrone can be an exceptionally pretty soup if you use a variety of vegetables. Start with the basic soup and vary by using any number of fresh, frozen, or canned vegetables. Add them so they will be just done at serving time. Chopped greens and sliced zucchini are especially attractive tasty additions. Be sure you add them only a few minutes before the soup is done in order to preserve the flavors, color, consistency, and nutrients.

2 cups dry beans
2 quarts water or stock
1 pinch rosemary
1 minced clove of garlic
salt and pepper
meat scraps or pieces of Italian
    sausage (optional)

½ cup grated cheese
1 tablespoon olive oil
1 cup high protein macaroni
vegetables as desired

Soak beans 12 hours. Put to boil in the water or stock for 2 hours. Add rosemary, garlic, salt and pepper, meat scraps, cheese, and olive oil. Start adding vegetables and macaroni according to cooking time needed. It is desirable to add at least 1 chopped tomato for color and flavor. Serve with grated cheese.

SALADS

CREATIVE TOSSED SALAD

(any number)

Tossed salad is my favorite contribution to any meal. I never make it exactly the same because I have no set recipe. It is invariably a success whether I concoct the dressing right on the salad or whether I make it separately (for a picnic or potluck supper) and add it. With the addition of cheese, meat, hard-cooked eggs, etc., it makes a filling luncheon main dish. Use any of the following ingredients in any combination (you should have some type of green as a base). You can use up leftovers in an attractive, tasty and nutritious way.

lettuce	cubes Cheddar cheese	kohlrabi
endive or escarole	well-drained cottage cheese	cucumbers
Chinese cabbage	marinated artichokes	dandelion leaves
carrots	chunks of tuna	radishes
onions	sardines	watercress
parsley	green or red sweet peppers	fresh basil
cauliflower	fresh zucchini	chives
fresh mushrooms	fresh spinach	celery
cooked green beans	hard-cooked eggs	cabbage
tomatoes	anchovies	peas
chopped cooked meat	olives	leftover vegetables
shredded chicken	avocado	

Cut vegetables into the size you prefer. Any raw vegetables and greens should have been washed and shaken dry first. Cut up enough to be eaten at one meal. Put in salad bowl. Add a generous sprinkle of oregano, a good shake of basil, sprinkle on some garlic powder and celery salt; add a good dash of pepper. You can use other herbs as desired—tarragon, for example. Add olive oil mixed with cold-pressed mild oil such as soybean, cottonseed, or corn oil (or omit olive oil if you wish). Add about one-third as much vinegar as you added oil. Vinegar may be mixed with few drops of honey if desired to augment flavor. Toss all together until all ingredients are thoroughly coated. Serve immediately. Experiment with new combinations. Go easy on new seasonings until you are sure you like them.

If you are making a salad for later use, prepare vegetables and other salad contents. Place in a large plastic bag and refrigerate to keep crisp. Concoct dressing separately using the above combination of oil and vinegar. Test-taste dressing to determine the best combinations of herbs and seasonings. Just before serving combine the salad dressing with the greens and toss thoroughly.

POTATO SALAD

(8 servings)

4 cups chopped, cooked potatoes
½ cup chopped celery
½ cup chopped dill pickle
½ cup diced cucumber
¼ cup minced parsley

1 minced onion
2 hard-boiled eggs, sliced
2 cups nutritious, boiled salad
  dressing

Combine potatoes, celery, pickle, cucumber, parsley, onion, and eggs. Mix in the salad dressing thoroughly. Refrigerate. Serve on salad greens.

NUTRITIOUS BOILED DRESSING

(1½ cups)

2 tablespoons butter or oil
2 tablespoons flour
1 cup milk
3 eggs

¾ cup vinegar
2 teaspoons salt
2 teaspoons dry mustard

Melt butter in heavy pan. Remove from heat and stir in flour. Return to heat; add milk while stirring. Beat eggs with vinegar, salt, and mustard. Add a little of the hot mixture to the egg mix, then stir it into the milk mixture. Cook until creamy. Refrigerate immediately.

COLE SLAW

(any amount)

cabbage
carrot
onion
mayonnaise, vinegar, honey

Coarsely grate cabbage into bowl—enough to use up at one meal. Grate one or more carrots and a few gratings of onion and add. Use enough mayonnaise to coat the slaw. Add a few drops of vinegar and a little honey to taste. Mix thoroughly.

Variation: Add chopped raisins, apples, or pineapple.

FRUIT SALAD

(any amount)

This is another opportunity to create according to the fruits you have on hand, what is cheap and available. This can be served at the end of the meal as a dessert, if you wish, with sherbert instead of dressing.

banana	*peach*	*grapes*
orange	*plums*	*strawberries*
grapefruit	*nuts*	*pear*
pineapple, fresh or	*melons—any in season*	*nectarines*
canned in juice	*apples*	*cherries*
raspberries	*blueberries*	*coconut*

Prepare fruit by cutting into good-sized attractive pieces. For example, split banana and slice crosswise; peel orange or grapefruit and with sharp knife remove skins on outside of sections. Leave pineapple in chunks; put berries in whole; make melon balls of varying sizes; cut apple, pear, or peach in sections and thence in chunks—leave peel in place. If serving as salad, add salad dressing and toss. If serving as compote, add pineapple and orange juice with a little lemon or lime juice to maintain color.

DRESSING FOR FRUIT SALAD

(2¼ cups)

1 cup mayonnaise or cooked salad
  dressing
½ cup honey
¼ cup lime juice

1 cup evaporated milk or heavy
  cream or ⅔ cup ice water
  combined with ⅔ cup instant
  milk, whipped

Combine dressing with honey and lime juice. Fold in whipped cream or milk. Refrigerate. When ready to serve, combine with fruit salad.

PEANUT BUTTER SALAD DRESSING

(1 cup)

4 tablespoons milk
4 tablespoons lemon juice
2 tablespoons water

4 tablespoons peanut butter
salt

Mix milk, lemon juice and water. Blend in peanut butter. Add salt to taste. Use with fruit salads.

SPINACH-MUSHROOM SALAD

(any amount)
Toss together fresh spinach in bite-size pieces, sliced fresh mushrooms and any oil and vinegar dressing. Serve immediately.

CARROT-RAISIN SALAD

(any amount)
Grate carrot and combine with raisins and mayonnaise to moisten.

CEREALS AND BREADS

CEREALS

OATMEAL PORRIDGE

(4 servings)

1 cup oatmeal
2 cups water
½ teaspoon salt

Combine oatmeal, water, and salt in saucepan. Place over medium heat. Bring to a boil. Lower heat, stir, cover, and cook 5 minutes. Serve with honey, molasses, or sugar and milk.

Variations: Add 1 tablespoon raisins before or after cooking.
Add 1 tablespoon unsulfured molasses before cooking.
Add 2 cut up, pitted prunes or dates before cooking.
Add a pinch of cinnamon prior to cooking.
Add 1 chopped apple prior to cooking.
Top with sliced banana or other fruit or berries.
Use 1¼ cups milk in place of water or use ½ milk and
½ water.

BULGAR

(4 servings)

This can be served as a breakfast dish with sweetening and milk, or it may be eaten at dinner with butter or as a base for spaghetti sauce.

1 cup bulgar (cracked wheat)
2 cups water
½ teaspoon salt

Combine bulgar, water, and salt in saucepan with a tightly fitting cover. Bring to a boil over a medium heat. Stir with a fork, cover, and continue cooking on low heat until all water is absorbed, about 15 minutes.

Variations: For dinner, cook in meat stock rather than water.

CORNMEAL MUSH

(4 servings)

½ cup cornmeal, undegerminated
½ cup cold water
½ teaspoon salt
2 cups water

Combine cornmeal, cold water, and salt. Bring the other two cups of water to a boil. Slowly stir the cornmeal mixture into the boiling water. Turn the heat to low, cover, and cook 30 minutes until thick and done. Serve with milk and sweetener, or with butter.

FRIED CORNMEAL MUSH

Pack leftover cornmeal mush in a small dish. Cover and refrigerate. Slice and sauté in butter, fat, or oil until crisp. Serve with molasses syrup, maple syrup, or honey.

POLENTA

(4 servings)

1 recipe for cornmeal mush
1 dash red pepper sauce
½ cup grated cheese

Prepare the cornmeal mush. Let it cook about 15 minutes. Add pepper sauce and slowly stir in grated cheese. Continue cooking another 15 minutes until done.

FRIED POLENTA

(serves 4)

Pack polenta into loaf pan. Cover with waxed paper and refrigerate. When cold, slice into ½-inch slices and sauté in olive oil. Serve with tomato sauce or any spaghetti sauce.

GRANOLA I

(5 or 6 servings)

2 cups rolled oats
½ cup wheat germ
1 cup raisins or currants, prunes, dates, dried pears, apricots, or apples, chopped

½ teaspoon cinnamon
2 tablespoons honey
2 tablespoons oil

Combine the rolled oats, wheat germ, raisins, and cinnamon in a bowl. Mix and heat the honey and vegetable oil to liquify. Add to the rolled oats mixture, stirring well to mix thoroughly. Spread on cookie sheet and bake at 350° F. about 10 minutes until lightly browned. Serve with milk, buttermilk, or yoghurt.

Variations: Use vanilla in place of cinnamon. Add ½ cup chopped nuts, hulled sunflower seeds, or sesame seeds.

GRANOLA II

(8 or more servings)

2 cups rolled oats	½ cup sunflower seeds
½ cup rye flour, or bran, whole wheat or wheat germ	½ cup soybean meal
	¼ cup oil
½ cup shredded coconut	¼ cup honey
½ cup chopped nuts	¼ teaspoon vanilla

Combine oats, flour, coconut, nuts, sunflower seeds, soybean meal in bowl. Heat oil and honey to about 110° F. or 120° F. Mix thoroughly with vanilla into the rolled oats mixture. Spread on cookie sheet and bake at 325° F. about 20 minutes. Stir at the end of 10 minutes. Serve with yoghurt, buttermilk, or sweet milk. Use plain as a snack.

Variations: Use rolled wheat in place of rye flour. Vary the other seeds and nuts as desired. Add ½ cup chopped dried fruit.

GNOCCHI

(4 servings)
This dish can be prepared the night before and heated for breakfast as a treat, or it can be used as a luncheon dish.

2 cups milk	½ cup grated cheese, either Italian or Cheddar
½ teaspoon salt	
pepper	2 tablespoons butter or margarine
½ cup enriched farina	1 egg, beaten

Heat milk, salt, and a little pepper in a heavy saucepan. Slowly add farina while stirring. Simmer 3 to 5 minutes until thick. Remove from heat and add ¼ cup of the grated cheese and 1 tablespoon of the butter. Place back on low heat, stirring for one or two minutes. Turn out on a 13½ x 9-inch pan, buttered, spreading to about ½-inch thickness. Let cool until set. Cut in 1½-inch squares or, if you prefer to be fancy, in silver-dollar-size circles.

Overlap them on buttered baking dish. Sprinkle with remaining cheese and dot with remaining butter. Bake at about 400° F. for 10 minutes. Put under broiler to brown lightly. Serve with tomato sauce if desired.

If you plan to have gnocchi for breakfast, cover with waxed paper and refrigerate. In the morning, place in a 400° F. oven until heated through, about 15 to 20 minutes. Run under a broiler a minute or so to brown, if desired.

CONVERTED RICE

(4 to 5 servings)

Converted rice retains more nutrients than regular enriched rice. If you must have white rice this is the kind to use.

1 cup rice
2 cups water
1 teaspoon butter or margarine
1 teaspoon salt

Combine rice, water, butter and salt in saucepan with close-fitting cover. Bring to a boil, stir lightly with a fork. Turn heat to low. Cover. Cook 15 minutes until rice is tender and liquid is absorbed. If necessary, remove cover and continue cooking to evaporate any excess water.

BROWN RICE

(5 to 6 servings)

1 cup rice
3 cups water
1 teaspoon salt
1 teaspoon butter or margarine

Combine rice, water, butter and salt as above. Bring to a boil. Turn heat to low and stir. Cover. Cook 45 minutes as above.

PILAF

(5 servings)

1 cup converted rice
2 tablespoons olive oil
1 clove garlic, minced
¼ cup chopped onion

2 cups stock or 2 cups water with
   2 bouillon cubes
1 chopped tomato

In a heavy covered saucepan, sauté rice, olive oil, garlic and onion until rice is translucent. Add stock and tomato. Bring to a boil. Turn heat to low. Simmer until liquid is absorbed and rice grains are tender, about 15 minutes. Serve with chicken, chicken livers, liver, lamb, fish.

Variations: To use brown rice, add an additional cup of water or stock. Cook 40 to 45 minutes. You may add 1 to 1½ cups cooked leftover meat, chicken or fish for a one-dish meal. Meat can be added with the tomatoes and bouillon. Add fish or shellfish when rice is cooked and heat through.

JAMBALAYA

(about 4 servings)
This is a creole dish and can be used with almost any type of meat or fish leftovers either individually or in combination.

1 tablespoon lard or oil
1 chopped onion
1 clove garlic
1 teaspoon flour
any amount of meat or fish
   leftovers
2 large tomatoes, chopped

1½ cups boiling water (2 cups for
   brown rice)
1 cup raw rice—brown or
   converted
1 teaspoon celery salt
¼ teaspoon pepper
dash liquid red pepper

Heat lard in dutch oven. Brown onion and garlic. Stir in flour. Add tomatoes and chopped leftovers. Add water. Cover, simmer 10 minutes. Slowly add rice. Stir once. Cover pot and simmer until done—about 20 to 40 minutes depending on the rice. Add celery salt, pepper, and red pepper.

Variations: If you wish to add oysters, add them when the rice is done and cook only until the edges are curled so they will be plump and tender.

PASTA

Macaroni is usually made with enriched, white flour. Consequently while trace minerals and some vitamins are not available, it at least has the vitamin and mineral content of the enriched flour. Noodles have the addition of egg which makes them more nutritious. Noodles may be homemade with whole-wheat flour. Macaroni and spaghetti made from whole-wheat and other grains are available at natural food stores. There is also high-protein macaroni available if you can find it. You may be able to locate some through a local wholesaler. It has soy flour base and is excellent in macaroni and cheese casserole and in soups. It is a good idea to use regular enriched pasta only occasionally as a treat. Be certain it is enriched.

NOODLES

(about 1 lb. dry noodles or 16 servings when cooked)

Homemade noodles taste great—far better than those you buy. They are fun to make, too.

1⅓ cups enriched unbleached
  flour
2 eggs

2 tablespoons water
¼ teaspoon salt
2 teaspoons oil

Heap flour on pastry board. Make a well in the middle. Combine eggs, water, salt and oil slightly with a fork. Pour into the well formed in the flour. Work with your hands, mixing and kneading until the ball of dough no longer sticks to your hands. Divide in two. Roll each piece of dough out very thin, stretching and pulling as you do. You may sprinkle lightly with flour as necessary to keep from sticking or forming holes. Try to get the dough paper-thin and translucent as you continue rolling and stretching. Let it dry for about 30 minutes. Roll up like a jelly roll and cut to the thickness you desire, very narrow to very wide (for lasagne). Use immediately, or dry another hour and store in cool place in a tightly covered container. Do not allow to dry before cutting if making ravioli.

Variations: To make green noodles, add about 6 tablespoons thoroughly drained and dried spinach, chard, or other cooked greens very finely chopped.

WHOLE-WHEAT NOODLES

(about 1 lb. noodles)

2 cups whole-wheat flour　　*1 teaspoon salt*
2 eggs　　*2 tablespoons water*
2½ tablespoons wheat germ

Proceed as for noodles, but allow to dry only 10 minutes before cutting. To store, dry out the noodles for about 2 hours. Place in tight containers and keep cool or freeze.

FLOURS————————————————————

Wheat flours are, of course, the ones we use most. Whole-wheat flour contains the germ of the wheat which has a wider variety of B vitamins and some trace minerals as well. Graham flour contains both the germ and the bran, the outer covering of the grain. The refining process strips wheat flour of most of its vitamins and minerals, with the bleaching process further raping the wheat. As I have pointed out previously, niacin, iron, riboflavin, and thiamine are put back into the flour to "enrich" it, but at the expense of other vital nutrients.

CORNELL TRIPLE-RICH FORMULA

You can compensate for the shortcomings of white flour to some extent by using the Cornell Triple-Rich Formula. In the bottom of each cup, place 1 tablespoon soy flour, 1 tablespoon nonfat, dry-milk powder, and 1 teaspoon wheat germ. Fill the cup with flour—whole wheat, enriched, unbleached white flour or any other type flour called for. Make your triple-rich mix ahead by combining 1 cup nonfat dry milk, 1 cup soy flour, and ¼ cup wheat germ with 13¾ cups enriched, unbleached flour. Mix thoroughly, store in tightly covered gallon container. Use in place of unbleached, enriched flour in any of the recipes. This mixture provides additional protein, calcium, B vitamins and other nutrients. You may also add ¼ cup of brewer's yeast and use 13½ cups flour.

Since most flours are now presifted, or in the case of whole grains should not be sifted, the recipes in the book are formulated for unsifted flour, unless otherwise indicated. Be sure to combine the dry ingredients thoroughly. Be especially careful that baking soda, if used, does not clump. One way to avoid that problem is to dissolve the baking soda in the liquid called for in the recipe.

There are a number of other types of flour available: rye, barley, buckwheat, rice, potato, corn, etc. The latter three are usually refined, the former ground from the whole grain. Oatmeal is used in the rolled form as a component of baked goods. Oatmeal flour is also available.

QUICK BREADS

Quick breads are easy to make, quick to cook, and very tasty. The secret of making successful muffins is to stir them very lightly, only until the ingredients are moistened. Combine all of the liquid ingredients and add to the combined dry ingredients, using about ten complete stirs with a large spoon. Use paper liners to line muffin tins. It saves time. You can use Teflon muffin tins or brush the tins with lecithin if you wish. An ice cream scoop is the ideal tool for filling the pans.

DOUBLE WHEAT MUFFINS

(about 1 dozen)

1 cup whole-wheat flour
1 tablespoon baking powder
½ teaspoon salt
1 cup rolled whole wheat

2 tablespoons honey
3 tablespoons vegetable oil
1 egg
1 cup milk

Combine thoroughly the whole-wheat flour, baking powder, salt, and rolled wheat. Combine vegetable oil, honey, egg, and milk, with a wire whisk or egg beater. Add to dry ingredients, stirring only until moistened. Fill prepared muffin pans ⅔ full. Bake at 425° F. about 20 minutes. Remove from pans and let cool a few minutes so paper liners will peel off more easily, if they were used.

CRUNCHY ORANGE MUFFINS

(1 dozen large muffins)

1 cup unbleached, enriched flour
    or C T-R mix
1 cup whole-wheat flour
2 tablespoons nonfat dry milk
1 teaspoon baking powder
½ teaspoon salt
1 cup Grape Nuts

2 eggs
1 cup orange juice
½ teaspoon soda
2 tablespoons honey
1 tablespoon grated orange rind
⅓ cup oil

Combine flours, nonfat dry milk, baking powder, salt, and Grape Nuts. Beat eggs lightly with a fork, dissolve soda in orange juice and add to eggs with honey, grated rind, and oil. Stir into dry ingredients until just moistened. Pour into prepared muffin tins to ⅔ full. Bake at 400° F. 20 to 25 minutes.

OATMEAL MUFFINS

(1 dozen)

1 cup unbleached, enriched flour
   or C T-R mix
3 teaspoons baking powder
½ teaspoon salt
1 cup rolled oats

1 egg
1 cup milk
2 tablespoons honey
3 tablespoons oil

Combine flour, baking powder, salt, and oats. Beat egg lightly with a fork and combine with milk, honey, and oil. Add to flour mixture, stirring to just moisten. Fill prepared muffin tins ⅔ full. Bake at 425 ° F. about 15 minutes.

CORN MUFFINS

(about 1 dozen)

1½ cups unbleached, enriched
   flour or C T-R mix
¾ cup undegerminated cornmeal
¾ teaspoon soda
1 teaspoon baking powder

1 teaspoon salt
1 egg
¼ cup unsulfured molasses
1 cup sour milk or buttermilk
2 tablespoons melted butter or oil

Combine flour, cornmeal, soda, baking powder, and salt. Beat egg lightly with molasses, milk, and butter. Add all at once to flour mixture stirring only until moistened. Fill prepared muffin tins. Bake at 400° F. about 20 minutes.

JOHNNY CAKE

Make the corn muffin recipe, but bake it in a shallow, buttered pan at 400° F. about 25 minutes.

GRAHAM MUFFINS

(12 muffins)

1½ cups graham flour
½ cup unbleached, enriched flour
   or C T-R mix
1 teaspoon soda
1 teaspoon salt

1½ cups sour milk
2 tablespoons unsulfured molasses
2 tablespoons oil
1 egg

Combine flours, soda, and salt. Stir together the milk, molasses, oil, and slightly beaten egg. Add to flour mixture. Fill prepared muffin tins. Bake at 375° F. about 25 minutes.

Variations: Fold in 1 cup blueberries or ½ cup chopped dates or prunes.

WHOLE-WHEAT CREAM OF TARTAR MUFFINS

(12 muffins)

2 cups whole-wheat flour
1 teaspoon soda
1 teaspoon salt
2 teaspoons cream of tartar

¼ cup molasses (unsulfured)
1 egg, slightly beaten
1 cup milk
1 tablespoon oil

Mix whole-wheat flour, soda, salt, cream of tartar. Combine molasses, egg, milk, and oil. Stir liquids into flour quickly. Pour into prepared muffin pans. Bake at 400° F. for 20 minutes.

SQUASH MUFFINS

(12 muffins)

These muffins are a beautiful gold color.

1 cup cooked strained squash or
  pumpkin
2 well-beaten eggs
1 cup milk
1 tablespoon honey

2 tablespoons oil
2 cups whole-wheat flour
3 teaspoons baking powder
½ teaspoon salt

Combine squash with eggs, milk, honey, and oil. Mix flour, baking powder, and salt. Stir squash mixture into the flour mixture until just combined. Bake at 400° F. about 25 minutes.

DOUBLE CORN MUFFINS

(makes 12)

1 cup undegerminated cornmeal
1 cup unbleached, enriched flour
  or C T-R mix
2 teaspoons baking powder
¾ teaspoon salt

1 beaten egg
1 cup cream-style corn
¾ cup milk
2 tablespoons oil

Mix cornmeal with flour, baking powder, and salt. Combine egg, corn, milk and oil. Add to cornmeal mix and stir to combine. Pour into prepared muffin tin. Bake at 425° F. about 20 minutes.

RYE MUFFINS

(about 12)

1 cup rye
1 cup unbleached, enriched flour
  or C T-R mix
¼ cup brown sugar

½ teaspoon salt
1 egg
1 cup milk

Mix rye, flour, sugar, and salt. Combine egg and milk, beating lightly with a fork. Butter cast-iron popover pan. Bake at 400° F. about 20 minutes.

RICE MUFFINS

(about 18)

1 cup cooked rice (either brown or
  converted)
2 eggs, separated
1 cup milk
¼ cup melted butter or margarine

2½ cups unbleached, enriched
  flour or C T-R mix
2 teaspoons baking powder
½ teaspoon salt

Beat egg yolks and add to rice with milk and butter. Beat egg whites until stiff. Mix flour, baking powder, and salt. Add rice mixture to flour, stirring to just mix. Fold in stiffly beaten egg white. Bake in prepared muffin tins at 400° F. about 30 minutes.

BARLEY BREAD

(8 pieces)

This should be served fresh and hot for best flavor. It is simple to make and flavorful.

2 cups barley flour
¾ teaspoon salt
2 teaspoons sugar
2 teaspoons baking powder

1 cup undiluted evaporated milk
  or double-strength reconstituted
  nonfat dry milk
2 tablespoons melted butter

Combine flour, salt, sugar, and baking powder. Stir in milk and butter. Butter a cookie sheet and turn dough on to it. Dip your hands in flour and pat out into a circle about ½ inch thick. Prick lightly with a fork and bake at 450° F. for 10 minutes until light brown. Serve immediately.

Variations: Use rye flour in place of barley.

POPOVERS

(8 popovers)

3 eggs
1½ cups milk
1 cup whole-wheat flour
¾ teaspoon salt

Beat eggs and add milk. Mix milk and egg mixture into flour and salt. Butter muffin tins or cast-iron popover pan or custard cups. Heat oven to 450° F. Heat pans in oven for 2 to 3 minutes. Fill pans ⅔ to ¾ full with popover batter. Bake for 20 minutes. Lower oven to 350° F. and continue baking about 15 minutes. If you like dry popovers, prick with a fork, turn off oven. Put popovers back into oven for a few minutes.

BISCUITS

After I was first married, I tried a number of times to make biscuits. Although I followed the recipes carefully, the biscuits were invariably tough. One day I followed my grandmother around while she was creating her superb biscuits. Her recipe was the result of years of practice with no need to measure anything. After watching her, I was able to turn out good biscuits. The solutions I found were: 1. Cut the shortening in thoroughly. 2. Use enough milk for a soft dough—not stiff. 3. Stir in milk quickly to just mix. 4. If you knead, do so for only about 30 seconds, lightly with your fingertips. 5. Pat out to about ½-inch thickness. 6. Cut straight down with biscuit cutter (or can). For crispy edges, separate biscuits on cookie sheet. For soft sides, place them close together in a shallow pan. The tops may be brushed with milk if you wish.

WHOLE-WHEAT BISCUITS

(8 to 10)

1 cup whole-wheat flour
1 cup enriched, unbleached flour
2 teaspoons baking powder
½ teaspoon salt

2 tablespoons butter or other solid
  shortening
¾ cup milk (about)

Mix flours, baking powder, and salt. Cut butter in with a pastry blender until mixture resembles coarse cornmeal. Add milk, stirring with a fork to form a soft dough. Turn out on floured board. Knead lightly with fingertips two or three times. Pat out to ½-inch thickness. Cut with biscuit cutter. Place on buttered cookie sheet or shallow pan. Bake at 425° F. 12 to 15 minutes.

Variations: Add ¾ cup grated cheese to flour mixture.

Roll biscuit dough out thinly and spread with mixture of ½ teaspoon cinnamon and 2 tablespoons honey or applesauce. Roll up and cut in slices ½ inch thick.

BUTTERMILK BISCUITS

(about 8 to 10)

2 cups enriched, unbleached flour
½ teaspoon soda
½ teaspoon salt

3 tablespoons butter
1 cup buttermilk or thick sour milk

Combine flour, soda, and salt. Cut in butter. Stir buttermilk in quickly. Turn out on floured surface. Knead lightly one or 2 turns. Pat out to ½-inch thickness. Bake at 425° F. 12 to 15 minutes.

IRISH SODA BREAD

(2 loaves)

This is a quick bread which is delicious with a hearty pea or bean soup meal. The bread is also excellent cold or toasted with butter.

2 cups enriched, unbleached flour
2 cups whole-wheat flour
1 teaspoon salt
3 teaspoons baking powder
1 teaspoon baking soda
2 tablespoons sugar

1½ teaspoons caraway seeds
¼ cup butter or margarine
1 egg
1¾ cups buttermilk
1½ cups currants or raisins

In large bowl, combine flours, salt, baking powder, soda, sugar, and caraway seeds. Cut in butter with a pastry blender until consistency of coarse cornmeal. Beat egg slightly with fork and combine with buttermilk. Stir into dry ingredients. Add raisins or currants. Knead lightly on floured board. Divide dough in half. Form into round loaves and place in 8-inch cake tins. Press down to fill pans. Cut crosses on tops of loaves with a sharp knife. Bake in 375° F. oven for 35 to 40 minutes.

Variations: Omit caraway and/or raisins and currants.

BROWN BREAD

(1 large or 2 small loaves)

By tradition, in New England, brown bread is served with baked beans on Saturday night. When families lived in the same towns, bean baking was a cooperative effort. One week grandmother prepared the beans and brown bread, the following week mother did. This cooperative feeding carried over into bread baking and any number of other foods—the food was divided and picked up or delivered. Friends can share these chores as well as families. It's no harder to prepare enough for two pots of beans, and this brown bread recipe will serve two families. Another possibility is to prepare enough for next week's meal.

Brown bread is steamed. I find this recipe fits nicely into a three-pound coffee can. It can be cooked in two smaller cans. Grease a piece of brown paper and tie tightly over the top with string. Place in a deep kettle partly filled with boiling water. Cover. Replace water as it boils away.

1½ cups undegerminated cornmeal	1 tablespoon sugar
1 cup graham flour	½ teaspoon salt
½ cup rye flour	¾ cup unsulfured molasses
2 teaspoons baking soda	2 cups sour milk or buttermilk
	¾ cups seeded raisins (optional)

Mix cornmeal, graham flour, rye flour, baking soda, salt, and sugar. Combine molasses, milk, and raisins. Add to the dry ingredients. Turn into buttered mold filled to ⅔ full. Steam 3½ hours for large mold, 1½ to 2 hours for small molds.

PEANUT BUTTER BREAD

(1 loaf)

1¾ cups unbleached, enriched
  flour or C T-R mix
1 tablespoon baking powder
1 teaspoon salt

⅓ cup brown sugar
1 cup peanut butter
2 eggs
1¼ cups milk

Mix flour, baking powder, salt, and sugar. Blend in peanut butter with a pastry blender or fork. Beat eggs slightly and combine with milk. Add the egg-milk mixture to the peanut butter mixture, stirring just to blend. Pour into greased 8-½ x 4-¾ x 2-inch loaf pan. Bake at 350° F. about 1 hour.

CORNMEAL PANCAKES

(about 1 dozen)
  These are crisp and nicely flavored.

1 cup boiling water
¾ cup yellow, undegerminated
  cornmeal
1 cup sour milk or buttermilk
2 eggs

1 cup enriched, unbleached flour
3 teaspoons baking powder
1 teaspoon salt
¼ teaspoon baking soda
¼ cup oil

Pour boiling water over cornmeal, stirring until thick. Add milk and beat in eggs one at a time. Mix flour, baking powder, salt, and baking soda. Add to the cornmeal mixture, stirring quickly. Lightly stir in oil. Bake on hot, ungreased griddle. Turn when bubbles have formed and tops start to dry slightly. Serve with syrup, honey, applesauce, or blueberries.

CORNMEAL WAFFLES

(about 10)

1 cup enriched unbleached flour
½ teaspoon salt
1 teaspoon baking soda
2 teaspoons baking powder

1 cup undegerminated cornmeal
2 beaten eggs
2 cups buttermilk
¼ cup oil

Mix flour, salt, baking soda, baking powder, and cornmeal. Combine eggs, buttermilk, and oil. Add to cornmeal mixture, stirring to just combine. Bake in hot waffle iron until steaming stops. Serve with syrup, honey, or fruit sauce.

WHOLE-WHEAT PANCAKES

(8 4-inch pancakes)

1¼ cups whole-wheat flour
3 teaspoons baking powder
½ teaspoon salt
1 tablespoon honey

1 egg
1 cup milk
2 tablespoons oil or melted fat

Mix flour, baking powder, and salt. Beat together the honey, egg, milk, and oil. Add to the flour mixture, stirring just to moisten. Bake on hot griddle.

WHOLE-WHEAT WAFFLES

(makes about 12)

1 cup whole-wheat flour
1¼ cups enriched, unbleached
   flour or C T-R mix
4 teaspoons baking powder
¾ teaspoon salt

1 tablespoon honey
2 eggs
2¼ cups milk
¾ cup oil

Mix the whole-wheat flour, unbleached flour, baking powder, and salt. Beat together the honey, eggs, milk, and oil. Add to the flour mixture, stirring just to moisten. Bake in a preheated waffle iron until steaming stops. Serve with fruit sauce, honey or syrup.

CORN CRISPS

(2 dozen 2-inch crisps)

½ cup cornmeal
½ teaspoon salt
¾ cup boiling water

2 tablespoons butter
poppy seeds, sesame seeds, or
   celery seeds as desired

Mix cornmeal and salt. Stir in the boiling water with the butter dissolved in it. Mixture will be thin and runny. Drop by teaspoonfuls on lightly buttered cookie sheets, only eight to a sheet to allow for spreading. Sprinkle with seeds as desired. Bake at 425° F. about 8 minutes or until lightly browned. When done they are easy to remove from cookie sheet and are very crisp.

PUFFS

These can be made any size up to 2½ inches in diameter, or they can be elongated into the shape of an eclair. Filled with a milk pudding, they make a nutritious dessert. Or they can be used as casings to serve creamed chicken, etc.

1 cup water
½ cup butter or margarine
1 cup unbleached, enriched flour
4 eggs

Bring water and butter to a boil in a saucepan. Add flour, beating well with a wooden spoon. Remove from heat. Beat in eggs one at a time, beating two minutes after adding each. Drop by dessert spoonfuls on buttered cookie sheet or put through pastry press to form eclairs. Bake at 375° F. until lightly browned, about 30 minutes.

CHEESE PUFFS

(about 2½ dozen 1-inch puffs)

These are a light, delicate puff, high in protein and very simple to make.

½ cup water
2 tablespoons butter
¼ cup unbleached, enriched flour
   or C T-R mix

¼ cup grated cheese
⅛ teaspoon salt
dash of paprika
1 egg

Combine water and butter in small saucepan. Bring to a boil. Add flour, cheese, salt, and paprika, stirring with a wooden spoon and cooking over low heat until it forms a ball coming away from the sides of the pan, about 3 minutes. Remove from heat. Beat in the egg thoroughly. Put ½ teaspoon batter on buttered cookie sheets. Bake at 375° F. 15 minutes.

YEAST BREADS

Making yeast bread is a creative undertaking. Breads can be formed into all kinds of fascinating shapes, and can be flavored with unbelievable varieties of ingredients. Even better than the shaping and flavoring, though, is the kneading and proving, watching the bread grow—knowing the live yeast is actually multiplying and giving off gases which cause the bread to rise.

Yeast grows best when the temperature is warm, right around body temperature or a little above. It is inactive at cold temperatures and is killed if temperatures get too hot. Yeast is available in cakes or dry. The cakes spoil rather quickly while the dry yeast will keep for long periods of time in the refrigerator. For some reason, Fleischmann's finds it necessary to add BHA to preserve freshness. El Molino Mills of Alhambra, California, puts out dry yeast which works very well and is far less costly than the regular brands available at the supermarket. It comes in 4-ounce, 8-ounce and 1-pound packages in natural food stores. One level tablespoonful is equal to one yeast cake or one packet of dry yeast.

Gluten is a protein contained in flour which helps to give it elasticity. Thorough mixing and kneading of bread develops the gluten. Because the gluten content varies from flour to flour and high-gluten flour rises better, bread recipes will not specify exact amounts of flour. You can start with the minimum called for and work in any additional as you knead to the desired smooth velvety elastic consistency. To knead, fold dough over and push down hard with the heels of your hands. Give it a quarter-turn and repeat. Continue kneading until the proper consistency is obtained.

Flours other than wheat may be used, but since they are low in gluten, they should be used with at least an equal amount of wheat flour. Soy and rice flour contain no gluten and must be used sparingly.

Bread made with water has a heavy crispy crust. Milk, besides adding nutrients, provides a soft, smooth grain, while sour milk or buttermilk give a very tender soft loaf. Unpasteurized milk must be scalded to kill enzymes which will cause the bread to be gummy. Water in which vegetables have been cooked is fine for baking bread, especially potato water. To make it more nutritious, add nonfat dry milk.

Fats are added to breads to improve flavor and texture. Sugars add flavor and improve the action of the yeast. They also produce a brown crust. Salt adds flavor and affects the action of the yeast. Eggs are flavorful, nutritious, add color, and improve the texture of the bread. Various other ingredients such as dried fruits, herbs, spices, nuts, and cheese may be added for flavor and food value. Since they slow the rising time, they should not be used in large amounts and should be added just prior to kneading.

Batter breads are especially easy to make, requiring no kneading and often only one rising. Consequently they call for more yeast. In fact, generally the more yeast you use, the shorter the rising times. Each time you let the bread rise, the less time it will take. To form loaves, stretch and roll dough to three times the length of baking pan. Fold over in thirds, pressing out bubbles. Fold in thirds again, pinching and pressing. Seal ends by pinching and rolling under to form smooth loaf shape. Ingredients should be at room temperature, liquids at 105 to 115° F., quite warm to touch but not hot.

Bread should rise at a temperature of about 80 to 85° F. unless it is a refrigerator bread. If you are interrupted while making bread, just punch it down and let rise again or refrigerate the dough to slow rising.

If bread is fully cooked, loaves will sound hollow when tapped. Unbaked bread may be frozen for short periods.

WHOLE-WHEAT CREAM
AND HONEY BREAD

(2 loaves)

This is an exceptionally light and flavorful bread. The eggs add nutrients. Cream provides the shortening as well as liquid.

1 cup heavy cream
⅓ cup honey
1 cup very warm water
2 tablespoons dry yeast

⅓ cup nonfat dry milk
6-7 cups whole-wheat flour
4 large eggs

Scald cream and pour over honey, stirring to dissolve. Dissolve yeast in warm water and add to cooled cream and honey mixture. Stir in nonfat dry milk. Add 2 cups of the whole-wheat flour, mixing thoroughly. Add the eggs one at a time, mixing after each addition. Add additional flour until mixture begins to come away from the sides of the bowl. Turn out on floured board and knead until smooth. Put into oiled bowl turning once. Set to rise in a warm place about 1 hour until doubled in bulk. Punch down. Let rise 15 minutes more. Turn out on floured surface. Divide in two and form into balls. Let rest covered while you prepare two pans. Oil or grease two 9 x 5 x 2-inch bread tins. Form loaves. Turn loaves in pans to slightly oil the tops. Set to rise, covered for about ½ hour, until doubled in bulk. Bake at 375° F. about 25 minutes.

Variation: Make the above bread using 1¾ cups scalded milk and ¼ cup very warm water and ⅓ cup of any type fat desired in place of the cream and water.

GRANDMA'S BREAD

(4 loaves)

This bread was developed by my grandmother over a period of years. It is relatively low in fat and adapts very nicely to changes. I have made it using milk for all but ½ cup of the liquid. I have substituted buttermilk for sweet milk with a lovely soft bread resulting. Whole-wheat flour has been used for up to ⅓ of the white flour—still with good results. I have used honey in place of sugar (use 3 tablespoons). Makes 3 loaves of bread and a pan of rolls.

2 cups milk, scalded
4 tablespoons sugar
1½ tablespoons salt
3 tablespoons shortening

2 tablespoons dry yeast
2 cups lukewarm water
about 12 cups unbleached,
enriched flour or C T-R mix

Combine milk, sugar, salt, and shortening. Stir until dissolved and let cool to lukewarm. Dissolve yeast in a little of the water; add with the remaining water to the milk mixture. Add flour to the yeast mixture, blending thoroughly, until batter leaves the sides of the bowl.

Turn out on floured surface and knead for 10 minutes or until smooth and elastic. Place in greased bowl, turning once to grease the top. Cover with clean dish towel, and set to rise in warm place (80-85° F.) for about 1½ hours or until the impression of your finger remains in the dough. Punch down. Cover; let rise again, about ½ hour.

Turn out on floured surface, flatten, cut and mold into 4 balls. Let rest 15 minutes, closely covered. Shape into loaves. Place in greased 9 x 5 x 3-inch pans, turning once to grease tops. Cover. Set in warm place until the dough fills the pans and center rises above top, about 1¼ hours. Bake in a hot oven about 400° F. for 40 minutes.

REFRIGERATOR BREAD

(2 loaves)

2 tablespoons dry yeast
½ cup very warm water
1¾ cups warm milk, scalded if
    unpasteurized
2 tablespoons sugar

1 tablespoon salt
3 tablespoons butter or margarine
5½ to 6½ cups C T-R mix or
    unbleached, enriched flour

Dissolve yeast in water and add with sugar, salt, and butter to warm milk. Add 2 cups flour and beat with egg beater or on low speed with electric mixer for about 1 minute. Add another cup of flour and beat hard for another 2 or 3 minutes (or at medium speed with electric mixer). When dough is smooth and elastic, stir in the rest of the flour until dough begins to leave the sides of the bowl. Turn out on floured surface. Knead for 5 to 10 minutes until smooth and elastic. Cover with plastic wrap and towel. Let set for 20 minutes.

Punch down. Form into 2 loaves. Place in a greased 8½ x 4½ x 2⅝-inch bread pans. Brush with oil. Cover with oiled wax paper and plastic wrap. Refrigerate for 2 to 24 hours. Before baking, remove from refrigerator, uncover and let stand for 10 minutes while oven is heating. Prick any bubbles which rise to the surface. Bake on the lower rack of oven at 400° F. about 30 to 40 minutes. Remove from pans and cool.

Variations: To make cheese bread, stir in ½ cup grated cheese with the final addition of flour.

Form one of the loaves into rolls if desired. Top with poppy seeds, sesame seeds, and chopped onions, if desired.

GRACIE'S OATMEAL BREAD

(2 loaves)

1 cup rolled oats
2 cups milk, scalded
2 teaspoons salt
1 tablespoon melted butter
⅔ cup molasses

2 tablespoons dry yeast
¼ cup very warm water
5 cups C T-R mix or unbleached,
    enriched flour

Add oats to scalded milk and let stand until lukewarm. Add salt, butter, molasses, yeast dissolved in water, and flour. Mix thoroughly but do not knead. Set in warm place to rise until double in bulk (about 1¼ hours). Turn out on floured surface. Knead until smooth and elastic. Form into 2 loaves. Let rise until doubled in bulk. Bake at 350° F. about 45 minutes. Turn out of pans and cool.

EGG BREAD

(2 loaves)

5½ to 6½ cups C T-R mix
2 tablespoons sugar
1 tablespoon salt
2 tablespoons dry yeast

2 tablespoons soft margarine
2 cups very warm water
3 eggs at room temperature

Thoroughly mix 1½ cups of the flour with sugar, salt and dry yeast, in a large bowl. Add margarine. Gradually add the water while beating at medium speed of electric mixer, or beating vigorously by hand. Scrape bowl occasionally. Add eggs and another ½ cup of the flour. Beat at high speed for 2 minutes. Stir in enough of the remaining flour to make a soft dough. Cover. Let rise in warm place until doubled, about 35 minutes. Stir down. Spoon into greased 1½-quart casseroles or into two 9 x 5 x 3-inch tins. Cover, let rise in warm place until double, about 40 minutes. Bake at 375° F., about 35 minutes. Remove from pans and cool.

RYE BATTER BREAD

(1 loaf)

1¼ cups very warm water (105 to
   115° F.)
1 tablespoon dry yeast
2 tablespoons soft shortening
2 tablespoons dark brown sugar

2 teaspoons salt
1 tablespoon caraway seeds
1 cup rye flour
2 cups C T-R mix or unbleached,
   enriched flour

Dissolve yeast in warm water. Add shortening, sugar, salt, and caraway seeds, ½ of the rye flour, and 1 cup of the white flour. With mixer at medium speed, beat 2 minutes. Add remaining flour, beating 1½ minutes, and scraping sides of bowl. Cover with towel. Let rise in a warm place until double, about 30 minutes. Beat hard by hand. Pour into greased 8½ x 4½ x 2⅝-inch pan. Cover with towel. Let rise about 40 minutes or until double. Bake at 375° F. about 45 to 50 minutes. Remove from pan to cool on wire rack. Brush crust with butter.

EGGS

SOFT-COOKED EGG

(any number)

Put desired number of eggs in a saucepan with a cover that fits. Add enough cold water to cover eggs. You may add a dash of vinegar to help prevent eggs from breaking, if desired. Cover and set on moderately high heat. Bring to a boil. Turn off heat. Let set 3 to 4 minutes. Rinse with cold water to stop cooking. Peel and serve.

HARD-COOKED EGG

Proceed as above, but let eggs set in hot water 10 to 12 minutes, depending on size.

SCRAMBLED EGGS

(any number)

Add 1½ to 2 tablespoons milk for each egg, a dash of pepper, and a pinch of salt. Beat lightly with a fork. Melt small amount of butter or margarine in pan over moderately low heat. Add egg(s). Cook, scraping to side of pan with a large spoon or spatula until set but fluffy and moist.

POACHED EGGS

(any number)

Heat water with a little salt in a flat saucepan or fryer to simmering. Break egg or eggs individually in saucer and slip into water. When white is partially set, gently spoon the water over the yolk to set nicely. Remove from water with slotted spoon. Serve on buttered toast.

OMELET I

(any number)

Choose pan of a size to fit the number of eggs you plan to use. Using 2 or more eggs, break them into small bowl. Beat until light and fluffy. Add a pinch of salt and a dash of pepper. Heat small amount butter or margarine in pan on moderate heat. Pour eggs into pan. Cook until the underside is browned. Place warmed plate over pan. Turn omelet out on plate and slip back into pan so the browned side is up. Cook until the other side is browned. Serve at once, plain or with tomato, cheese, mushroom, or fish sauce.

OMELET II

(any number)

Choose pan as for Omelet I, but be sure it is oven-proof. Separate eggs. Beat egg whites until stiff but not dry. Add a pinch of salt and dash of pepper to taste to egg yolks. With same beater, beat yolks until light. Gently fold yolks into whites, blending until combined. Heat butter or margarine in pan over moderate heat. Pour omelet into pan. Cook until bottom is lightly browned. Run omelet under broiler to brown top. Or you may preheat oven to 350° F. and bake omelet for 10 minutes or until lightly browned. Serve as for Omelet I.

Variations: Add crisply cooked, crumbled slice of bacon to egg yolks for each egg.

Add 1 tablespoon grated cheese or 1 tablespoon sieved cottage cheese to egg yolks for each egg.

Add 1 teaspoon minced onion for each egg.

Add 1 teaspoon minced sweet pepper for each egg.

DOUBLE-BOILER EGGS

(2-3 servings)

4 eggs
¾ teaspoon vegetable salt
¼ teaspoon pepper

3 tablespoons milk
2 tablespoons butter or margarine

Beat eggs, salt and pepper until light and fluffy. Gradually beat in milk. Melt butter in top of double boiler over hot water. Add eggs and cook covered for 10 minutes. Remove cover and stir. Replace cover and continue cooking for 10 more minutes or until set.

SPANISH EGGS

(3 servings)

6 eggs
2 tablespoons butter or margarine
1 clove garlic, minced
1 small onion, minced
1 large chopped tomato

½ teaspoon salt
½ teaspoon celery salt
dash liquid red pepper
1 teaspoon chopped parsley

Melt butter in frying pan over moderate heat. Add minced garlic and onion, sautéing until transparent. Add chopped tomato, cook five minutes. Combine eggs with salt, celery salt, pepper, and parsley, beating slightly with a fork. Add to pan, stirring with large spoon or spatula until set and fluffy. Serve on buttered toast.

SHIRRED EGGS

(1 serving)

1 egg
1 tablespoon undiluted evaporated
  milk or light cream

1 teaspoon butter
1 tablespoon tomato sauce or
  ketchup

Place cream, butter, and tomato sauce in custard cup. Break egg over the tomato sauce mix. Set in shallow pan of hot water. Bake at 350° F. about 15 minutes or until egg is set.

BAKED EGGS WITH MEAT

(any number servings)
   For each serving desired, use:

1 egg   salt, pepper, butter
¼ cup cooked leftover meat   gravy or milk
¼ cup dry, whole grain crumbs

   Combine meat and crumbs in small saucepan. Season with salt
and pepper as desired. Dot with butter. Add enough gravy or milk
to moisten thoroughly. Heat over moderately low heat, stirring
until hot and well combined. Place in buttered muffin tin cup or
custard cup. Break egg on top. Bake at 350° F. until eggs are set,
about 15 minutes.

EGG TIMBALES

(3-4 servings)

6 eggs
1 cup milk
½ teaspoon salt
dash liquid pepper

   Beat eggs until light. Beat in the milk and salt and pepper. Pour
into buttered muffin tins or custard cups. Set in pan of hot water
and bake at 350° F. about 15-20 minutes or until firm. Serve with
tomato sauce or cheese sauce.

CURRIED EGGS

(up to 3 or 4 servings)

SAUCE:

3 tablespoons butter	*1 tablespoon cornstarch*
2 chopped apples	*4 chicken bouillon cubes*
1 minced onion	*1 cup boiling water*
½ teaspoon ground cloves	*1½ cups milk*
1 tablespoon curry powder	*¼ cup raisins (optional)*
3 teaspoons lemon juice	

Melt butter in heavy saucepan on moderate heat. Sauté apples and onion until tender. Combine cloves, curry powder, lemon juice and cornstarch, stirring until smooth. Dissolve bouillon cubes in boiling water. Stir a little of the bouillon into the curry powder mixture. Add with remaining water to saucepan, stirring until smooth. Slowly add the milk, stirring constantly until thickened. (Add optional raisins.)

Prepare two hard-cooked eggs for each serving. Peel and cut in wedges. Place on hot rice and pour curry sauce over all.

DEVILED EGGS

(any number)

Cut hard-cooked eggs in half. Remove yolks and mash. Moisten with mayonnaise. For each egg add: a dash of mustard, a sprinkle of pepper, a sprinkle of garlic powder, chopped chives if available, celery salt to taste.

EGG SALAD

(any amount)

Chop or coarsely mash hard-cooked eggs. For each egg add: 1 tablespoon mayonnaise, 1 teaspoon chopped onion, dash garlic powder, 1 teaspoon chopped green pepper, 1 teaspoon chopped celery, 2 drops lemon juice, celery salt to taste. Serve on greens or in sandwich with lettuce.

CHEESE DISHES

CHEESE WITH EGGS

(2-3 servings)

4 eggs
4 tablespoons grated cheese
1½ cups milk

1 teaspoon salt
⅛ teaspoon pepper

Beat eggs slightly. Add grated cheese, milk, salt, and pepper. Pour into casserole dish. Set in pan of hot water. Bake at 325° F. about 40-45 minutes or until firm. Let stand 3 minutes and unmold. Serve with tomato sauce if desired.

MACARONI AND CHEESE

(4 servings)

3 cups hot, cooked macaroni (high
   protein if available)
⅓ pound sharp Cheddar cheese
   grated or cubed

salt and pepper
milk
bread crumbs
butter

Toss hot, drained macaroni with cheese. Sprinkle with salt and pepper. Pour in enough milk to just reach the top layer of cheese. Sprinkle bread crumbs over all. Dot with butter. Bake at 350° F. about 35 minutes until cheese is melted.

Variations: Add 1 tablespoon grated onion, 1 tablespoon green pepper, and/or ¾ teaspoon dry mustard.

CHEESE PIZZA

(2 12-inch)

SHELL:

1 cup very warm water

1 tablespoon dry yeast

1 teaspoon sugar

2 tablespoons oil

3½ cups unbleached, enriched
  flour

1 teaspoon salt

In bowl, dissolve yeast in water. Add sugar, oil, 2 cups of the flour, salt. Beat until smooth. Stir in remaining flour. Turn out on floured surface. Knead until smooth and elastic. Put into greased bowl, turning to grease top. Cover. Let rise in warm place until double (about 45 minutes). Punch down; divide in two. Form balls and place each in center of greased cookie sheets. Flatten dough with palms and push out—pulling and pushing to form 12-inch circles. Form ridge at outside edges. (Or, if you wish, place all of dough on one jelly roll pan and form pastry to fit pan.) Let rise while you prepare filling.

FILLING:

⅔ cup tomato paste

½ cup water

1 teaspoon salt

pepper

1 teaspoon oregano

½ teaspoon basil

¼ pound mozzarella cheese

2 tablespoons olive oil

4 tablespoons Parmesan cheese

Mix tomato paste, water, salt, pepper, oregano, and basil. Heat to boiling point. Spread on prepared pizza pastry. Add mozzarella or other cheese, coarsely grated or thinly sliced—distributing over the surface of the shell. Sprinkle with olive oil and Parmesan cheese. Bake at 400° F. about 25 minutes. Serve immediately.

COTTAGE CHEESE

(any amount)

Prepare buttermilk from nonfat dry milk (see recipe). Keep warm until curds separate from whey. Strain through cheesecloth. Rinse with lukewarm water. Tie corners of cheesecloth together and let drain for about 2 hours. Add salt to taste. Chill. If you wish to have creamed cottage cheese, mash in a little cream and butter.

WELSH RAREBIT

(6 servings)

Though this recipe should serve six, it only provides two teenage-boy-size servings.

3 tablespoons butter
1 pound sharp Cheddar cheese
1 teaspoon cornstarch
1 teaspoon salt
½ teaspoon mustard
½ teaspoon paprika
1 cup beer or ale
2 eggs

Melt butter over low heat (in double boiler over hot water if you have a gas stove). Grate or dice cheese into butter and sprinkle with the cornstarch, salt, mustard, and paprika. When cheese has melted stir in the beer, a little at a time, always stirring in the same direction (this is important—for some reason—as it does not come out right otherwise). Stir *vigorously* until thoroughly blended. When sauce bubbles, add eggs one at a time, stirring vigorously until of a creamy consistency and sauce is no longer stringy. Cover. Simmer until thick. Serve on whole grain toast or warmed hard-tack. The hard stirring makes the difference between success and failure. This is a superb rarebit and really quite easy once you know how.

EASY BAKED CHEESE FONDUE

(4 servings)

6 slices whole grain bread
butter
½ pound Cheddar cheese, grated

3 eggs, beaten
2 cups milk

Butter the bread. Place in shallow pan and cover with the cheese. Combine the eggs and milk and pour over bread and cheese. Bake at 350° F. about 30 minutes. Serve with tomato sauce.

LASAGNE

(6-8 servings)

½ pound lasagne noodles
2 tablespoons olive oil
1 clove garlic, minced
½ pound lean ground beef
1 teaspoon salt
2 8-ounce cans tomato sauce

oregano
basil
½ pound drained cottage cheese or
  ricotta
½ pound mozzarella cheese
¼ pound grated Parmesan cheese

Cook lasagne noodles in water with a little oil added to prevent them from sticking together. Sauté minced garlic in olive oil. Add ground beef, stirring until no red shows. Add salt and tomato sauce. Sprinkle generously with oregano and basil and heat to boiling point.

In 13½ inch x 8 inch x 1-inch pan, put a little of the meat sauce mix. Arrange layer of noodles, half the cottage cheese, half the mozzarella and ⅓ the Parmesan cheese. Top with ⅓ tomato sauce. Make another layer of noodles with cottage cheese, mozzarella and Parmesan. Top with remaining noodles and tomato meat mix. Sprinkle with remaining Parmesan cheese. Bake at 350° F. about 35-45 minutes. Serve.

LIVER

For best nutrition at lowest price, buy pork liver. Lamb liver is tender and delicate; beef liver, robust; calves liver, expensive. Chicken livers are often good buys.

LIVER LOAF WITH GRAVY

(6 servings)

1½ pounds liver
1½ cups boiling water
2 ounces salt pork
1 medium onion
¼ cup chopped parsley

2 cups soft bread crumbs
2 eggs
1 teaspoon salt
¼ teaspoon pepper
2 tablespoons flour

Rinse liver. Remove any tough membranes. Pour boiling water over it and let stand 10 minutes. Remove rind and chop salt pork. Grind with liver and onion. Add the water, parsley, bread crumbs, slightly beaten eggs, salt and pepper. Mix thoroughly. Pack into bread tin and bake at 350° F. about 1 hour. Turn out on platter. Stir flour into pan drippings. Heat to brown. Stir cold water in slowly and cook, stirring to thicken. Add salt and pepper to taste. Pour over loaf.

Variations: Leave out water, use only 1 cup crumbs. Shape into patties, wrap with bacon and broil. Use liver water to make gravy as above and serve with patties.

CHICKEN FRIED LIVER

(4 servings)

1 pound liver, thinly sliced	dash pepper
¼ cup flour	2 tablespoons or more fat for
1 teaspoon salt	sautéing

Remove membranes from liver. Combine flour, salt, and pepper. Coat liver slices thoroughly with seasoned flour. Heat heavy iron skillet. Melt fat (bacon fat, oil, butter, or margarine). When hot, quickly lay liver slices in pan. When well-browned on underside, turn. Cook until that side is browned. Remove to platter. Pour hot water to barely cover bottom of pan. Pour gravy over liver slices. Garnish with parsley or broiled tomatoes if desired. Serve.

LIVER LUNCHEON TURNOVER

(4 servings)

½ pound liver	salt and pepper
4 slices bacon	⅛ teaspoon sage
1 large onion	recipe, pie shell

Fry bacon until crisp. Drain. Quickly fry liver and onion in bacon fat. Drain. Put through grinder or chop fine. Add salt and pepper to taste and sage. Roll pastry into a long oblong about 6 inches wide. Spread filling along one side of pastry leaving ½- to ¾-inch edge. Moisten the edge with water. Fold the other half of pastry over, pressing the edges together firmly to seal flat. Slide on to baking sheet. Mark off servings firmly with side of knife. Prick top to let steam escape. Bake at 450° F. about 20 minutes. Serve either hot or cold.

LIVER WITH TOMATO SAUCE

(4-6 servings)

1 pound thinly sliced liver
2 tablespoons olive oil
1 clove garlic, minced
2 quarts canned tomatoes
1 6-ounce can tomato paste
1 6-ounce can hot water

1 bay leaf
2 teaspoons dried oregano
½ teaspoon dried basil
¼ teaspoon rosemary
salt and pepper

Remove membranes from liver. Heat heavy, covered pot with olive oil. Sear liver on both sides. Cut into bite-size pieces. Add minced garlic, tomatoes, tomato paste, water (rinse can out), bay leaf, oregano, basil, and rosemary. Turn heat to low. Simmer covered 30-40 minutes until liver is tender. Season with salt and pepper to taste. Serve over spaghetti or rice if desired.

CHICKEN LIVER SAUTÉ

(2 servings)

This makes a delicious luncheon dish served over buttered toast with a tossed green salad on the side.

½ pound chicken livers
2 tablespoons flour
½ teaspoon salt
pinch pepper

2 tablespoons butter or margarine
1 cup water
1 teaspoon dry sherry (optional)

Toss chicken livers in combined flour, salt and pepper, until thoroughly coated. (If they are large ones, you may want to split them.) Melt butter in heavy skillet. Sauté livers until well browned, turning. Pour in water and sherry and stir lightly. Simmer for 3-5 minutes. Serve immediately.

Liver can be ground and combined with hamburger in any meat loaf recipe. Cover with boiling water, as in Liver Loaf with Gravy, to facilitate grinding.

Ground liver can also be combined with mashed potato prepared with butter and milk. Pack in bread tin. Bake at 350° F. until heated through.

HEART

Heart is low in price and very flavorful. Use it in any beef stew recipe in place of the beef cubes.

To prepare heart: Slit, inserting knife into the large artery at the top. Carefully insert knife under valve strings, loosening and cutting them out. Remove the artery and vein tissue. Rinse thoroughly.

STUFFED HEART

(3-4 servings)

2 veal or pork hearts or a small
  beef heart
1 tablespoon butter or other fat
2 tablespoons chopped onion
1½ cups dried whole grain bread
  crumbs
¾ teaspoon salt
¼ teaspoon pepper

¼ teaspoon celery salt
3 tablespoons flour
2 tablespoons butter or other fat
1½ cups boiling water
2 bouillon cubes
2 whole cloves
3 peppercorns
1 bay leaf

Prepare the hearts as above. Brown onions. Add bread crumbs, salt, pepper, celery salt and ¼ cup of the boiling water. Mix well. Fill heart cavities with stuffing mixture. Roll hearts in flour. Sauté in butter until lightly browned. Add rest of boiling water combined with bouillon cubes, cloves, peppercorns, and bay leaf. Simmer 1½ to 2 hours until tender. Serve.

SAUTÉED HEART

(3-4 servings)

1 beef heart or 2 pork or veal or 3
  lamb hearts
¼ cup flour
1 teaspoon salt

¼ teaspoon pepper
2 tablespoons butter
½ cup hot water

Prepare the hearts and slice crosswise into ½-inch slices. Combine flour, salt, and pepper. Coat slices with flour mixture. Heat butter in skillet. Add heart slices, sautéing on both sides until brown. Add water. Cover. Simmer about 1½ to 2 hours, turning occasionally until fork tender. Add water if needed. Remove lid last 5 minutes of cooking, turning slices. Serve.

BRAISED HEART

(6 servings)

5-6 pounds any type heart
boiling water
¼ cup diced carrots
¼ cup chopped celery with leaves
½ cup chopped onion
½ teaspoon salt
¼ cup chopped green pepper
  (optional)

3 tablespoons butter or other fat
3 tablespoons flour
1½ cups stock
2 tablespoons lemon juice or dry
  sherry
½ teaspoon of marjoram
2 tablespoons chopped parsley

If a beef heart is used, slice in ½-inch slices. If small hearts are used, slice or halve. Pour about ¾ inch boiling water into saucepan. Add carrots, celery, onion, salt, and green pepper. Place heart slices on rack above the water in the pan. Cover. Steam 1½ to 2 hours. Melt butter in pan. Stir in flour. Add stock, slowly stirring. Add meat and vegetables, lower heat and add lemon juice, marjoram, and parsley. Serve with rice, noodles, or dumplings.

TONGUE

Tongue, whether beef, veal, pork, or lamb is tender and flavorful. It is especially good in sandwiches and far cheaper than the processed meats.

BOILED FRESH TONGUE

(6-8 servings)

about 2 pounds tongue
1 onion
1 carrot
2 stalks celery with leaves

2 tablespoons chopped parsley
8 peppercorns
1 teaspoon salt
boiling water

Place tongue in saucepan with onion, carrot, celery, parsley, peppercorns, and salt. Pour boiling water in to barely cover. Simmer about 3 hours for beef tongue; about 2 hours for smaller tongues. Skin and trim the tongue for serving. If planning to eat cold, let cool in broth after skinning. Remove from broth and slice on the diagonal. Serve with hot mustard sauce, horseradish, or mustard pickles if desired.

CORNED TONGUE

(6-8 servings)

This is especially good in sandwiches and keeps better than fresh tongue.

Rub tongue with coarse salt (kosher salt is ideal). Make a brine of salt and water, adding salt until an egg will float. Immerse tongue in brine. Weigh down with heavy plate. Put in cool place. Let stand 1 or 2 days. Remove from brine. Rinse. Cover with fresh water and simmer 2 to 3 hours until tender.

BLOOD SAUSAGE

These are nutritious and high in iron. They are a contribution of French Canada so are generally available in the northern border states.

To cook sausage, melt butter or other fat in heavy skillet. Prick skin with fork to prevent it from bursting. Put in sausage. Sauté, turning until cooked through.

KIDNEY

Small kidneys, those of lamb and veal, are delicate and delectable when properly prepared. They should not be overcooked and are especially good broiled. Beef, pork and mutton kidneys need slow cooking.

To prepare kidneys, remove membranes and white vessels or tubules. Use partially split for broiling. Beef, pork or mutton kidneys may need to be soaked in cold, salted water to lessen strong flavor.

BROILED KIDNEYS

(any number)

1 lamb kidney per serving
butter
lemon juice
salt and pepper

Split kidneys part way through and lay open on grill. Brush with butter and broil 5 minutes. Turn; brush with butter again; broil another 5 minutes. Serve with lemon juice or slices. Salt and pepper to taste.

MIXED GRILL

(any amount)

Broil a mixture of any of the following meats and/or vegetables. Serve attractively on a platter garnished with fresh parsley and/or lemon slices.

lamb kidney	*liver*
lamb chop	*steak*
sausage	*bacon*
halved fresh tomatoes	*fried egg*
mushroom caps	*pork chop*

Start the meat which takes the longest cooking time first (example: pork chop, sausage). Thickness is a factor also. Brush any meat lacking fat, and vegetables with oil or butter prior to broiling. Try to have them all ready at once.

STEAK AND KIDNEY PIE

(4 servings)

¾ to 1 pound stewing beef	*2 tablespoons flour*
¼ pound kidney	*1 teaspoon salt*
dash pepper	*pastry for pie shell*

Cut beef in 1-inch cubes. Dice kidney. Toss in flour combined with salt and pepper. *1st method:* Brown prepared meat in a little melted fat in skillet. Add 2 tablespoons water or stock. Simmer, tightly covered on low heat until tender 45-60 minutes. Pour into pie dish or casserole. Cool while preparing pastry. Roll pastry to fit top of dish. Lay on, pressing at edges to seal. Prick top with fork. Bake at 450° F. about 20 minutes or until pastry is well browned. *2nd method:* Put prepared raw meat into pie dish, adding stock or water. Cover with prepared pastry. Bake at 425° F. about 35 minutes to brown pastry. Lower oven to 325° F. and continue baking 2 more hours. If necessary cover pastry loosely with foil to prevent burning.

CHOPPED KIDNEYS ON TOAST

(2 servings)

2 *lamb or veal kidneys*	*dash pepper*
2 *tablespoons flour*	2 *tablespoons fat*
1 *teaspoon salt*	2-3 *tablespoons water*

Chop kidneys coarsely. Toss in flour combined with salt and pepper. Shake off excess. Brown quickly in the melted fat, stirring. Add water. Heat to serving temperature. Serve immediately on whole grain toast.

Chicken Giblets:
Dice chicken giblets and cook in boiling water or chicken broth for about 1 hour or until tender. Drain. Make a gravy with the stock. Add giblets to gravy and reheat. Serve on whole-wheat toast.

KIDNEYS WITH MUSHROOMS

(6 servings)

6 *lamb kidneys*	1 *tablespoon flour*
3 *tablespoons lemon juice*	1 *cup bouillon*
2 *tablespoons butter*	¼ *teaspoon pepper*
1 *cup chopped mushrooms*	*salt to taste*

Prepare kidneys. Chop coarsely and mix with lemon juice. Melt butter in skillet. Sauté kidneys and mushrooms 5 minutes. Sprinkle with flour and stir in bouillon and pepper. Add salt if necessary. Serve on toast.

TRIPE

The tripe you buy in the store is usually pickled tripe. To remove the sourness, boil in two changes of water for 15 to 20 minutes.

TRIPE CASSEROLE

(4 servings)

1 pound honeycomb tripe
1 tablespoon butter
1 minced onion
1 tablespoon minced green
  pepper

¼ teaspoon salt
⅛ teaspoon pepper
1 tablespoon flour
1 cup hot water
¼ teaspoon Worcestershire sauce

Prepare tripe. Cut tripe in 2-inch pieces. Melt butter. Sauté onion and green pepper until soft but not brown. Add tripe. Pour into casserole and add salt, pepper, sprinkle with flour and add hot water. Bake at 300° F., 1½ hours. Add Worcestershire sauce after cooking.

SAUTÉED TRIPE

(4 servings)

1 pound tripe
3 tablespoons flour
½ teaspoon salt
⅛ teaspoon pepper
1 egg

1 tablespoon milk
½ cup fine bread or cracker
  crumbs
fat for frying

Prepare tripe. Cut in serving-size pieces. Mix flour, salt, and pepper. Toss tripe in flour. Beat egg slightly with milk. Dip floured tripe in egg then in crumbs. Heat fat in pan, just enough to cover the bottom. Fry tripe until golden. Turn. Fry the other side. Serve.

Broiling or frying: Generally, the cuts you choose for broiling or frying should be well marbled with fat which helps to assure tenderness. Certain low fat cuts do broil nicely however—the tenderloin being a prime example. Less tender cuts or lower quality meat can also be broiled if it is tenderized or marinated in oil and vinegar or lemon juice prior to cooking. To tenderize, buy one of the plain or seasoned meat tenderizers and follow directions. Be sure your broiled meat is cooked to medium or well done to guard against toxoplasmosis.

GRILLED OR BROILED STEAK

(any amount)

Have steak at room temperature. Brush with oil or butter if desired. Preheat broiler. Cook quickly under broiler 2 or 3 minutes on a side to brown. Either move steak rack down so surface is 4 inches below broiler or lower broiler temperature setting. Continue broiling 5 or 6 minutes for medium, longer for well done.

FLANK STEAK OR LONDON BROIL

(4-6 servings)

Flank steak is inexpensive and versatile with no waste.

1 flank steak, 1½ pounds or more
1 clove garlic
oil

With sharp knife, score flank steak crisscross about 1 inch apart and ¼ inch deep. Rub both sides with garlic. Place on greased broiler pan. Brush with oil. Broil 2 inches from heat about 5 minutes or more until well browned. Turn. Brush with oil. Broil 5 minutes more until browned. Cut diagonally into very thin slices. Serve.

PAN-BROILED STEAK

This method can be used effectively for less fatty cuts of steak, sliced less than ¾ inch thick. It is a very good method for cooking venison steak. If steak is not tender, pound thoroughly with tenderizing mallet or hammer. Heat heavy iron skillet to hot. Sprinkle with salt. Quickly lay in steak, searing thoroughly and cooking until brown (if the pan is hot enough, the juices will remain in the meat). When brown on one side, turn and brown the other side. Serve with butter and lemon if desired.

SAUERBRATEN

(10 servings)

4 pounds pot roast	2 tablespoons lemon juice
2 tablespoons flour	1 cup water
2 teaspoons salt	3 tablespoons ketchup
¼ teaspoon pepper	3 bay leaves
2 onions	3 whole cloves
½ cup vinegar	6 gingersnaps

Rub meat with flour, salt, and pepper. Sear in dutch oven. Add onions, vinegar, lemon juice, water, ketchup, bay leaves, and cloves. Cover. Simmer 2 hours. Add gingersnaps and simmer another hour. Serve with dumplings.

SPAETZLE

(4 servings)

The first time I had these was in Munich served in a venison stew. They are excellent with veal dishes and with the Sauerbraten (above).

2 eggs	½ teaspoon salt
1½ cups unbleached, enriched flour	¼ teaspoon baking powder
½ cup water	¼ cup bread crumbs
	¼ cup butter

Beat eggs. Add flour, water, salt, and baking powder and beat well. Drop in small bits from spoon into boiling, salted water or stock or push through a colander or spaetzle maker. They should be light and tender. When done, drain them. Heat butter in skillet. Toss bread crumbs with spaetzle. Sauté spaetzle and bread crumbs in butter until heated through. Serve.

If using in stew, omit the last step.

PAN-BROILED HAMBURG

(serves 4)

1 pound lean ground beef made
 into patties
If desired, add chopped onion

Heat heavy iron skillet. When hot, place patties in pan. Cook on one side until well browned. Turn. Cook on the other side until browned. Remove to hot platter. Dot each with butter or margarine.

Pour a little boiling water into the pan. Scrape and pour over patties.

GOURMET HAMBURG PATTIES

(3 to 4 servings)

1 pound lean ground beef
½ pound fresh mushrooms
1 tablespoon butter
½ tablespoon cornstarch

¼ cup burgundy
¼ cup boiling water
1 bouillon cube

Prepare hamburger as above. While cooking, melt butter in small saucepan. Wipe mushrooms; slice lengthwise. Sauté in butter. Stir burgundy into cornstarch. After removing hamburg patties from fry pan, lower heat and pour in water combined with bouillon cube. Stir, scraping any hamburger from bottom of pan. Quickly stir in burgundy and mix. Add mushrooms. Pour over Hamburg Patties.

MEAT LOAF

(8 servings)

1½ pounds ground beef
1 cup oatmeal
1 egg
¼ cup chopped onion
2 teaspoons salt

¼ teaspoon pepper
1 teaspoon chili powder
1 tablespoon ketchup
1 tablespoon Worcestershire sauce
1 cup milk

In large bread tin, mix beef, oatmeal, egg, onion, salt, pepper, chili powder, ketchup, Worcestershire sauce, and milk. Pack it down in the tin. Bake at 350° F. 1 hour. Serve with tomato sauce.

QUICK MEAT LOAF PATTY

(4 servings)

1 pound hamburger
¼ teaspoon basil
1 teaspoon parsley
½ teaspoon oregano
1 small onion, chopped

½ teaspoon salt
dash pepper
dash Worcestershire sauce
¼ cup milk or 1 egg
1 cup boiling water

Mix hamburger, basil, parsley, oregano, onion, salt, pepper, Worcestershire sauce, and milk or egg thoroughly. Form one large patty. Brown in large skillet on both sides. Add 1 cup water. Lower heat. Cover. Cook until partly done (about 20 minutes). Add frozen vegetables—green beans and corn or peas and wax beans—1 10-ounce package of each. Cook until patty is done and vegetables just tender. If using fresh vegetables, add them sooner. If canned, use vegetable water to cook patty and add vegetables when meat is done. Heat through and serve.

Variation: Add 1 tablespoon ketchup if desired.

SARMA (STUFFED CABBAGE)

(4 servings)
This is a Yugoslavian dish.

1 head cabbage
1 chopped onion
2 tablespoons lard
½ pound lean ground beef
½ pound ground pork
1 egg
¼ cup raw rice

salt, pepper, garlic powder or
  garlic salt
1 teaspoon vinegar or wine
sliced bacon (about 4 slices)
boiling water
2 tablespoons flour

Cut leaf by leaf off cabbage and lay on plate. Sauté onion in 1 tablespoon lard until brown. Mix beef and pork. Add browned

170

onions, egg, and rice. Season well with salt, pepper, and garlic. Add vinegar or wine. Sauté the mixture slightly in the lard used for the onion. Place a heaping tablespoonful of mixture on each cabbage leaf, rolling and tucking in sides of leaf around meat. Arrange in dutch oven. Lay slices of bacon over cabbage rolls. Pour boiling water in to level of bacon. Cover. Simmer 20 minutes if converted rice is used; 30 minutes if brown rice is used. Melt 1 tablespoon lard in small skillet and brown flour in it. Slowly add 1 cup of the liquid from the dutch oven, stirring. Pour this mixture over Sarma without stirring. Continue cooking for 30 minutes. When done, serve with thickened broth poured over it.

BEEF GOULASH WITH NOODLES

(4-6 servings)

1½ pounds stew beef
⅛ pound salt pork
1 tablespoon flour
½ teaspoon salt
dash pepper
1 minced clove garlic

½ cup chopped onion
1 cup water with 2 bouillon cubes
1 8-ounce can tomato sauce
12 peppercorns
1 tablespoon paprika

Dice salt pork. Sauté in skillet. Drain and save. Cut beef in 1-inch cubes. Combine flour, salt, and pepper. Toss with beef cubes. Brown beef on all sides in pork fat. Add garlic, onion, bouillon, tomato sauce, peppercorns, and paprika. Cover tightly and simmer 1½ hours or until tender. Add more liquid if needed. Thicken with 1 tablespoon flour mixed with a little cold water to make thin paste. Serve on cooked noodles.

CORNED BEEF

(any amount)

Select a pot roast of beef or beef brisket. Rub with coarse pickling salt (kosher salt is an excellent choice). Salt enough water to cover the beef. Add salt until an egg will float in it. Put a weight on the meat to keep it down in the water and let set for 1 or 2 days.

To cook: Drain and rinse the corned beef. Place in large kettle. Cover with water. Simmer until fork-tender—between 1½ to 4 hours depending on the size and cut of meat. Cool in broth. Save broth.

NEW ENGLAND BOILED DINNER

(any amount)

Corned beef	turnip
Corned beef broth	cabbage
carrots	(optional) beets, parsnips
potatoes	

Prepare vegetables—scrub and quarter carrots lengthwise or cut in pieces. Cut cabbage in wedges. Slice turnip or cut in cubes. Scrub potatoes, cut out eyes and halve. Scrub parsnips. Prepare beets for cooking, if fresh. You may prefer to use canned sliced beets.

Bring corned beef broth to a boil. Add carrots and potatoes. Simmer about 10 minutes. Add turnip. Simmer another 10 minutes. Add cabbage. Simmer until tender (about 10 minutes). Cook or heat beets in a separate pan. You may add cut-up parsnips to broth after adding cabbage if desired—however due to their distinctive sweet flavor, I prefer to cook them in a little broth removed from pot. They will be done in minutes depending on size. Remove all vegetables from broth and arrange on platter with corned beef. Serve with mustard or mustard pickle. Save broth for cooking beans, peas, or lentils.

CORNED BEEF HASH

(4 servings)

4 potatoes
1 onion
3 cups leftover corned beef

Boil potatoes in their skins. Cool, peel and put in chopping bowl. Slice onion and add to potatoes with corned beef. Chop very fine (or put through fine blade of food grinder). Melt about 2 tablespoons butter in hot frying pan. Add 4 tablespoons water and hash. Cook, stirring slightly until heated through. Lower heat. Cook until crust forms on bottom. Fold over. Serve with ketchup and poached egg if desired. A tossed green salad makes an excellent accompaniment to this dish.

Variations: For red-flannel hash, add beets to the ingredients.

CORNED BEEF
ESCALLOPED POTATOES

(4-6 servings)

4 thinly sliced potatoes
¼ cup flour
salt and pepper

3 tablespoons butter
leftover sliced corned beef
1 cup milk

Place layer of potatoes in bottom of casserole. Sprinkle lightly with flour, salt, and pepper. Dot with butter. Add layer of corned beef. Repeat layers. Add a last layer of potatoes. Pour in milk. Bake at 350° F. about 45 minutes.

ROAST BEEF

(any amount)

An oven roast of beef is now rather a luxury dish. But if you have extra money to spend on food, this method of roasting is unsurpassed.

1 good cut beef (rib, loin, sirloin
 tip)
salt and pepper

Let beef stand at room temperature for 1 hour. Wipe and rub with salt and pepper. Place beef on rack in roasting pan; standing— not on the cut side, but as in the case of a rib roast, on the ribs with fat uppermost. Put ½ inch water in pan. Heat oven to 500° F. Roast at this temperature for 20 minutes. Lower heat to 300° F. Baste 3 times the first hour of cooking at this temperature. Allow 22 minutes per pound for medium, 30 minutes per pound for well done.

COLD BEEF IN MARINADE

This recipe can be used for oven roast of beef or even for pot roast if you wish.

Cold, thinly sliced, cooked beef
3 tablespoons olive oil or other oil
4 tablespoons lemon juice
1 chopped onion

½ teaspoon red pepper
1 teaspoon salt
½ teaspoon dry mustard

Beat together the oil, lemon juice, onion, pepper, salt, mustard. Arrange beef on platter and pour marinade over it. Refrigerate until serving time.

SWISS STEAK

(6 servings)

2 pounds lean round steak
salt and pepper
½ cup flour
2 tablespoons butter or other fat
1 small onion, chopped

¼ cup green pepper, chopped
2 cups stewed tomatoes
juice, ½ lemon
1 teaspoon mustard
1 tablespoon horseradish

Combine salt, pepper, flour. Rub into steak and pound. Melt butter in heavy pan. Brown meat. Add onion, green pepper, tomatoes, lemon juice, mustard, and horseradish. Cover, simmer 2 hours. Turn occasionally. Add water if needed.

EASY CHILI CON CARNE

(6 servings)

¾ pound ground beef
2 tablespoons olive oil or other oil
1 large onion, chopped
1 large clove of garlic, minced
1 large can tomatoes

1 tablespoon or more chili powder
1 teaspoon salt
⅛ teaspoon pepper
1 large can cooked dry beans
  (about 1 quart)

Heat olive oil in heavy skillet. Add onion and garlic. Sauté lightly. Crumble beef into pan. Cook, stirring until red is gone. Add tomatoes, chili powder, salt, pepper. Heat. Simmer 15-20 minutes. Add beans. Heat through and simmer 5 minutes more. Serve with grated cheese on the side.

HAMBURG CURRY

(6-8 servings)

1 tablespoon oil
1 large onion, finely chopped
½ teaspoon turmeric
½ teaspoon black pepper
1 bay leaf
2 teaspoons curry powder
½ teaspoon powdered ginger
½ teaspoon garlic powder
2 cloves

½ teaspoon cinnamon
½ teaspoon cardamom
1 teaspoon salt
1½ pounds ground beef
½ cup water
1 cup fresh or frozen peas
1 teaspoon lemon juice
parsley

Brown onion in oil. Add turmeric, pepper, crumbled bay leaf, curry powder, ginger, garlic powder, cloves, cinnamon, cardamom, and salt and sauté 2 minutes. Add beef and sauté, stirring, 5 minutes. Add water. Simmer 15 minutes. Add peas (if using fresh peas add with water). Simmer 5 minutes. Serve hot with Pooris (below) or rice.

POORIS

2 cups whole-wheat flour
1 cup unbleached, enriched flour
1 teaspoon salt

1 tablespoon butter or margarine
water

Combine wheat flour, flour, and salt. Add butter, rubbing in with hands. Knead in enough water to make a stiff dough. Cover and let set at least 1 hour. Pinch into small balls of dough about 1 inch in diameter. Roll out on floured surface to form circles. Heat ½ inch of oil in skillet to 375° F. Fry Pooris quickly, pressing down into oil with perforated spoon or spatula to make them puff. Turn once. Remove. Drain on paper towels. Serve hot. Store unused ones in refrigerator and reheat in oven.

MEAT SAUCE FOR SPAGHETTI

(3 to 4 servings)

¼ pound prosciutto or bacon,
 sliced
1 tablespoon butter
1 medium onion, minced
1 carrot, minced
¼ stalk celery, minced
½ pound lean ground beef
¼ pound minced chicken livers
1 cup dry, white wine

1 cup beef bouillon
2 tablespoons tomato paste
salt and pepper
⅛ teaspoon ground nutmeg
2 teaspoons grated lemon rind
2 cloves
1 cup heavy cream or undiluted
 evaporated milk

On cutting board or in chopping bowl, combine prosciutto (bacon), butter, onion, carrot, and celery. Mince together to make almost a paste. In dutch oven, cook over low heat until slightly brown. Add beef and brown evenly. Add chicken livers and cook 2 minutes. Combine wine, bouillon, and tomato paste. Blend well. Add to meat mixture. Season with salt and pepper to taste. Stir in nutmeg, grated lemon rind and cloves. Simmer on low heat covered for 45 minutes, stirring occasionally. Just before serving, scald cream without boiling and stir into hot sauce.

MEAT SAUCE FOR PASTA, RICE, OR CORNMEAL

(4 servings)

1½ to 2 ounces dried mushrooms
 or ½ pound fresh mushrooms,
 diced
1 pound lean beef
½ cup butter
1 medium onion, minced
1 medium carrot, minced

1 stalk celery, minced
½ cup minced parsley
⅔ cup burgundy or claret
1 cup beef bouillon
salt and pepper
1 teaspoon grated lemon rind

Crumble mushrooms and soak in water to cover. Dice meat as finely as possible. Melt butter in dutch oven. Add onion, carrot, celery, and parsley. Cook, stirring over medium heat for three minutes. Add mushrooms and water, wine, and bouillon. Season to taste. Add lemon rind. Cover tightly. Simmer on low heat about three hours until meat is completely melded into the sauce. If the sauce is not thick enough, cook uncovered to thicken. Serve over rice, spaghetti, or cornmeal.

EASY SPAGHETTI
WITH MEATBALLS

(6-8 servings)

MEATBALLS:
1 pound lean ground beef
1 garlic clove, minced
½ small onion, minced
½ cup dry bread crumbs
1 teaspoon oregano
½ teaspoon basil
2 tablespoons grated Parmesan
  cheese
½ cup milk
1 egg
⅛ teaspoon pepper
1 teaspoon salt

SAUCE:
2 garlic cloves, minced
1 tablespoon olive oil
2 large cans tomatoes
1 6-ounce can tomato paste
2 teaspoons oregano
1 teaspoon basil
⅛ teaspoon rosemary
1 bay leaf
1 teaspoon salt
pepper

Prepare meatballs by mixing thoroughly the beef, garlic, onion, bread crumbs, oregano, basil, cheese, milk, egg, salt, and pepper. Form into balls about 1½ inches in diameter.

Sauté garlic lightly in olive oil. Add tomatoes, tomato paste (rinse can in water and add), oregano, basil, rosemary, bay leaf, salt, and pepper. Bring to boil. Drop in meatballs. Reheat. Lower heat to simmer. Cook about 45 minutes. Serve on spaghetti with Parmesan cheese. Be sure you use *lean* ground beef in this recipe. If the beef is *not* lean, brown the meatballs, pouring off excess fat before adding to sauce.

VEAL

Veal is quite expensive in the United States, although in Europe it is a staple meat. That is because veal takes little feed to raise in the crowded lands of Europe. Since veal has little fat, it may in some cases be a better buy than beef if it is on special. Because of its low fat content, veal is generally pot-roasted or braised.

BREADED VEAL CUTLET
VEAL SCALLOPINI
OR WIENER SCHNITZEL

(4-6 servings)

1½ pounds veal cutlet, sliced thin	2 tablespoons milk
2 tablespoons flour	¾ cup fine bread crumbs
1 teaspoon salt	4 tablespoons oil, butter or other
⅛ teaspoon pepper	fat
1 egg	1 lemon

Pound cutlets until thin, removing any membranes or fat. Dust with flour, salt, and pepper mixture. Dip in egg, beaten with milk. Coat with crumbs. Sauté in hot fat until well browned, turning. Serve with lemon wedges and parsley as a garnish.

Variation: Add 1 teaspoon mixed Italian herbs to bread crumbs. After quickly browning meat, add 1 8-ounce can tomato sauce with a dash of cloves and allspice added. Simmer, covered on low heat about ½ to ¾ hour. Serve with lemon if desired.

VEAL PAPRIKA

(4 servings)

1 pound veal stew meat
2 tablespoons flour
½ teaspoon salt
dash pepper
1½ tablespoons butter or other fat
1 large chopped onion

1 minced clove garlic
1 cup boiling water, vegetable
    water or chicken stock
2 tablespoons paprika
½ cup sour cream

Cut veal in 1-inch cubes, removing connective tissue. Toss in combined flour, salt, and pepper. Brown in butter with chopped onion and garlic. Add water and paprika. Simmer, covered, until fork tender. About 1½ hours. Stir in sour cream. Serve with noodles or rice.

Variation: Either of these veal recipes can be used with venison. You can also use venison in preparing most lamb recipes.

PORK

Pork has suddenly become one of the more expensive meats. It is, however, very versatile, lending itself to a variety of cooking methods. It is rich in B vitamins, especially thiamine (vitamin B_1). Because pork may be host to trichina, an organism which can cause illness in man, it should be well cooked (to 137° F.). Curing meats, freezing and holding for specified periods at below 5° F. are also methods of killing trichinae. A pork product stamped USDA "Ready to Eat" is safe to eat without cooking—at least with respect to trichinae. Of course one must consider age, storage, packaging, and other factors.

ROAST PORK WITH SAGE STUFFING

1 *pork loin*	*sage if desired*
salt and pepper	*stuffing*
flour	

Wipe meat. Season thoroughly with salt and pepper and rub with flour. If you plan to stuff the roast, be sure to have your butcher cut partway through the bone at the base to provide a pocket for stuffing. Stuff with sage and onion stuffing (see following recipe). Sprinkle with sage. Heat oven to 500° F. Place pork in roasting pan. Roast for 15 minutes at 500° F. Lower heat to 325° F. Cook 50 minutes per pound. Add 1 cup hot water at the end of the first hour. Baste occasionally. Serve with gravy made from pan drippings.

SAGE AND ONION STUFFING

2 *cups dry whole-grain bread*	1 *tablespoon butter*
crumbs	¾ *cup boiling water*
1 *teaspoon dried sage*	¼ *teaspoon salt*
1 *chopped onion*	*dash pepper*

Combine bread crumbs, sage, onion, butter, boiling water, salt, and pepper. Add more water if needed. Use to stuff pork.

Variation: Add a chopped apple.

ROAST PORK

3-4 pound pork roast
3 cloves garlic
1 teaspoon dried rosemary

3 whole cloves
salt and pepper
dry wine, water

Trim excess fat from pork. Make three pockets in meat with tip of knife. Wet cloves of garlic and roll in rosemary. Insert a garlic and whole clove in each pocket. Rub meat with salt and pepper. Place on rack in roasting pan. Pour about 2 inches of half wine, half water into pan. Bake at 300° F. about 45 minutes per pound, basting occasionally. Cool in the juice. May be eaten hot or cold.

Variations: Use veal, lamb, venison, or kid roast in place of pork.

PORK CHOPS WITH PINEAPPLE AND RICE

(4 servings)

4 pork chops
1 cup uncooked rice
1 medium onion, chopped
1 can crushed pineapple,
    unsweetened

1½ cups boiling water
1 teaspoon salt
dash pepper
1 tablespoon honey
1 green pepper, sliced

Brown pork chops. Remove from pan. In fat from chops, sauté the rice and onion. Add pineapple, water, salt, and pepper and honey. Simmer 30 minutes. Add green pepper and chops. Simmer 10-15 minutes more until chops and rice are tender and most of the water is absorbed. Serve plain or with soy sauce if desired.

PORK CURRY

(4 servings)

4 pork chops
¼ cup flour
1 tablespoon fat
2 cups sliced mushrooms
¼ cup chopped onion
1 tablespoon butter or margarine

1 tablespoon salt
dash pepper
½ or more teaspoons curry
  powder
1¼ cups milk

Coat chops with flour. Save remaining flour. Brown chops in fat in large heavy skillet. Pour off excess fat. Place chops in baking dish, and cover with mushrooms. Sauté onion in butter until light brown. Stir in rest of flour and salt, pepper, and curry powder. Slowly stir in milk. Cook to thicken, stirring constantly. Pour over chops in baking dish. Bake at 350° F. 1 hour or until tender.

CHOW MEIN

(4 servings)

2 cups cooked pork cut in strips
1 cup thin strips celery or Chinese
  cabbage
1 small onion, thinly sliced
1 tablespoon fat or oil
1½ tablespoons cornstarch
1 cup water, vegetable water, or
  stock

½ teaspoon salt
dash pepper
1⅓ teaspoons soy sauce
1 pound can bean sprouts, drained
chow mein noodles if desired

Cook pork with celery and onions in fat until vegetables begin to get tender. Blend cornstarch with a little liquid. Stir in with remaining liquid and salt, pepper, and soy sauce. Cook to thicken. Add bean sprouts. Heat through. Serve over noodles or rice.

PORK SOUFFLE

(6 servings)

4 eggs, separated
¼ cup flour
1½ cups milk
2 cups cooked, diced pork

2 tablespoons finely chopped onion
¼ cup chopped green pepper
½ teaspoon salt

Beat egg yolks. Beat whites stiffly. Blend flour with a little milk in saucepan. Heat slowly, stirring in remaining milk. Cook, stirring, until thickened. Stir a little of milk mixture into egg yolks. Add yolks to milk, stirring. Remove from heat. Add pork, onion, green pepper, and salt. Fold in egg whites. Pour into casserole. Set in pan of hot water. Bake 1 hour at 325° F. until set. Serve.

PORK WITH VEGETABLES

(6 servings)

1½ pounds lean pork
1 tablespoon fat
¼ cup flour
1¾ cups water
1½ cups diced potato
1 cup sliced carrots

2 cups fresh or frozen lima beans
1 tablespoon chopped onion
2 teaspoons salt
pepper
1 cup yoghurt

Cut pork in 1-inch cubes. Brown in fat. Sprinkle with flour, stirring. Add water slowly, stirring until thickened. Simmer, covered, about 45 minutes or until tender. Add potato, carrots, lima beans, onion, salt, and pepper. Cook about 20 minutes until vegetables are tender. Serve topped with yoghurt.

PORK CHOPS WITH SAUERKRAUT

(4 servings)

4 pork chops
1 pound sauerkraut
2 teaspoons paprika

2 chopped apples
½ teaspoon caraway seeds

Sear pork chops in hot skillet. Add sauerkraut, paprika, apples, and caraway seeds. Simmer, covered, 30-45 minutes until tender.

LAMB

Lamb is flavorful. It combines beautifully with a number of vegetables and with rice. One secret of cooking lamb is using lemon juice to bring out the flavor.

ROAST LAMB

(10 servings)
This is my husband's favorite roast lamb.

5-pound leg of lamb
salt and pepper
slivered clove of garlic

2 tablespoons lemon juice
butter

Wipe lamb. Place in pan. Combine salt, pepper and garlic slivers. Make skewer holes in lamb at random. Put slivers of seasoned garlic into skewer holes. Rub with butter and sprinkle with salt, pepper, and lemon juice. Roast uncovered at 300° F. for 2½ hours.

BROILED LAMB CHOPS

Rub chops with lemon juice. Sear close to hot broiler on each side then continue broiling until well browned. They should be slightly pink inside. The length of time to cook depends on thickness, 1-inch chops taking about 5 minutes.

LAMB STEW

2 pounds boneless lamb cut in
   1-inch cubes
¼ cup minced, lean bacon
1 small minced onion
1½ tablespoons lard
salt and pepper
2 tablespoons flour

½ cup dry, white wine
boiling water
3 egg yolks
1½ tablespoons lemon juice
¼ cup minced parsley
½ teaspoon dried marjoram

In dutch oven, heat lard over medium heat. Add lamb, bacon and onion. Cook, stirring constantly until golden brown. Season with salt and pepper and sprinkle with flour. Cook 2 minutes longer. Add wine and cook uncovered until wine evaporates. Add enough boiling water to nearly cover meat. Cover. Simmer covered over low heat, stirring occasionally 35 minutes until tender. Before serving, beat egg yolks; add lemon juice, parsley, and marjoram to yolks. Add a little hot liquid from lamb to yolk mixture. Stir yolk mixture into lamb liquid. Keep warm for about 5 minutes until sauce is thickened but not curdled.

Variations: Use kid, veal or venison in place of lamb.

MINCED LAMB WITH VEGETABLES

(4 servings)
   This meal-in-a-dish is delicious.

1 pound ground lamb
1 tablespoon olive oil
1 minced clove garlic
1 cup raw brown rice
3 cups water
1 teaspoon salt
dash pepper

1 sliced onion
1 thinly sliced green pepper
2 small or 1 medium zucchini
   unpeeled, quartered, and sliced
   in ½-inch slices
2 chopped tomatoes

Heat olive oil in deep skillet with tightly fitting cover. Sauté garlic and crumbled lamb. Sauté brown rice. Add water, salt, pepper, and onion. Bring to a boil. Lower heat. Simmer 40 minutes. Add green pepper, zucchini, chopped tomatoes. Simmer 5 to 8 minutes or until zucchini is tender but not soggy. Serve with a tossed green salad.

Variations: Add eggplant cut in ½-inch slices. Add other vegetables if desired.

LAMB-BEAN STOVE-TOP CASSEROLE

(6 or more servings)
   This dish is excellent, low in cost, and a good source of protein.

2 pounds lamb combinations
2 tablespoons oil
1 small onion, sliced
1 minced clove garlic
1 can tomatoes, #303
1½ teaspoons salt
oregano
dash pepper

1 bay leaf
¼ pound fresh mushrooms
2 medium zucchini cut in ½-inch slices
2 1-pound, 4-ounce cans canneloni (white kidney beans or other cooked dry beans)
½ cup pitted dry olives

   In dutch oven, heat oil. Brown lamb. Pour off fat. Add onion, garlic, tomatoes, salt, oregano, pepper, and bay leaf. Cover. Simmer ¾ hour. Add mushrooms (cut any large ones in quarters, leave small ones whole) and zucchini. Cook until vegetables and lamb are tender—about 10 minutes. Add kidney beans and olives. Cook about 5 minutes to heat through.

TOMATOES STUFFED WITH LAMB

(4 servings)

4 large tomatoes
1 tablespoon butter
1 tablespoon flour
½ cup evaporated milk
1 cup leftover cooked lamb, ground

⅓ cup chopped mushrooms
salt and pepper
¼ cup grated Parmesan or
Romano cheese
2 tablespoons butter, melted

Cut out stem-end of tomatoes and scoop out. Drain. Melt butter. Blend in flour. Add evaporated milk, stirring constantly until thickened. Combine with lamb and mushrooms. Add salt and pepper to taste. Stuff into tomatoes. Place stuffed tomatoes in shallow pan. Sprinkle with the cheese (1 tablespoon per tomato) and melted butter. Bake at 375° F. 25-30 minutes until top is slightly browned.

CURRIED LAMB

(4 servings)

2 cups leftover lamb, diced
1 tablespoon fat
1 medium onion, chopped
1 minced clove garlic
1 apple, chopped
2 tablespoons raisins
¼ cup grated coconut (optional)

1 tablespoon flour
2 teaspoons curry powder
1 chicken bouillon cube dissolved
in ½ cup boiling water
1½ cups milk
salt and pepper

Melt fat. Sauté onion and garlic until transparent but not brown. Add apple, raisins, and coconut. Sauté 5 minutes. Add lamb. Sprinkle with combined flour and curry powder, stirring. Slowly add chicken bouillon and milk while stirring. Heat and stir until thickened. Add salt and pepper to taste. Serve over cooked rice.

POTTED LAMB

(4 servings)

2 pounds lamb combinations
2 tablespoons flour
1 teaspoon salt
⅛ teaspoon pepper
2 tablespoons butter or margarine
½ cup boiling water
2 peeled tomatoes, sliced

2 medium onions, sliced
2 celery stalks with leaves, diced
4 large carrots cut in pieces
2 tablespoons flour, moistened
   with cold water to make thin
   paste

Toss the lamb with the combined flour, salt, and pepper. Melt butter in dutch oven. Brown meat. Add boiling water, tomatoes, onion, and celery. Cover and simmer until meat is tender, about 1 hour. Add carrots and cook until tender (about 15-20 minutes). Stir a little of the hot liquid into flour-water paste. Then add to pot, stirring until thickened. Serve.

LAMB WITH EGGPLANT

(4 servings)

1 cup cooked lamb, ground
1 small eggplant
¼ cup oil or butter
¼ pound mushrooms, sliced
2 cups uncooked rice

dash pepper
1 cup grated cheese
1⅓ cups boiling water with
   1 chicken bouillon cube,
   1 beaten egg

Peel and slice eggplant into ¼-inch slices. Sauté in butter or oil to brown. Sauté mushrooms, add rice and lamb. Layer rice and lamb mix, eggplant, and cheese in large casserole or baking pan. Press down firmly. Beat egg into bouillon mixture. Pour over layers. Add top layer of cheese. Bake at 350° F. 35 minutes. Serve with tomato sauce.

POULTRY

Though the price has nearly doubled, as it has on almost everything, poultry is still a good buy. Buy whole chickens and cut them up yourself to save money. Use the neck, backbone, giblets, and wings to prepare a chicken broth. Freeze and use for soup or as a stock when chicken bouillon or stock is called for in a recipe.

To cut up chicken: Place chicken on its back on cutting board. Insert a large sharp knife just to the side of the sharp breast bone starting from the opening between the legs and working toward the neck. Pull open a bit and insert knife just to the side of the tail. Cut along edge of backbone with knife (or cleaver if you have one). Insert knife on the other side of tail and cut again along backbone. Chicken will now be in three parts: two sides and the backbone.

To cut up further, cut through wing joint where it joins breast, twisting as you cut. Insert knife between breast and hind quarter, cutting through (take the path of least resistance). Turn hind quarter, holding drumstick in left hand (if right-handed). Cut down through joint between drumstick and thigh. Repeat with the other half chicken. You now have one back with tail, two drumsticks, two thighs, two breast halves, two wings—also the neck and giblets. If the chicken is relatively large, you can cut each breast half in half again.

In any recipe calling for a cut-up chicken, use the breast, drumsticks, and thighs. You may use other parts as desired.

If you buy a number of chickens on special, cut them up and wrap for freezing, separating out the livers. You can package them by the amounts you need to serve your family, by white or dark meat, or however you wish.

To make broth from necks, backs, wings, giblets: Place parts in saucepan. Cover with cold water. Add bay leaf, pinch of thyme, salt and pepper, celery and onion. Bring to boil. Lower heat and simmer about two hours or so. Strain. Pick out bits of meat and replace in broth. Refrigerate.

SWEET AND SOUR BAKED CHICKEN

(4 servings)

1 broiler fryer, cut up
½ cup flour
1 teaspoon salt
¼ teaspoon pepper
¼ cup vinegar

1 tablespoon soy sauce
½ cup crushed, unsweetened
 pineapple
2 tablespoons honey

Combine flour, salt, and pepper. Put in bag. Rinse chicken pieces and shake, a few at a time, in the seasoned flour. Place skin side down on 13 x 9 x 2-inch pan. Bake at 350° F. 15-20 minutes until skin side is brown. Turn. Cover with sauce made by mixing vinegar, soy sauce, pineapple, and honey. Bake 35 more minutes.

OVEN-FRIED CHICKEN

(4 servings)

1 broiler fryer, cut up
½ cup fine bread crumbs or wheat
 germ
¼ teaspoon garlic powder
1 teaspoon salt
¼ teaspoon pepper

1 teaspoon oregano
¼ teaspoon basil (or 1 teaspoon
 Italian seasoning or Romano
 cheese)
¼ cup grated Parmesan cheese

Combine crumbs, garlic powder, salt, pepper, oregano, basil, and Parmesan cheese. Wet chicken pieces and roll in crumb mixture to coat. Place on baking sheet, skin side up. Bake at 375° F. about 1 hour. (You may want to turn pieces after 30 minutes.)

Variations: Shake in ½-cup flour combined with salt and pepper.

BAKED CHICKEN PUFF

(4-6 servings)
  This is chicken baked in a Yorkshire pudding.

1 cut up broiler fryer	3 eggs
salt, pepper, mace	¼ cup flour
boiling water	½ teaspoon salt
2 cups milk	2 tablespoons butter

  Rub chicken with salt and pepper and sprinkle with mace. Place in deep saucepan. Add about ½-inch water. Cover. Simmer about 25-30 minutes until partly cooked. Make a batter of the milk, eggs, flour, and salt. Melt butter in baking pan. Place chicken in pan. Pour batter over chicken. Bake at 375° F. about ½ hour until batter has puffed up and is browned. Thicken the liquid in which the chicken was cooked by adding a thin paste of 2 tablespoons flour and a little cold water. Serve with the pudding.

CHICKEN FRICASSEE

(8 or more servings)

1 fowl (stewing chicken, cut up)	1 teaspoon salt
bay leaf	½ cup flour
1½ teaspoons salt	¼ cup butter
6 peppercorns	

  Wash fowl. Place in dutch oven. Add bay leaf, salt, and peppercorns. Simmer until tender (2-3 hours). Roll chicken pieces in ¼-cup flour mixed with salt. Sauté in butter until lightly browned. Remove to warm platter. Add remaining flour to butter, blending. Slowly stir in chicken broth, simmering until thick. Pour gravy over chicken. Serve.

CHICKEN CROQUETTES

(2 servings)

1 cup chopped cooked chicken
½ cup whole-grain bread crumbs
½ cup evaporated milk
1 teaspoon melted butter

¼ teaspoon salt
⅛ teaspoon pepper
1 egg, slightly beaten
oil or fat

Pour evaporated milk over bread crumbs and combine with chicken. Add butter, salt, pepper, and egg. Form into oval rolls. Heat enough oil to cover bottom of skillet. Sauté. Drain. Serve with tomato sauce or leftover gravy.

CHICKEN PAPRIKA

(4 servings)

1 fryer broiler, cut up
2 tablespoons flour
½ teaspoon salt
1½ tablespoons paprika

½ cup sliced onion
2 tablespoons butter or other fat
½ cup hot water
½ cup yoghurt

Combine flour, salt, and 1 tablespoon paprika. Coat chicken in seasoned flour. Heat butter in dutch oven. Brown onions. Add chicken pieces and sauté, turning until browned. Add water. Simmer slowly until tender (about 45 minutes). Add remaining paprika. Simmer 5 more minutes. Lift chicken to warm platter. Add yoghurt to liquid in pan. Heat through, stirring. Pour over chicken.

CHICKEN WITH VEGETABLES

(4 servings)

1 broiler fryer, cut up
3 tablespoons butter or other fat
2 medium onions, thinly sliced
1 minced clove garlic
3 tomatoes, peeled and quartered
¼ cup raw rice (brown or
  converted)

1 teaspoon salt
dash pepper
½ teaspoon thyme
2 cups hot chicken bouillon
1 cup peas (fresh or frozen)

In dutch oven, brown chicken in hot butter until golden. Sauté onion and garlic until lightly browned. Add tomatoes, rice, salt, pepper, and thyme. Pour in bouillon. Cover and simmer ¾ hour. Add peas. Heat to simmer. Simmer until peas are done and chicken is tender, about 10-15 minutes.

BASQUE CHICKEN

(4 servings)

1 broiler fryer, cut up
2 tablespoons olive oil
1 tablespoon flour
1 tablespoon tomato paste
1 tablespoon white Concord wine
  or other sweet white wine

1 cup chicken bouillon
¼ pound sliced mushrooms
8 stuffed olives
1 sliced green pepper
salt to taste
2 pimientos or 1 red pepper, diced

Heat olive oil in dutch oven. Brown chicken, add flour, blending. Add combined tomato paste, wine, bouillon, stirring. Add mushrooms, olives, green pepper, salt and pepper. Cover. Simmer about 45 minutes until chicken is tender.

CHICKEN WITH RICE

(4 servings)

1 broiler fryer, cut up
2 tablespoons flour
1 teaspoon salt
⅛ teaspoon pepper
3 tablespoons olive oil
1 sliced medium onion

1 minced clove garlic
1 cup brown or converted rice
1 1-pound can tomatoes
1 cup chicken bouillon
1 teaspoon powdered saffron
salt and pepper to taste

Put flour, salt, and pepper in bag. Add chicken pieces one or two at a time, shaking to coat. Heat olive oil in dutch oven. Sauté onion, garlic, and chicken pieces. Add rice and sauté for 2-3 minutes. Add tomatoes and bouillon. Heat to simmering. Simmer 45 minutes or until chicken and rice are tender. Add saffron. Simmer 5 more minutes. Serve.

TURKEY

There is no question that *fresh* turkey is superior to frozen, but it is available only at premium prices. The prebasted turkeys cost more for the addition of water and a little fat. A good regular frozen turkey is far less expensive and you are not paying extra for water and grease. Sometimes you can get a turkey at bargain prices after a holiday. If your family is small, freeze some of the cooked meat and gravy for later use. Use leftover turkey meat in recipes calling for cooked chicken or cooked turkey.

ROAST TURKEY

(any amount)

1 turkey
dressing

Preheat oven to 450° F. Stuff body cavity and neck of turkey. Tie legs to tail or tuck under flap. Turn neck skin under back and pin with skewer. Place bird on rack in uncovered roasting pan. Put in oven. Lower heat to 350° F. if bird weighs up to 16 pounds. If bird weighs over 16 pounds, lower heat to 300° F. After 30 minutes drape the bird with cloth (doubled cheesecloth or an old linen dish towel will do) soaked in butter, margarine, or other shortening or bland oil. Remove cloth about ½ hour before turkey is done to brown. Baste with drippings (or roast uncovered, basting with butter or margarine until brown. Then cover lightly with foil and continue roasting.) Allow 20-25 minutes per pound for turkey weighing under 16 pounds. If over 16 pounds, allow about 15 minutes per pound. Make gravy with pan drippings and broth made from cooking neck and giblets (cover with water; bring to boil; lower heat; simmer 1½ hours). Use flour or cornstarch to thicken. Add chopped giblets. Season to taste.

CORNBREAD-SAUSAGE STUFFING

(for 10- to 20-pound bird)
This stuffing is a family favorite.

¼ cup butter or margarine
¾ cup chopped onion
½ cup chopped celery
½ cup chopped green pepper
⅔ cup hot chicken bouillon
5 cups firm (not dry) bread, diced
5 cups crumbled cornbread (see recipe below)

½ pound fresh pork sausage links (fine spiced country or English style sausage are best)
¼ teaspoon salt
⅛ teaspoon pepper
½ teaspoon poultry seasoning
2 beaten eggs
¾ cup coarsely chopped pecans

Heat butter in skillet. Sauté onions, celery, and peppers until tender. Combine bread crumbs in large bowl. Pour sautéed vegetables and bouillon over them. Toss. Cut up sausage and sauté until browned. Add salt, pepper, and poultry seasoning to crumb mixture. Add sausage and drippings. Stir in the eggs and pecans. Stuff lightly into turkey. Any excess can be refrigerated and baked the last ¾ hour with turkey.

CORNBREAD

1 cup cornmeal
1 cup enriched, unbleached flour
4 teaspoons baking powder
1 teaspoon salt

1 tablespoon oil
1 egg
1 cup milk

Combine cornmeal, flour, baking powder, and salt. Combine oil, milk, and egg. Stir into cornmeal mixture. Bake in greased pan at 375° F. about 30 minutes.

TURKEY SCRAPPLE

(10 or more servings)
This keeps well for some time.

4 cups turkey meat
4 cups stuffing
bones of turkey, simmered 1 hour
   (water to cover)

gravy
1 teaspoon salt
1 teaspoon poultry seasoning
1½ cups cornmeal

Put meat and stuffing through fine grinder (or chop fine). Strain liquid from bones. Add water to make 12 cups. Pick off meat and add to liquid. Add meat and stuffing, gravy, salt, and seasoning. Heat over medium heat to boil. Stir in cornmeal gradually. Cook, stirring until thick. Pour into buttered pans. Refrigerate, covered with plastic. Slice as desired and brown in butter.

SHELLFISH

SCALLOPED OYSTERS

(4 servings)

We almost always prepare oysters this way.

1 pint fresh, shelled oysters
1½ cups fine crumbs (bread or
  cracker)
1 teaspoon salt
¼ teaspoon pepper
4 tablespoons butter or margarine,
  melted

½ cup evaporated milk or light
  cream
Worcestershire sauce
pinch mace or nutmeg
Roquefort or blue cheese
  (about 1 tablespoon)

Check oysters for bits of shell. Drain off liquid and reserve. Blend crumbs, salt, pepper and butter. Put ⅓ of the crumbs in bottom of 1½ quart casserole. Put on half the oysters. Combine evaporated milk with reserved oyster liquor. Pour half of milk mixture over oysters. Add a few drops of Worcestershire sauce. Make a second layer of crumbs, oysters, milk, and Worcestershire sauce. Put remaining crumbs on top. Sprinkle with mace. Crumble cheese over top. Bake at 350° F. for ½ hour.

CURRIED OYSTERS

(4 servings)

1 pint (pound) oysters
2 tablespoons butter or margarine
oyster liquor and milk to make 1
  cup
2 tablespoons butter or margarine

1½ tablespoons flour
dash salt
dash pepper
¼ teaspoon curry powder

Sauté oysters in butter until edges curl. Remove. Measure liquid in pan, liquor and milk to make 1 cup. Set aside. Melt butter in saucepan. Blend in flour, salt, pepper, and curry powder. Slowly stir in milk mixture, stirring until thickened. Add oysters. Heat and serve over rice.

CLAM CASSEROLE

1 7½-ounce can minced clams	1 cup clam liquid with milk
1 can whole kernel corn or 2 cups thawed frozen corn	1 egg
	¼ cup Parmesan cheese
2 tablespoons minced onion	¼ cup fine crumbs
2 tablespoons minced green pepper	butter

Combine drained clams, corn, onion and green pepper. Measure clam liquid and add milk to make 1 cup. Beat in egg and cheese. Pour into casserole. Top with crumbs. Dot with butter. Bake at 350° F. about 35-45 minutes until set.

DEVILED CLAMS

(4-6 servings)

1 pint clams, chopped	2 tablespoons butter
clam liquor	2 hard-cooked eggs, chopped
1 tablespoon chopped onion	¾ cup fine dry crumbs
1 tablespoon chopped green pepper	1 teaspoon salt
¼ cup chopped celery	⅛ teaspoon pepper

Cook clams in their liquor. Cool. In skillet, heat butter. Sauté onion, green pepper, celery for 5 minutes. Add to clams. Stir in eggs, crumbs, salt, and pepper. Put into individual oven-proof dishes. Bake at 400° F. for 20 minutes.

CLAM CASSEROLE

(4 servings)

2 7½-ounce cans minced clams
2 cups cooked rice
¼ cup butter
3 tablespoons flour
1 cup dry white wine
½ cup mushrooms

2 egg yolks
1 cup evaporated milk
½ teaspoon salt
dash pepper
½ cup Parmesan cheese

Drain clams, saving liquid. Mix clams with rice. Melt butter. Blend in flour. Stir in combined wine and clam liquid, stirring until thickened. Add mushrooms, cooking about 3 minutes, stirring. Beat egg yolks with milk and add to sauce. Add salt and pepper. Heat but don't boil. Pour into casserole. Sprinkle with cheese. Bake at 375° F. about 20 minutes until brown.

SHRIMP

We are fortunate to be able to get sweet, tender, green shrimp in late winter. If you are lucky enough to have a supply of fresh shrimp available, try the following recipes. It is possible to use drained, rinsed, canned shrimp in cooked recipes if you add them last and just heat through. Frozen shrimp can, of course, be used.

SHRIMP CURRY

(6 servings)

This is my husband's favorite curry.

4 cups cooked cleaned shrimp
¼ cup butter or margarine
½ cup minced onion
6 tablespoons flour
2½ teaspoons curry powder
1¼ teaspoons salt

¼ teaspoon ginger
1 cup hot chicken bouillon
1 teaspoon honey
2 cups milk
1 teaspoon lemon juice

Melt butter over medium-low heat. Add onion. Sauté until transparent but not brown. Combine flour, curry powder, salt, and ginger. Remove pan from heat and stir flour mixture into butter, blending thoroughly. Stir in the chicken bouillon. Return to low heat. Add milk and honey slowly while stirring. Cook until thick. Add shrimp and lemon juice. Heat to serving temperature. Serve with rice. Chutney, coconut, banana slices, almonds, and pineapple chunks make good accompaniments. Cooked fresh or frozen green peas is the ideal vegetable to serve with this curry.

BROILED HERBED SHRIMP

(4 servings)

1 pound uncooked, shelled shrimp
  fresh or frozen
½ cup dry bread crumbs
1 teaspoon oregano
¼ teaspoon basil
¼ teaspoon garlic powder
¼ teaspoon salt
dash pepper
oil
lemon wedges

Combine bread crumbs, oregano, basil, garlic powder, salt, and pepper. Roll shrimp in these. Spread on large baking sheet in 1 layer. Sprinkle with oil. Run under preheated broiler until shrimp begins to curl. Remove from broiler. With spatula, turn shrimp. Sprinkle with oil. Broil on other side for a minute or two. Serve with lemon wedges.

SHRIMP WIGGLE

(6 servings)

2 cans drained rinsed shrimp
3 tablespoons butter
6 tablespoons flour
3 cups milk
½ teaspoon salt
dash white pepper
1 cup cooked peas

Melt butter. Blend in flour. Add milk slowly, stirring. Add salt and pepper. Stir until thick. Add shrimp and peas. Heat through. Serve on toast or crackers.

SHRIMP NEWBURG

Make as above but after thickened, remove from heat. Add 1 teaspoon lemon juice, shrimp and peas. Reheat and add 3 tablespoons sherry. Serve with rice or on puffs.

SCALLOPS————————————————————

SAUTÉED SCALLOPS

(4 servings)

1 pound scallops
dry bread crumbs
¼ cup butter or margarine

Roll scallops in bread crumbs. Sauté in butter, turning until browned. Serve with tartar sauce or lemon.

FISH————————————————————————

Salmon is delicious, either fresh or canned. Fresh salmon can be poached, steamed, or broiled. In Maine, the traditional Independence Day (Fourth of July) fare has always been fresh salmon and green peas, probably because the first fresh peas of the season are ready by the first of July and fresh-run Atlantic salmon are moving up the rivers. In any event, the combination of pink salmon with lemon wedges, green peas, mashed potatoes, molded aspic salad or crisp greens and strawberries (all native Maine foods) is as pretty to look at and as delicious to eat as it is nutritious. Eating on the screened-in porch of a cottage on a lake or at the ocean with relatives and friends, the water shimmering in the sun, has made the Fourth a truly memorable day for me. Try it some time.

BROILED SALMON

(½ pound per person)

Place salmon steaks on broiler pan. Dot with butter. Put under heated broiler. Broil one side until lightly browned. Turn. Dot with butter. Broil until browned. Serve with lemon.

POACHED SALMON

(any amount, ½ pound per person)

A chunk of fish may be used or a cleaned whole fish without head or tail (or as in Europe prepared and served with the head still intact, then filleted at the table). To poach, you may wrap fish in a piece of cheesecloth, if desired. Place in water with salt, peppercorns, a stalk of celery, a slice of onion, a clove of garlic if desired. Simmer until done (it flakes easily with a fork and comes away from the bone). The length of time depends on whether the fish is a piece of a thick fish or a smaller, slimmer one. It should take about 10 minutes for a pound. If the fish is very thick, turn it once. Serve with lemon and butter.

Note: Haddock, pollock, bass, trout, and other whole fish can be prepared in this way.

STEAMED SALMON

(any amount, ½ pound per person)

Proceed as for poached salmon, but place salmon on rack out of water (or in top of steamer). Cover lightly.

BAKED STUFFED SALMON
OR WHITEFISH

(any amount, ½ pound per person)

1 cleaned fish or part of fish	¼ pound salt pork, thinly sliced
1 recipe for stuffing	lemon
1 onion, sliced	

Wash, wipe, and stuff fish. Place in baking pan. With sharp knife, make slashes, slanting, about 1 to 1½ inches apart, through skin about ½ to ¾ inch deep. Lay ½ slice of onion into each slash. Lay a slice of salt pork over onion in each slash. Bake at 325° F. about 40 minutes for a 3-pound fish. Longer if it weighs more.

STUFFING:

1½ cups dry bread crumbs	*½ teaspoon salt*
2 tablespoons chopped onion	*dash paprika*
½ cup chopped celery	*½ teaspoon dill seed*
2 tablespoons chopped parsley	*milk or water to moisten*
1 tablespoon butter or margarine	

Sauté onion, celery, and parsley in butter or margarine until transparent. Add to crumbs with salt, paprika, and dill seed. Moisten with water to desired wetness.

BAKED UNSTUFFED SALMON
OR WHITEFISH

(any amount, ½ pound per person)

Proceed as for stuffed salmon, but cook only about 30 minutes for a 3-pound fish, proportionately longer if heavier.

SALMON LOAF

(4 servings)

1 pound can salmon
1 cup bread crumbs
¼ chopped onion

1 egg
¼ cup milk

Mix salmon and juices with bread crumbs, chopped onion, egg, and milk. Pack into buttered bread tin. Bake at 350° F. for about 40 minutes. It can be packed in custard cups or muffin tins placed in pan of hot water for 20 minutes or until set. Serve with cheese or tomato sauce.

ON BROILING OTHER FISH

Tuna steak, shark steak, and halibut steak all can be broiled as salmon is broiled.

BROILED FILLETS

(any amount, ⅓ pound per person)

Arrange fillets on broiler pan. Dot with butter or brush with oil. Drizzle with lemon. Broil 1½ minutes. Serve garnished with parsley.

SAUTÉED FILLETS

(3 servings)

1 pound fillets
¼ cup dry bread crumbs
½ teaspoon salt

dash pepper
butter or other fat or oil

Rinse fillets. Roll in crumbs seasoned with salt and pepper. Melt butter in skillet. Place fillets in hot skillet. Cook until brown on one side. Turn. Cook until browned. Serve with lemon or tartar sauce.

Variation: Add ½ teaspoon oregano, ¼ teaspoon basil, pinch of garlic powder to bread crumbs. Serve with tomato sauce.

CORNED FISH DINNER

(any amount, ⅓ pound per person)

Buy a piece of corned fish (hake, pollock or other) or corn it yourself for 12 hours as in Corned Beef. Fry out diced salt pork on low heat until crisp. Boil fish. Boil potatoes in skins. Chop an onion finely. Place fish on platter with potatoes. Put pork scraps with their fat in small pitcher. Make layer of potato and fish on your plate. Sprinkle with onion and drizzle with a little of the pork scraps. Green peas or beans are a good vegetable with this meal, along with a tossed salad.

FISH CAKES

(any amount)

Use equal amounts leftover potatoes and corned or other leftover flaked fish. Combine thoroughly. Form into cakes. Heat a little fat or oil in skillet. Sauté on each side until browned. Serve with ketchup.

CODFISH CAKES

Soak salt cod several hours in cold water (to freshen). Crumble. Heat to boiling in fresh water, drain. Repeat until fish tastes fresh. Form fish cakes as above.

FISH NEWBURG

Use any white fish with Shrimp Newburg recipe.

EEL

Eel is a delicious fish, juicy and delicate. It must be skinned prior to cooking, which takes muscles and pliers. Clean. Cut in slices if large.

BAKED EEL

Cut in pieces and bake at 350° F. until done, about 20-30 minutes.

STEWED EEL

(6 servings)

2 large cleaned skinned eel, cut in
  sections
1 cup water
1 cup red wine
1 clove garlic
1 sliced onion
bay leaf

pinch thyme
3 whole cloves
1 teaspoon celery salt
parsley
1 tablespoon butter
1 tablespoon flour

Pour water, wine, garlic, onion, bay leaf, thyme, cloves, celery salt, parsley over fish in saucepan. Simmer until done. Remove fish. Strain sauce. Melt 1 tablespoon butter in saucepan. Stir in 1 tablespoon flour, blending. Add stock slowly, stirring and heating to thicken. Toast and butter slices of bread. Place fish pieces on bread. Pour sauce over it.

MACKEREL

Mackerel is a fatty fish, usually quite inexpensive. It is very good broiled or baked. To split and clean, cut through backbone side (not belly) so it lays flat.

BROILED MACKEREL

(1 small fish, 1 serving; 1 large fish, 2 servings)
Have mackerel cleaned and split. Lay on oiled broiler pan, skin side down. Drizzle with lemon. Broil small fish only on flesh side about 5-7 minutes. Larger fish should be turned and broiled skin side up until skin is crisp.

MACKEREL LOAF

Prepare as for Salmon Loaf, using canned mackerel.

SMELTS

Smelts are available frozen or fresh if you live in smelt country. They are in season in winter when they are taken through the ice and in spring during their spawning runs. Their meat is sweet and delicate.

Clean smelts by cutting off head where it meets the backbone. If you do so carefully, the intestines will come out with the head and your cleaning is complete. Rinse.

Frozen smelts are usually cleaned.

SAUTÉED SMELTS

Coat smelts in a mixture of flour, salt, and pepper. Sauté in butter, oil, or other fat until crisp. Only the backbone has to be removed. The rest of the smelt is perfectly edible.

TUNA

TUNA LOAF

Canned tuna can be prepared as a loaf, using the recipe for Salmon Loaf.

TUNA-EGG CASSEROLE

(4 servings)

1 7-ounce can tuna
1 tablespoon lemon juice
2 sliced hard-cooked eggs
1 cup cooked peas
2 tablespoons flour
1 cup milk

½ teaspoon salt
dash pepper
½ cup grated sharp cheese
½ cup buttered toasted bread
    finely diced

Drain tuna if oil packed. Flake, adding 1 tablespoon lemon juice. Layer fish, eggs, and peas in casserole. Melt butter. Blend in flour. Add milk, slowly stirring. Add salt and pepper. Stir in cheese. Heat, stirring, until thickened and cheese is melted. Pour over mixture in casserole. Top with bread. Bake at 400° F. about 20 minutes.

TUNA-STUFFED PANCAKES

(6 or more servings)

PANCAKES:
1 egg
½ teaspoon salt
1 cup evaporated milk

½ cup flour
butter or margarine

Beat egg, salt, and milk together. Beat in flour. Heat 7-inch skillet with enough butter or margarine to grease bottom. Pour 2 tablespoons of batter into skillet, tilting to cover bottom. Lightly brown. Flip over. Brown the other side. Lay on paper towel. Repeat with the rest of the batter, separating pancakes with paper towels or waxed paper (make ahead of time if desired).

TUNA FILLING:
2 7-ounce cans tuna
¼ pound sliced mushrooms
2 tablespoons butter
2 tablespoons flour
1½ cups milk
½ teaspoon salt

dash pepper
2 tablespoons chopped parsley
½ cup grated cheese (Swiss cheese is good)
paprika

Sauté mushrooms lightly in butter. Sprinkle on flour, blending. Slowly stir in milk. Add salt and pepper, stirring until sauce comes to a boil. Add tuna and parsley. Remove from heat. Put some of tuna mixture on each pancake, rolling it around filling. Lay in buttered baking pan. Sprinkle with cheese and paprika. Bake at 400° F. about 15 minutes until cheese is melted. Serve.

SMOKED FILLETS WITH EGG SAUCE

(2-3 servings)

1 pound smoked fillets	*2 tablespoons flour*
water	*1 cup milk*
2 tablespoons butter	*2 or more hard-cooked eggs*

Cook fillets in water to cover until they flake. Meanwhile, melt butter in saucepan; stir in flour, blending. Slowly stir in milk. Stir to thicken. Add flaked fillets and sliced hard-cooked eggs, folding in. Serve on buttered toast.

VEGETABLES

ASPARAGUS————————————————————————

Asparagus is a delicious early spring vegetable. If you're lucky, you may be able to find wild asparagus.

In buying fresh asparagus be sure it is dark green with light buds which have not begun to open or spread. Snap off the stock so you will use all of the tender parts of the asparagus. The little scales on the stalk sometimes harbor dirt, so check when cleaning. Asparagus is a reasonably good source of vitamin A, B vitamins, and C. It also contains a little iron and calcium.

Rinse about 1½ pounds for 4 servings. Leave asparagus as stalks or slice on bias into 1½ to 2-inch lengths. Cook in small amount of boiling salted water, 8-10 minutes until just tender. Remove asparagus to platter. Stir a little cold water into 1 tablespoon cornstarch to make a paste. Stir a little hot asparagus mixture into the cornstarch paste. Add to asparagus mixture, stirring to thicken. Add 1 teaspoon of butter and ½ teaspoon lemon juice. Pour over asparagus and serve.

ORIENTAL ASPARAGUS

Prepare as above but put chicken bouillon cube in water rather than salt. Add a teaspoon of soy sauce in place of lemon juice.

CHINESE STIR-FRY ASPARAGUS

(4 servings)

1½ pounds asparagus cut on bias   ½ teaspoon salt
  in 1-inch lengths   dash pepper
1 tablespoon oil

Heat covered skillet. Add oil. Add asparagus, salt and pepper, stirring to start cooking. Cover. Lower heat to medium. Shake pan often. Cook until crisp-tender, about 4-5 minutes. Serve.

BEANS

Green beans and wax beans are fair sources of some B vitamins and contain a little calcium and iron. Lima beans are far better sources of B vitamins and iron. Bean sprouts provide calcium and vitamin C, and soy sprouts are also a good source of B vitamins.

Letting beans grow to maturity greatly increases their food value. Dried beans contain three times as much of the B vitamins, phosphorus, iron and protein as the green ones do.

To cook green or wax beans (1 pound equals 4-6 servings): Fresh green beans should be topped and tailed, cut up or left whole, and simmered about 20 minutes in boiling, salted water. You can make a sauce of water as described under asparagus.

MARINATED GREEN BEANS

(4 servings)

2 cups cooked green beans
3 tablespoons oil
1 tablespoon vinegar
1 tablespoon chopped onion

dash garlic powder
dash pepper
¼ teaspoon salt
¼ teaspoon paprika

Combine oil, vinegar, onion, garlic powder, pepper, salt, and paprika. Toss with beans. Refrigerate covered. Serve cold.

CALICO SALAD

(serves 8-10)

1 can whole green beans, drained
1 can wax beans, drained
1 can kidney beans, rinsed
½ cup chopped green pepper
1 medium onion sliced

DRESSING:
¾ cup vinegar
⅔ cup honey
⅓ cup salad oil
1 teaspoon salt
pepper to taste

Combine vinegar, honey, salad oil, salt, and pepper. Add drained green and wax beans and rinsed kidney beans; add chopped green pepper and sliced onion. Marinate overnight or for several hours. Cover. Drain dressing off before serving. (Reserve dressing for leftover vegetables.) Good with steaks or fish.

GREEN BEANS AMANDINE

(4 servings)

1 package fresh, frozen or canned
  French-style green beans, cooked
  (heated, if canned)
⅔ tablespoons blanched slivered
  almonds

1 tablespoon butter or margarine
pinch salt

Sauté almonds in butter to brown slightly. Add a pinch of salt. Pour over drained beans. (Save liquid for soup, etc.)

GREEN BEANS WITH HERBS

(4-6 servings)

1 pound fresh green beans, cut up
1 tablespoon butter or margarine
¼ cup chopped celery
¼ cup chopped onion

1 minced clove of garlic
½ teaspoon basil
¼ teaspoon rosemary

Cook beans in a little boiling salted water until nearly tender, about 10-15 minutes. Stir in butter, onion, celery, garlic, basil, and rosemary. Cover. Cook about 10 minutes longer or until beans are tender. Serve.

To grow sprouts: Buy *untreated* bean seed (mung beans, soy beans, or other type seeds for other sprouts such as alfalfa or wheat).

Place two tablespoons bean seeds in 1 quart bottle. Soak overnight. Drain and rinse with clean water. Place piece of cheesecloth over top and secure with rubber band. Lay on side in dark place. Rinse with fresh water about 3 times a day, draining. It takes about 10 days to form full sprouts. Rinse, place in plastic bag, and store in vegetable crisper. Use in salads or add to cooked vegetable dishes, chop suey, etc.

Green lima beans: You are more apt to find frozen and canned green lima beans than fresh unless you grow your own. Fresh limas must be shelled and cooked 20-30 minutes until tender. Lima beans are delicious with a little butter or margarine. They are also good combined with cheese or tomatoes.

Fava, Windsor, or broad beans: These beans are delicious fresh or canned. They should be shelled and cooked like lima beans. However, if young and tender, they take very little cooking time. If you are of Italian or Mediterranean descent, however, do a bit of checking before you buy them if you have never eaten them before. Some susceptible people from the Mediterranean areas react to fava beans, developing a hemolytic anemia as a result of eating them.

BEETS

Beet greens are a valuable part of the beet. They are especially delicious when young with tiny, tender, sweet beets attached. But the greens from mature beets are also excellent when fresh.

The greens are a superb source of vitamin A, ½ cup containing as much as 22,000 IU. They are also a good source of vitamins C and B_2. Though they contain good amounts of iron and calcium, the oxalic acid in their leaves may bind these. The root contains iron and a little calcium, as well as traces of other vitamins and minerals.

BEET GREENS

(any amount)

Wash greens thoroughly to get off any attached dirt. Remove wilted leaves. Place in large covered pan with just the water which clings from washing them. Add salt and a slice of bacon if desired. Cover. Cook on medium heat until it starts to boil. Remove lid and turn greens with fork or tongs. Recover. Lower heat. Cook until just tender (about 5-10 minutes depending on size of greens). Serve with a little butter or margarine and a dash of vinegar if desired.

HARVARD BEETS

(4 servings)

2 cups cooked, diced beets
1 tablespoon honey
1 tablespoon cornstarch
¼ teaspoon salt

⅓ cup beet liquid
3 tablespoons vinegar
2 tablespoons butter or margarine

In saucepan, combine honey, cornstarch and salt. Stir in beet liquid, vinegar, and butter. Cook, stirring until mixture thickens. Add beets. Heat.

BRASSICA FAMILY

Consists of broccoli, brussels sprouts, cabbage, cauliflower, kale, Chinese cabbage, collards, kohlrabi, mustard greens and even turnip and radish. With the exception of radish, they are all very nutritious. Most of them are excellent sources of vitamin A and good-to-excellent sources of vitamin C. They also provide some of the B vitamins, iron and calcium. For nutritive value, you really can't beat the brassica family.

BROCCOLI

Choose broccoli with florets that are still tight buds and deep green. Rinse thoroughly. Cut off only the woody part of the stem. The leaves and tender stems can be cooked right along with the heads. Split the stems into 3 or 4 sections from the branches to the base. Place in saucepan with a little water, salt, and a dash of garlic powder if desired. Cover. Bring to a boil. Lower heat. Cook 5 to 7 minutes until tender. Serve with a little butter or margarine and lemon juice or vinegar.

CHINESE STIR-FRY BROCCOLI

(4 servings)

½ bunch fresh broccoli
1 tablespoon oil
½ teaspoon salt
dash pepper

Prepare broccoli as above, then cut on bias into 1 to 1½ inch slices. Heat skillet. Add oil. Quickly stir in broccoli stalk pieces, then add florets and salt and pepper. Stir quickly until bright green. Cover. Lower heat to medium. Shake occasionally, cooking about 4-5 minutes until tender-crisp.

BROCCOLI SOUFFLÉ

(4-6 servings)

½ bunch fresh broccoli, cooked
2 tablespoons butter or margarine
2 tablespoons flour
½ teaspoon salt
½ cup milk

¼ cup grated Parmesan cheese
4 eggs, separated
mushroom sauce (recipe on the following page)

Drain and chop broccoli. Put in saucepan with butter, heating and stirring until butter is melted. Stir in flour and salt. Add milk while stirring. Cook, stirring, until it thickens and comes to a boil. Add Parmesan cheese. Let cool while preparing eggs. Beat egg whites stiff. Beat yolks until thick and lemon-colored. Add the broccoli mix to egg yolks, blending thoroughly. Fold yolk mixture into egg whites. Put in ungreased soufflé dish or large casserole. Bake at 350° F. about 35 minutes until knife inserted comes out clean.

MUSHROOM SAUCE

¼ *pound sliced mushrooms*   *dash salt and pepper*
3 tablespoons butter or margarine   *1 cup chicken bouillon*
2 tablespoons flour

Sauté mushrooms in butter until golden. Sprinkle with flour, salt and pepper. Stir. Add bouillon, heating and stirring until thickened. Serve with soufflé.

BRUSSELS SPROUTS
Wash and cut a cross through stem end. Place in saucepan with a little water and salt and cook about 8-10 minutes. Thicken liquid as for asparagus. One pound serves 4 people.

CABBAGE
Cabbage is versatile, being equally at home in a raw salad, as a cooked vegetable, or as sauerkraut. Obviously cabbage which is pale and has been long stored is lower in nutrients than darker cabbage or than when it is fresh. Sauerkraut also is lower in nutritive value than fresh cabbage.

STIR-FRY CABBAGE

(4 servings)

½ *small head cabbage*
1 tablespoon oil
salt
pepper

Shred cabbage with sharp chef's knife. Heat oil in skillet. Add cabbage. Stir with salt and pepper. Cover. Lower heat. Cook 4-5 minutes. Serve with vinegar if desired.

CAULIFLOWER

Cauliflower is excellent raw in salads as well as cooked. It should be separated into florets and cooked in a little water until barely fork-tender. Cauliflower should still be a lovely white. If you overcook it, it will turn pinkish to gray.

Cauliflower is delicious served with a cheese sauce or just with a little butter or margarine. If you use only a little water, all the water should have evaporated by the time it is tender. Toss with a little butter and put in a warm serving dish.

CHINESE CABBAGE

Chinese cabbage can be shredded and added to Chinese dishes. It needs very little cooking. It is good raw in salads, or can be prepared as for cabbage above.

COLLARD GREENS

Clean collards and put in saucepan with a piece of bacon, salt pork, or a little ham. Simmer until just tender (time depends on size of greens). Serve with vinegar or lemon juice if desired.

KALE

Kale is one of the most nutritious vegetables you can eat. Wash the leaves quickly; strip the leaves from the stem and rib with your thumb and finger. Put in kettle with a little oil, bacon, or other fat. Cook until just tender. The flavor is outstanding, a bit like broccoli but more definite. It is good served with lemon or vinegar (as are most greens).

KOHLRABI

Kohlrabi can be sliced and eaten raw like celery or in a salad. It can also be cooked. Peel, dice and cook in a little boiling salted water until tender.

TURNIP GREENS

Prepare as for collard greens.

TURNIP OR RUTABAGA

Mild turnips can be diced and small amounts added to salads. To cook turnips, pare and cut in cubes. Cook in a little salted water until tender, 15-20 minutes. Mash, adding a little nonfat dry milk and butter if desired.

CARROTS

Carrots are an excellent raw snack and a delicious cooked vegetable. They should be cooked only until barely tender. Many children have been put off by overcooked carrots. They are beautiful to look at and can be enhanced in a number of ways.

GLAZED CARROTS

(4 servings)

3 cups sliced carrots
1 tablespoon butter or margarine
3 tablespoons honey

2 tablespoons prepared mustard
¼ teaspoon salt
1 tablespoon parsley

Cook carrots in a little water until barely tender. Melt butter in skillet. Add honey, mustard, salt. Add carrots, stirring until well coated. Sprinkle with parsley. Serve.

HERBED CARROTS

(4 servings)

3 cups sliced or quartered carrots
1½ tablespoons butter or
    margarine
salt and pepper

2 or 3 tablespoons water
1 teaspoon parsley
pinch thyme
¼ teaspoon summer savory

Combine carrots, butter, salt, pepper with water in saucepan. Simmer on low heat until carrots are barely tender. Add parsley, thyme and savory. Shake over heat to coat carrots. Serve.

CELERY

Celery contains tiny amounts of vitamins, green celery and the leaves being better sources. It also contains some calcium. Celery is good to eat plain or in salads. It also is good braised and in soups. Stuffed with cheese, it makes a good protein-rich addition to a meal.

To prepare celery, separate stalks. Scrub stalks with vegetable brush to get every last vestige of dirt from between the ribs. This is important since celery can harbor salmonella, the organism responsible for food poisoning.

To braise celery, cut up or chop. Place in saucepan with a little butter, water, salt and pepper. Cover and simmer until tender.

To add to Chinese dishes, slice celery on the bias very thinly. Add to chow mein, chop suey, etc., cooking only until partly tender. It should still be crisp and not limp.

STUFFED CELERY

(any amount)

Pick attractive stalks. Clean thoroughly. Stuff with well-drained cottage cheese to which you can add a little chopped chives and garlic powder to taste. Sprinkle with paprika. Cut into 2- to 4-inch lengths. Arrange on plate. Garnish with parsley and olives if desired.

These are good as appetizers, snacks, or served with the meal on a relish tray.

CORN

Corn contains B vitamins and some vitamin A. Fresh corn on the cob should, ideally, be completely fresh. Now that we raise our own, it comes straight from the garden and into the pot with never more than an hour between picking and cooking. The cooking time for such fresh corn is only about 5 minutes, and the sweetness and flavor is perfect even without the addition of butter. Older or less-fresh corn needs longer cooking, up to 10 minutes, and much of the sugar will have turned to starch.

Corn freezes beautifully (but not on the cob). The blanching time needed for freezing corn on the cob is so lengthy that the corn is sure to be mushy or soggy and lacking flavor. However, if it is blanched only a few minutes, cut off the cob, and packed in the freezer, the kernels will have the fresh sweet flavor of garden corn.

Corn lends itself to a variety of dishes, puddings, soufflés, with beans as succotash, escalloped with tomatoes and bread crumbs, and as fritters.

SUCCOTASH

(4 servings)

1 cup corn cut from cob
2 cups shell beans
salt and pepper to taste

1 tablespoon butter or margarine
enough liquid to cook

If fresh, cook beans until nearly tender with salt, pepper, butter and liquid. Add corn, cook 5 minutes. Or combine canned corn, canned beans, salt, pepper, butter or margarine. Heat.

BAKED CORN PUDDING

(4 servings)

2 cups whole kernel corn (fresh or
  frozen, separated)
2 eggs
2 cups milk

1 tablespoon butter or margarine
½ teaspoon salt
dash pepper

Beat eggs, add milk, butter, salt, pepper and beat to combine. Stir in corn. Pour into greased casserole. Bake at 375° F. about 35-40 minutes.

CRESS

There is more than one variety of cress. Watercress is a pleasant peppery little green that grows in running water. It makes a good addition to salads or in sandwiches. Peppercress is one of the first of the wild greens available. It is shiny, dark green, and an excellent source of vitamin C. Clean. Cook in a little water until tender. Serve with butter or margarine and lemon or vinegar if desired.

CUCUMBER

Cucumbers are 95 percent water and not particularly high in nutrients. When cucumbers are cheap and readily available, they are a great thirst quencher and add enjoyable crunch to a salad. When they are expensive, your money can be better spent on more nutritious vegetables. Cucumbers can be cooked, if you wish, and made into cream soup, following the basic cream soup recipe. Float a slice on the soup as a garnish.

DANDELIONS

A field of dandelions in bloom is not only a delight to the eye in spring, but dandelions dug and cooked prior to blossoming are a delight to the palate. Digging greens is an excellent spring exercise. It gets you out in the fresh air and sunshine in a natural position for "pelvic rock." Add to that the excellent nutritive value of dandelions plus the fact that they are free (although stores do carry them), and you can understand why they are emphasized. One-half cup of cooked dandelions provides 15,000 units of vitamin A, some B vitamins, including folic acid, 6 mg. of iron, some calcium, and up to 100 mg. of vitamin C.

To dig greens, use a sharp knife and a paper bag. The tastiest greens are those with buds of the blossoms formed in the center of the rosette of leaves. Do not use any with open blossoms. Define the edge of the dandelions and the earth. Holding the dandelion in one hand, insert knife and cut around the base, releasing it from the deep root. Scrape off excess dirt, cut off extra root, leaving plant intact, and remove any yellow leaves. Drop into bag.

Wash greens thoroughly in a number of changes of cold water, spraying if possible. Pack in large saucepan with fitting cover. Add a piece of scored salt pork or one or two slices of bacon. Add a little water to the pot and simmer until tender, about 15-20 minutes, turning occasionally with a fork. Serve with butter and vinegar. Some people blanch dandelions before cooking to remove bitterness. This seems an abomination to me; however, if you find they are too robust for you, by all means blanch rather than avoid them.

Dandelions can also be used fresh in salads. Or if you wish, cook them as my friend from Sicily does. Fry a little diced salt pork or bacon in a heated covered skillet. Add chopped cleaned greens and stir thoroughly. Cook, simmering until greens are tender. Serve.

Dandelions or other greens can be used in a delicious pizza also. Prepare pizza crust (see recipe). Cook chopped fresh greens lightly in olive oil as above with a minced clove of garlic until barely tender. Spread on prepared pizza crust. Sprinkle with additional olive oil and salt and pepper. Bake as directed for pizza.

EGGPLANT

While eggplant is not especially high in nutrients, it does combine well in a number of dishes. It adds pleasant flavor and is attractive to look at. Eggplant can be cut up and simmered until tender in a little water. It is also very good sautéed. Roll slices in seasoned flour or bread crumbs and sauté until brown in a little oil or margarine.

CHEESE EGGPLANT

(4 servings, a high-protein dish)

1 medium eggplant cut in ¼-inch slices
1 egg
1 tablespoon flour
1 tablespoon milk
olive oil

8 ounces mozzarella cheese
Parmesan cheese
2 cups tomato sauce
½ teaspoon sweet basil
½ teaspoon oregano

Mix egg with flour and milk. Dip eggplant slices in it. Heat olive oil in heavy skillet. Brown quickly on both sides. Put a layer of tomato sauce in bottom of baking dish. Add layer of eggplant, a layer of diced mozzarella cheese, and some Parmesan cheese. Sprinkle with basil and oregano, add tomato sauce. Repeat layers ending with tomato sauce. Bake at 350° F. 1 hour.

RATATOUILLE

(6 servings)

2 thinly sliced onions
1 minced clove garlic
3 tablespoons olive oil
1 green pepper, thinly sliced
1 small eggplant, diced
1 medium zucchini, sliced

2 tomatoes peeled and sliced
fresh basil leaves or ½ teaspoon
   dried basil
1 teaspoon salt
dash pepper

In dutch oven, lightly sauté onions, garlic and green pepper in olive oil. Add eggplant, zucchini, tomatoes, basil, salt and pepper. Cover. Simmer about 20 minutes until tender. Stir gently, occasionally. Serve.

ENDIVE OR ESCAROLE

Endive comes in two forms, the curly variety so often labeled chicory by produce departments, and the escarole or straight-leafed variety. Either makes a welcome addition to salads, and both can be cooked following the directions for dandelions. Their flavor is a little like that of the dandelion and they are higher in vitamin A, though not quite as high in some other nutrients. They form an excellent vegetable for the winter diet since they are available fresh and quite reasonably priced.

FIDDLEHEAD GREENS

Fiddlehead greens are the unopened shoot of the ostrich fern. They are available fresh in early spring when flooded swamps drain. You may be able to buy them canned or frozen in your market.

Clean thoroughly to remove brown scales. Boil in salted water until tender, about 20 minutes. Serve with butter or margarine and lemon or vinegar if desired.

Fiddlehead greens are excellent cold with oil and vinegar dressing.

If you want to try gathering fiddlehead greens in the spring, contact your local extension service or state university for positive identification of the ostrich fern.

GARLIC

Garlic has long held an esteemed place in Mediterranean cookery. It is gradually coming into its own in the United States. Garlic has been touted as a panacea for a number of ills of mankind. It has maintained an important place in herbal medicine. Oddly enough, current news from British scientists indicates that garlic may, indeed, be an important herb for health. They point out that garlic may have a protective role in preventing cholesterol buildup. It will be interesting to watch developments in this research.

HORSE RADISH

The roots of this perennial are excellent as a very hot condiment. The leaves are a delicate spring green, cooked according to the directions for dandelions.

DRIED LEGUMES

Dried legumes—peas, beans, lentils, peanuts—provide an important source of protein in the diet. While the protein is incomplete, it can be enhanced by the addition of milk, cheese, eggs, a little meat or fish, or by combining complementary proteins with the meal.

For complete information, if you are a vegetarian, be sure to use *Diet for a Small Planet* (see bibliography). Protein is so vital to your baby's welfare and to your health that it is important that you get all of the protein value from whatever you eat.

BAKED BEANS

(8-10 servings)

1 quart pea, yellow eye, soldier, kidney, or any other type dry beans

½ pound lean salt pork (if you are a vegetarian, use oil or margarine)

1 onion

3 tablespoons molasses

2 tablespoons celery salt

1 teaspoon dry mustard

1 teaspoon pepper

Soak beans overnight in cold water. Parboil 30 minutes or until the skin cracks when you blow on them. (Or, alternatively, put dry beans in 2 quarts of water. Bring to a boil. Turn off heat. Let stand one hour. Then parboil, adding water if necessary.) Put onion in the bottom of bean pot (or large covered oven-proof casserole). Add most of the beans. Put in the salt pork and remaining beans. Add molasses, celery salt, dry mustard and pepper. Pour boiling water to just cover beans. Bake covered about 6 to 8 hours in very slow oven 275-300° F. From time to time, check and add a little boiling water to replace that which has boiled away. If you let the water boil away, the beans will be greasy. You can remove the cover for the last ½ hour to 45 minutes if you want the top of the beans brown and a bit crisp. Serve with brown bread which provides complementary proteins.

BEANHOLE BEANS

(40 servings)

There is nothing that can beat beans cooked in a beanhole. If you are so disposed, one large lot can be cooked and frozen in meal-size lots for winter eating. They make a great inexpensive feast for a crowd. You do need land available.

You need a 2½ by 2½ foot hole dug in dry ground lined with small rocks. Build a brisk fire with hardwood. Prepare the beans as above (quadruple the recipe), preparing them in a heavy iron pot or other heavy pot which will hold at least 3 gallons. The lid must fit tightly. When the fire has burned down to hot coals, shovel out part of the coals. Set pot in on the coals. Cover it with the coals you removed. Replace the gravel or dirt. Leave pot all day to cook. You can, of course, do this on a smaller scale, but it is more wasteful of wood.

QUICK BAKED BEANS

1 3-pound can New England–style
    baked beans
1 chopped onion
1 tablespoon bacon fat or oil

1 teaspoon dry mustard
1 teaspoon Worcestershire sauce
2 tablespoons maple syrup

Sauté onion in fat until browned. Put beans in casserole with onion, mustard, Worcestershire sauce, and syrup. Mix thoroughly (or mix in skillet and put in individual casserole dishes). Bake at 350° F. about 45 minutes (for individual casseroles, 30 minutes). Top with crumbled crisp bacon if desired.

ITALIAN BEANS

(4 servings)

1½ cups dried white beans
3 tablespoons olive oil
¾ teaspoon sage
½ teaspoon salt

dash pepper
⅓ cup tomato paste
1 teaspoon oregano

Soak beans overnight (or use alternate method described under Baked Beans). Simmer in just enough water to cover until tender, about 1 hour (do not add more water). Add oil, sage, salt, pepper, tomato paste, and oregano. Simmer about 5-10 minutes. Serve.

BEAN CASSEROLE

½ pound beef, diced
2 tablespoons diced salt pork
1 minced clove garlic
1 can (about 1½ pounds) any type beans (or about 3 cups cooked beans)
¼ cup chopped stuffed olives

2 pimientos, chopped
½ cup grated Cheddar cheese
2 teaspoons chili powder
2 teaspoons soy sauce
1 1-pound can Italian tomatoes
1 teaspoon celery salt
½ teaspoon dry mustard

Sauté salt pork with beef. Add garlic. Mix with beans, olives, pimientos, cheese in bean pot or covered casserole dish. Heat tomatoes with salt, mustard, chili powder and soy sauce. Pour over beans. Cover and bake at 250° F. about 1 to 1½ hours. Serve with cornbread.

If you wish, omit the beef and salt pork. Add 1 tablespoon margarine or oil. Cornbread made with milk and cheese complements the bean protein.

PURÉED LENTILS

(4-6 servings)

1½ cups dried lentils
5 cups bouillon or broth
1 small sliced onion
2 tablespoons butter

salt (do not use if corned beef
  broth is used)
dash pepper
⅛ teaspoon nutmeg

   Combine lentils, liquid, and onion. Simmer until lentils are soft
(about 2 hours). Put through strainer or puréer. Cook to thicken
slightly. Add butter, salt and pepper, and nutmeg to taste.
Note: Soy beans can be used in any of the dry bean recipes.

CHICK PEAS

These delicious peas can be eaten heated from the can or cold as a
snack. They are also delicious sautéed in a little olive oil and
chopped onion.

CHICK PEAS WITH SPICE

(4 servings)

2 cans chick peas
1½ tablespoons oil
½ teaspoon cumin seed
1 medium onion, chopped finely
1 teaspoon garlic powder
¼ teaspoon turmeric
¼ teaspoon ginger

½ teaspoon salt
¼ teaspoon red pepper
¼ teaspoon black pepper
1¼ teaspoon coriander or ¾
  teaspoon curry powder
3 teaspoons lemon juice
2 medium tomatoes, chopped

   Drain chick peas, reserving liquid. Heat oil, add cumin seed,
onion, garlic powder, turmeric, ginger, salt, peppers, coriander,
and curry. Add chick peas. Cover and cook 2-3 minutes. Add
liquid, tomatoes, and lemon juice. Simmer 5-10 minutes. Serve.

BLACK-EYED PEAS

(4-6 servings)

2 cups black-eyed peas　　　　　parsley
½ pound of corned beef or a ham　1 onion, chopped
　bone

　Soak peas as for beans. Combine peas with meat and onion.
Cook until tender, about 2 to 2½ hours.

DRIED PEA SOUP

(4-6 servings)
　Soak 2 cups peas (or beans or lentils) in 8 cups of water overnight
(or boil in water, turn off heat; let set 1 hour and continue recipe).
Add 1 bay leaf, a ham bone or 1 cup nonfat dry milk, a celery stalk,
chopped parsley, and 1 onion, chopped. Simmer 2 to 3 hours until
tender. Press through puréer if you desire. Serve with cornbread.
　The milk and cornbread help complete the protein.

BEAN PATTIES

(4 servings)

2 cups cooked beans　　　　　　½ teaspoon oregano
1 tablespoon chopped onion　　　1 egg
1 teaspoon apple cider vinegar　¼ cup wheat germ
2 tablespoons chopped parsley　1 tablespoon oil

　Grind or purée beans and combine onions, vinegar, parsley, and
oregano. Mix thoroughly. Make into patties. Dip into beaten raw
egg and roll in wheat germ. Heat oil in skillet. Sauté until heated
through.

Variation: Add ¼ cup grated cheese. The cheese will help to balance
protein.

231

BEAN LOAF

(6 to 8 servings)

4 cups cooked beans
2 tablespoons oil
2 celery stalks, chopped
1 large onion, chopped
1 raw carrot, grated
1 tablespoon parsley

½ cup tomatoes
½ cup wheat germ or a cup of
    whole wheat bread crumbs
2 eggs
1 teaspoon oregano
1 teaspoon basil

Cook onions and celery in oil to brown. Add to beans with carrot, parsley, tomatoes, wheat germ, eggs, oregano, and basil. Pack into a greased loaf tin. Bake at 350° F. for 1 hour. Serve with tomato sauce if desired.

LETTUCE

Lettuce has only moderate amounts of vitamins in the green outer leaves and lesser amounts in the blanched inner leaves. It is a source of some trace minerals. Lettuce is almost universally used in salads. It can also be used in cream soup or as a bed for cooking green peas.

MUSHROOMS

Mushrooms are good sources of B vitamins. They enhance a salad and are excellent sautéed, in sauces, combined with meat, and in soups.

STUFFED MUSHROOMS

(4 servings)

12 large mushrooms
1 tablespoon butter
1½ cups dry bread crumbs
¼ cup finely chopped nuts
1½ tablespoons chopped chives or
  onion

2 tablespoons evaporated milk or
  meat stock
¼ teaspoon salt
dash paprika
4 tablespoons grated Parmesan
  cheese

Wipe mushrooms with damp towel. Chop mushroom stems and sauté in butter until tender. Combine with crumbs, nuts, chives, milk, salt, and paprika. Stuff mushrooms with mixture. Sprinkle with Parmesan cheese, pressing it down into the stuffing. Set mushrooms, cap side up, on broiler tray. Brush with oil or butter. Broil 5 minutes under preheated broiler. Turn caps over and run under broiler to brown stuffing. Serve on buttered whole-grain toast. Or bake at 400° F. for 15 minutes.

MUSTARD

Mustard is another green of the brassica family. It also grows wild. It should be cooked while young and tender. It is high in vitamins A, B_2, C, and iron.

OKRA

Okra contains moderate amounts of vitamins and minerals. It is good boiled as a vegetable—cook in a little water until tender. It is often added to soups and is common in Creole cookery. The pods can also be breaded and sautéed in oil. Slice large pods, cook small ones whole.

ONIONS

Onion, like garlic, is an enhancer. It adds flavor to dishes. It can also be served as a side dish, boiled with butter or a cream sauce. It can be stuffed with other vegetables or leftover meats and baked.

PARSNIPS

Parsnips really need to be frozen to have the best flavor. Those which have lived through a long winter and are dug in the spring are superb in flavor. They are as sweet as candy, but not so dangerous. Parsnips contain some calcium and a little vitamin C and B_1.

To cook parsnips, put a little oil or butter in a saucepan. Add scrubbed, sliced parsnips, and cook over low heat covered until tender, stirring occasionally. They cook very quickly.

You can make a delicious parsnip stew.

PARSNIP STEW

(4 servings)

3 to 4 parsnips	3½ cups milk
2 tablespoons butter or margarine	salt and pepper to taste
2 tablespoons flour	

Cook parsnips, sliced, in butter or margarine until tender. Sprinkle flour over them. Stir. Stir in milk a little at a time. Heat, stirring until the milk reaches the boiling point. Season.

PEAS

Green peas are delicious. They contain some A and B vitamins as well as a little vitamin C.

Fresh peas must be shelled. Cook in a little water until just tender. If you overcook, then they will look as unappetizing as the canned peas do. They usually take 15 to 20 minutes, though tiny peas may take as little as 5 minutes. Frozen peas take only 2 or 3 minutes to cook. If frozen peas begin to wrinkle when you remove the lid to the pot, they are done. They should have a lovely bright green color.

SUGAR PEAS

These peas are also called Chinese peas. They are picked before the peas are formed in the pods. They are superb stir-fried. They need to be cooked only 2 to 3 minutes and are truly delectable. Add them to mixed vegetables, to Chinese dishes, or serve them as the main vegetable. They are hard to buy in the market fresh, though they are available frozen. If you have room for a garden, they are well worth growing as they produce throughout the summer if you keep them picked.

PEPPERS

Green and red sweet peppers are excellent sources of vitamin C. They are also excellent in salads or as an addition to cooked foods for flavor. They are also good stuffed.

STUFFED PEPPERS

(4 servings)

4 large green peppers	1 teaspoon parsley
1 cup raw brown rice	1 chopped tomato
1 cup grated cheddar cheese	¼ cup finely chopped onion
½ teaspoon thyme	2 cups tomato sauce

Cook rice according to recipe. Combine hot rice with cheese, thyme, parsley, tomato, and onion. Cut off stem end and scoop seeds out of peppers. Pack with rice mixture. Put peppers in pan with a little hot water on the bottom. Bake at 350° F. about 45 minutes. Heat tomato sauce and serve over peppers if desired.

BEAN-STUFFED GREEN PEPPERS

(6 servings)

2 tablespoons butter or margarine
½ cup finely chopped onion
½ cup chopped celery
1 cup dry beans, cooked
1 cup tomato sauce
¾ teaspoon Italian seasoning or ½
  teaspoon basil and ½ oregano

1 cup shredded Cheddar cheese
1 teaspoon salt
pepper
6 green peppers

Heat butter and sauté onion and celery until barely tender. Mash the beans. Add beans to onion and celery. Add tomato sauce and seasoning mixture. Stir. Add cheese, salt and pepper. Place the halved and seeded peppers in a baking pan. Fill with the bean mixture. Pour hot water around the peppers. Bake at 400° F. about 30 minutes, or until peppers are tender.

POTATO————————————————

The potato has been a much maligned vegetable of late, with so much emphasis on diet. Actually, potato is inexpensive and a reasonably good source of vitamin C. In addition, it contains some iron and a number of B vitamins as well as trace minerals. Be sure the potatoes you buy are firm and free from blight and from the green color on the skin. Potatoes should not be stored in the sun or light. Consequently, clear plastic bags are not good containers unless they are kept in a dark place. The light, besides destroying certain B vitamins, causes the formation of the toxic green coloration.

BOILED POTATO

(4 servings)

4 potatoes
Boiling salted water

Scrub potatoes and cut out any spots. Halve. Add water part way to the top of the potatoes. Cover tightly. Simmer until cooked (about 10 to 15 minutes). You can leave them whole, but cooking time is increased. Peel by holding potato on fork and slipping off only the thin skin with a paring knife. The skin pulls off very easily after the potatoes are cooked.

BAKED POTATOES

(4 servings)

To bake, rub potatoes with a little oil or butter. Place in a preheated 350° F. oven for about 1 hour. You may bake them along with meat, adding them 1 hour before the meat is done.

BAKED POTATO WITH YOGHURT

(4 servings)

Bake 4 potatoes. Remove from oven. Cut cross in top. Scoop out contents; mash, adding 1 tablespoon butter, a sprinkle of salt and pepper, 3 tablespoons yoghurt, and 1 tablespoon minced onion if desired. Stuff back into the skins. Sprinkle with parsley. Broil about 2 minutes to brown.

SCALLOPED POTATOES

(4 servings)

Pare thinly and slice 4 potatoes. Put a layer of potato in casserole, 2 thin slices of onion; dot with butter and sprinkle with salt and pepper. Repeat layers. Pour milk over the layer just to the top of the potatoes. Bake at 350° F. about 1 hour.

Variations: (A high-protein dish.) Add ½ pound cheese slices, layering with the potato and onion. Cook and serve.

You can also add leftover meat, beef, ham, corned beef, or you can add a layer of pork chops if you wish.

SWEET POTATOES

Sweet potatoes contain vitamin A in addition to the other vitamins and minerals. They may be boiled or baked. They also are good in casseroles. They are especially good served with pork.

SCALLOPED SWEET POTATOES AND APPLES

(6 servings)

6 boiled sweet potatoes (not quite tender)	1½ cups sliced apples
⅓ cup honey	¼ cup butter
	½ teaspoon salt

Peel and slice the potatoes in ¼-inch slices. Put a layer of the sweet potatoes in a casserole, then a layer of apples. Sprinkle with honey and salt and dot with a little butter. Repeat to fill dish. End with a layer of apple. Bake at 350° F. about 50 minutes.

PUMPKIN

Pumpkin is a squash and can be cooked and eaten as winter squash is. One way to cook pumpkin is to place it whole on a baking pan in a 350° F. oven and bake until tender, 1 hour or more depending on size. Cool slightly, peel. Purée the pulp and use for pies, cakes, or any other pumpkin recipe. Wash seeds, dry and shell, and eat as snacks or add to granola.

RHUBARB

Rhubarb is also called pie plant. It is a good source of vitamin A. Although it contains calcium, the oxalic acid in rhubarb binds it. The leaves are poisonous because of their high oxalic acid content. Rhubarb is used mostly for sauce and in making pies.

For sauce, cut up and cook rhubarb in a little water until nearly tender. Add honey to taste and cook until tender.

SALSIFY

Salsify is a root vegetable which, like parsnip, improves by freezing in the ground. It cooks very quickly (cook as for parsnips) and has a milky oysterlike flavor.

SPINACH

Spinach is valuable because of its vitamin A content. It also contains C and B vitamins including folic acid. Because of oxalic acid, you cannot depend on spinach for calcium and iron even though it contains them. Use spinach uncooked in salads or as a cooked vegetable.

To cook spinach: Wash and put in saucepan. Cover. Bring to a boil and simmer until tender, no more than 5 minutes. Serve.

To stir-fry: Chop spinach and add to hot oil in skillet. Stir, cover, and shake 1 to 2 minutes.

Spinach is good combined with fish, eggs, and meat. It also makes an attractive addition to soups and mixed vegetable dishes.

SQUASH

Winter squash is a very good source of vitamin A.

To cook, peel and cut in pieces. Put in a little boiling water, salted. When tender, mash if desired, adding a little butter and pepper.

BAKED SQUASH

(4 servings)

2 *medium acorn squash*
4 *tablespoons honey*
4 *teaspoons butter*

1 *teaspoon salt*
dash pepper

Halve squash. Place upside down on baking pan. Bake at 350° F. for 30 minutes. Remove from oven. Turn squash over. Add 1 tablespoon honey and 1 teaspoon butter to each squash. Sprinkle with salt and pepper. Return to oven. Bake another 20 to 30 minutes until tender.

Variation: Add chopped nuts if desired.

SUMMER SQUASH

Summer squash contains less vitamin A than winter squash, but it does contain a little vitamin C and calcium. Summer squash has a high water content and should never be cooked in additional water.

The various types are versatile and add color to any dish. The varieties are legion, but unless you grow them yourself, you are not likely to find many different kinds in the stores. Use any of them, when small, raw in salads. They are more nutritious than cucumber. You can also substitute them for cucumber in relish recipes.

Summer squash can be baked, fried, or boiled. They are excellent stuffed and baked with cheese, rice or meat, cheese or tomato mixtures. Use your imagination; the combinations are unending.

To cook, cut in thin slices and place on medium heat, stirring occasionally so they won't burn. Cook until barely tender.

Stir-fry by slicing into thin slices. Add oil to hot skillet. Put squash in and cook, stirring about 1 minute. Put on lid. Shake occasionally. When tender-crisp, add 1 tablespoon soy sauce. Shake to coat and serve.

VEGETABLE MEDLEY

(any amount)

Heat 2 tablespoons olive oil in large covered skillet. Add 1 or more minced garlics. Add 1 onion, thinly sliced. Sauté for 2 to 3 minutes. Add sliced green pepper and any of the following vegetables, thinly sliced or diced:

eggplant *celery*
zucchini *mushrooms*
tomatoes *cooked green beans*

Cook, stirring occasionally until just tender. If adding cooked green beans, add when vegetables are done. Heat through.

ZUCCHINI AND CHEESE

(4 servings, a high-protein dish)

2 small zucchini
½ pound Cheddar cheese
8 ounces tomato sauce

Slice zucchini. Place layer in baking dish. Add a layer of sliced cheese. Pour tomato sauce over all. Bake at 350° F. about 35 to 40 minutes until tender (or cook in covered dutch oven). Serve.

TOMATOES

Tomatoes are a good source of vitamins A and C. The C content is variable, however, depending on whether the tomato matures on the vine. Their vitamin content is highest before they have become fully ripe. Oddly enough, they are sweeter then, too, since the acid has not fully developed. The C content of tomatoes is barely affected by cooking since it is stabilized by the acid content of the tomatoes. Of course, if you cook them in cast iron, the C will be lost.

Tomatoes are delicious eaten out of hand with salt (some use sugar) or in salads. They make a refreshing juice drink and combine with an amazing number of cooked dishes.

Tomatoes can also be stuffed, fresh, with a meat, fish, or egg-salad mixture; or baked with a rice, meat, or cheese mixture as in stuffed peppers.

FRUITS AND DESSERTS

ELDERBERRY

Elderberry is high in vitamin C. You can use these berries to make jelly or pie (use a fruit pie recipe, adding a little extra sweetener, some lemon juice and 4 tablespoons of flour to the fruit). They are also good made into a syrup. Simmer the fruit until it is tender. Strain. Add honey to taste and heat to boiling. Bottle.

CRANBERRY

Cranberries are not especially nutritious, but they can be pretty added to muffins or used as a sauce accompanying meat.

CANTALOUPE

Cantaloupe is very high in vitamin C and contains A and a little calcium as well. It is only good served fresh, either as a part of a fruit compote or eaten as is.

BLUEBERRY

Blueberries contain small amounts of a number of vitamins and minerals. They are delicious and sweet, needing no sweetener to be eaten out of hand. The smaller wild blueberries are far more flavorful than the large cultivated ones and are better in muffins.

Blueberries are a very pretty addition to a fruit compote. They are excellent in pie, cake, muffins, pancakes and waffles. They make a pretty juice also.

BLUEBERRY CRISP

(6 servings)

3 cups fresh blueberries or frozen
1 tablespoon lemon juice
⅓ cup whole-wheat flour
1 cup oats

½ cup brown sugar
½ teaspoon salt
1 teaspoon cinnamon
⅓ cup butter or margarine

Put blueberries in shallow baking dish. Sprinkle with lemon juice. Combine flour, oats, brown sugar, salt, cinnamon, and butter. Mix until well combined and crumbly. Sprinkle over blueberries. Bake at 375° F. about 30 minutes. Serve warm or cold.

BANANA

Bananas have moderate amounts of vitamins and minerals. They are available all year and quite low in price. They combine well with other fruits in a compote, providing a sweet, bland flavor and consistency to offset the tangy taste of others.

Bananas can be cooked. They go well with peanut butter (make a sandwich of a split banana spread with peanut butter). They also make a good addition to puddings and ice cream.

AVOCADO

Avocado is high in fat content and vitamin E. It also contains small amounts of other vitamins and minerals. While avocado is a fruit, it is at home with vegetables in tossed salad. It also combines prettily with citrus fruit salads, topped with salad dressing.

APRICOT

Apricots are high in vitamin A. They are good eaten out of hand, dried, or used in recipes calling for peaches.

APPLES

Apples provide a good winter standby. They contain only small amounts of vitamins and minerals. Most of these are located just under the skin, a good reason not to peel your apples. They go well in compotes, cooked as a sauce, in jellies, and in various other cooked dishes. They are excellent baked.

APPLE CRISP

(4 to 6 servings)

Use four cups sliced apples in place of the blueberries in the Blueberry Crisp recipe.

BAKED APPLES

(4 servings)

4 large baking apples (Cortland or
  others)
4 tablespoons honey

2 teaspoons butter
4 pinches cinnamon
water

Cut cores from apples. Place in shallow pan. Fill cavity with honey (1 tablespoon in each), butter, and a pinch of cinnamon. Put a little boiling water in the bottom of the pan. Bake at 350° F. about ½ hour or more until tender.

APPLESAUCE

(4 servings)

6 red apples
water
1 teaspoon cinnamon
honey to taste

Cut up apples, removing cores. Put in saucepan with just a little water. Simmer until tender. Add cinnamon. Stir. Put through a puréer to remove skins. Add honey to taste.

WALDORF SALAD

(4 servings)

2 apples, cored and cut up
½ cup raisins
½ cup chopped walnuts

½ cup chopped celery
½ cup mayonnaise

Combine apples, raisins, walnuts, celery, and mayonnaise. Serve on lettuce.

FIGS

Figs have small amounts of A and some B vitamins and calcium. Dried ones are good chopped and added as sweeteners.

GOOSEBERRY

Gooseberries have some vitamin C and calcium. They are good cooked as a sauce or in pie.

GOOSEBERRY SAUCE

(6 to 8 servings)

Put 1 quart gooseberries in saucepan with a little water. Add ½ to ¾ cups honey. Simmer until tender.

GRAPES

Grapes are delicious eaten out of hand. They also make an attractive addition to compotes. They contain small amounts of vitamins A and C as well as some minerals. Raisins (dried grapes) are a good source of iron.

PEACHES

Peaches are excellent eaten fresh. They contain moderate amounts of vitamins and minerals. They are good in compotes and are delicious in pie, shortcake, and in various cooked dishes. Substitute 4 cups peaches for blueberries in Blueberry Crisp recipe.

BAKED PEACHES

(4 servings)

2 *large peaches*
¼ *cup ground almonds*
2 *tablespoons candied fruit,
  chopped fine*

4 *blanched almonds*
4 *tablespoons white wine*

Halve peaches. Remove stones and scoop out a little of the pulp from the cavity left by the stone. Mash the pulp you scooped out and combine with almonds and fruit. Fill cavities with the mixture. Garnish each with an almond. Place in buttered baking pan. Sprinkle each half with 1 tablespoon of wine. Bake at 350° F. for 15 to 20 minutes until tender.

PEARS

Pears are about on a par with apples nutritionally. They are also available throughout much of the winter. They go well in compotes and can be cooked in a few recipes.

PEAR-CHEESE PIE

(1 9-inch pie)

6 *pared, medium Bartlett pears*
3 *tablespoons lemon juice*
⅓ *cup honey*
2 *tablespoons flour*
1 *teaspoon grated lemon peel*
1 *9-inch pastry shell, unbaked*

CRUMB TOPPING:
½ *cup whole-wheat flour*
½ *cup sugar*
½ *teaspoon ginger*
½ *teaspoon cinnamon*
¼ *teaspoon mace*
2 *tablespoons butter or margarine*
3 *thin slices Cheddar cheese*

Slice five of the pears. Cut the last one into six equal slices. Sprinkle pear slices with lemon juice. Mix honey, flour, and lemon peel. Stir into the pears (reserve the six slices). Spoon evenly into pastry shell. Arrange the six slices in pinwheel pattern on the pie. Combine flour, sugar, ginger, cinnamon, and mace. Rub in butter. Sprinkle over pie. Bake at 400° F. until the pears are tender. It will take about 45 minutes. Cut cheese slices diagonally and arrange on pie in pinwheel effect. Serve.

PINEAPPLE

Pineapple contains some vitamins and minerals. The juice is not a good source of C even when fortified. Fortification makes it a fair source (30 mg./half cup). It is available canned in its own juice which forms an excellent base for fruit compote. It combines well with dates and bananas.

AMBROSIA

(4 servings)

1 orange
2 bananas
5 marshmallows or 1 tablespoon
  honey

1 can unsweetened pineapple
⅓ cup shredded coconut

Peel and slice the orange. Arrange slices in bowl. Slice bananas over orange. Add sliced marshmallows or drizzle honey over. Add pineapple, then the coconut. Chill.

Variation: Add 4 or 5 cut-up dates with the pineapple layer.

PLUMS

Plums contain some vitamin A and B vitamins. Prunes are a good source of iron.

Plums or prunes can be eaten out of hand or stewed. Prunes are an excellent laxative, so be sure you don't overdo a good thing. Fresh plums make a good addition to a fruit compote.

RASPBERRY

Raspberries contain some vitamins and minerals. They are only a fair source of vitamin C. They make a pretty addition to a fruit compote.

STRAWBERRY

Strawberries are a good source of vitamin C and also contain some minerals. They are excellent served fresh, as an addition to a compote, or in strawberry shortcakes.

STRAWBERRY SHORTCAKE

(6 or more servings)

1 recipe biscuits
1 quart strawberries
½ to ⅔ cup honey
½ pt. cream, whipped

Slice strawberries and pour honey over them. Refrigerate. Make biscuits timed to coincide with serving time. Split hot biscuits. Dot with butter. Heap on strawberries and top with a little whipped cream.

WATERMELON

Being mostly water, watermelon is a good thirst quencher. It does contain small amounts of vitamins and minerals.

Watermelon balls look pretty added to fruit compote.

FRESH FRUIT WITH
CHEESE AND BISCUIT

Place an attractively arranged tray of fresh fruit, mixed whole-grain crackers, and one or more types of cheese. Serve for dessert.

PEANUT COOKIES

(3½ dozen)

1½ cups sugar
¼ teaspoon salt
½ cup milk
¼ cup corn syrup

½ cup peanut butter
1 teaspoon vanilla
1½ cup oats
¾ cup chopped salted peanuts

In saucepan, combine sugar, salt, milk, and corn syrup. Heat on medium until sugar is dissolved. Cook, stirring occasionally, until a little dropped into cold water makes a soft ball.

Remove from heat. Stir in peanut butter and vanilla. Add oats and peanuts. Combine thoroughly. Drop onto waxed paper by spoonfuls. Cool.

HONEY CHOCOLATE COOKIES

(about 6 dozen)
These are relatively crisp for honey-based cookies.

1 cup margarine
1¼ cups honey
2 eggs
2 squares chocolate
1½ cup oats
2¼ cups unbleached, enriched
flour

1 teaspoon baking powder
¼ teaspoon baking soda
1 teaspoon salt
1 teaspoon cinnamon
1½ cups raisins
½ cup chopped nuts

Blend shortening and honey. Add eggs, melted chocolate, and oats. Combine flour with baking powder, baking soda, salt, and cinnamon. Add to oat mixture. Blend in raisins and nuts. Bake at 325° F. about 15 to 20 minutes.

PIE CRUST

Make pies with only one crust. Put a top crust on what is usually a two-crust pie. To make one crust or pie shell:

*1½ cups whole-wheat flour or
    unbleached, enriched flour
¼ cup lard or ⅓ cup other
    shortening*

*½ teaspoon salt
cold water*

Cut lard or shortening into the flour and salt until mixture resembles cornmeal. Add cold water by tablespoons, sprinkling it into the flour mixture, tossing with a fork, until just moistened enough to barely hold together. Turn out on floured surface. Form flattened ball. Dent ball at right angles with rolling pin, about 3 times each way. Quickly roll out to desired size, starting rolling in the center and rolling toward the edges. Your pie crust will be tender and flaky if you follow these directions. You may not get a perfect round like the pictures in the book, but it will not be tough.

BASIC FRUIT PIE

(one 9-inch pie)

*1 quart fruit
⅔ to ¾ cup honey*

Prepare fruit (peel and cut up apples, peaches, etc.). If the fruit is an especially juicy type, toss it with 2 tablespoons of flour. Pour honey over it, add 1 or 2 tablespoons lemon juice if desired. Put on top crust. Bake at 450° F. for 10 minutes. Lower heat to 375° F. and continue cooking 40 to 50 minutes, depending on the type fruit. Use the longer time for apples, shorter time for blueberries, etc.

BAKED APPLE PUDDING

(4 servings)

4 medium apples, pared and sliced
1 cup graham cracker crumbs
½ cup water

⅓ cup honey
3 tablespoons lemon juice

Combine apples, crumbs, water, honey, and lemon juice. Put in buttered baking dish. Bake at 375° F. 30 minutes or until apples are tender. Serve hot with cream or evaporated milk.

BLUEBERRY BETTY

(6 servings)

3 cups blueberries
¾ cup sugar
⅛ teaspoon salt

1 tablespoon lemon juice
6 pancakes
nutmeg

Cook blueberries, sugar, salt, and lemon juice until the blueberries are just tender. Pour into shallow baking pan, arranging pancakes on top. Sprinkle with nutmeg. Bake at 425° F. about 20 minutes.

APPLE BETTY

(6 servings)

3 cups apples, pared and sliced
1½ cups soft bread crumbs
⅓ cup brown sugar
1 teaspoon cinnamon

4 tablespoons melted butter or
   margarine
¾ cup hot or cold milk

Mix apples and 1 cup of the bread crumbs with the brown sugar and cinnamon in a buttered casserole dish. Pour milk and butter over the apple mixture. Sprinkle with the remaining crumbs. Bake at 350° F. about 45 minutes. Serve hot or cold with milk or cream if desired.

RICE AND PINEAPPLE

(4 servings)

2 cups cooked rice
butter
4 slices pineapple, halved

½ cup brown sugar
juice from pineapple

Place a layer of rice in the bottom of baking dish. Dot it with butter. Arrange the pineapple slices attractively over the top. Sprinkle with sugar. Pour in pineapple juice. Bake at 350° F. 20 minutes.

RICE PUDDING

(6 servings)

½ cup rice
½ teaspoon cinnamon
⅛ teaspoon salt

½ cup molasses
4 cups milk

Put washed rice in a buttered casserole dish. Add cinnamon, salt, molasses, and milk. Bake at 325° F. about 3 hours. Stir it occasionally. If desired, add 1 cup raisins about ½ hour before cooking is complete.

INDIAN PUDDING

(8 servings)

1 pint milk
¼ cup undegerminated cornmeal
½ cup molasses
2 tablespoons butter
½ cup sugar

½ teaspoon salt
½ teaspoon cinnamon
1 egg
½ cup raisins
3 cups milk

Boil a pint of milk and stir in the cornmeal, cooking 10 minutes to thicken. Add molasses, butter, sugar, salt, cinnamon, beaten egg, raisins, and 2 more cups milk. Bake at 250° F. for 2 hours. After the first half hour, add the final cup of milk, stirring.

SPICED CRUMB PUDDING

(8 servings)

1 cup dry bread crumbs
1 cup sour milk
¼ cup shortening
1 cup brown sugar
2 tablespoons molasses

½ cup whole-wheat flour
½ teaspoon cloves
½ teaspoon cinnamon
1 teaspoon baking soda
¾ cup raisins

Soak the crumbs in sour milk for about ½ hour. Cream the shortening and sugar, add molasses and beat. Mix flour, cloves, cinnamon, and baking soda. Add to the creamed mixture, stirring in well. Add the crumb-milk mix and raisins and beat thoroughly. Bake in a buttered mold or ring pan at 300° F. for 45 minutes. Serve hot or cold with pudding sauce, evaporated milk, or whipped cream.

BREAD PUDDING

(4 servings)

1 cup bread crumbs　　　　¼ teaspoon salt
¼ cup butter　　　　　　　2 eggs
¼ cup sugar　　　　　　　 2 cups milk
½ teaspoon cinnamon　　　 ½ cup raisins
¼ teaspoon nutmeg

Arrange the bread crumbs in a buttered baking dish. Dot with butter. Combine the sugar, cinnamon, nutmeg, and salt. Add to slightly beaten eggs. Heat milk. Pour slowly into eggs, stirring. Pour all with raisins over the crumbs. Set in a pan of hot water and bake at 350° F. for 40 minutes until firm.

BLUEBERRY COBBLER

(6-8 servings)

1 quart blueberries　　　　　　　　¼ teaspoon salt
⅔ cup honey　　　　　　　　　　　pinch nutmeg
2 tablespoons butter　　　　　　　　3 tablespoons shortening
1 tablespoon lemon juice　　　　　　1 egg
1 cup enriched, unbleached flour　　¼ cup milk
3 teaspoons baking powder

Put blueberries, honey, and butter with lemon juice in a baking pan. Mix together the flour, baking powder, salt, and nutmeg. Cut in the shortening until the mixture resembles coarse cornmeal. Combine milk and egg and stir into the flour mixture. Spread this mixture over the blueberries. Bake at 350° F. about 40 minutes.

CHAPTER SEVEN

TOWARD A HEALTHY FAMILY

The hour of the miracle has come. For each and every new baby is truly a miracle. You are suspended in space, a participant and an observer. The voices come from afar—a doctor, a nurse, your husband—cheering you on, encouraging, soothing. All is red and silver and shimmering as, with a last tremendous effort, your baby passes from within your body into your world.

"What is it?" you gasp.

"A beautiful big girl," comes the answer.

You laugh and cry at once, in love, in joy, in relief.

An eternity, that second before the infant cries—the thrilling lusty squall which turns the bluish doll-like being into a beautiful pink, breathing, kicking, arm-waving baby. The cord is cut, the baby—your baby—is wrapped and put in your arms. The true miracle—half her heritage has come from you, and half from her father.

Already you can see that she has her father's chin, your small flat ears. Each day you will discover new things about her—an expression like her great grandmother's, a sleeping position like your sister's. Each day she will gain in her awareness of you, of her environment and her place in it.

Whoever said a baby does nothing but eat and sleep probably didn't know much about babies. They eat, urinate, defecate, cry, cuddle, kick, wiggle, respond, and learn. Your baby learns constantly.

She has reflexes at birth which help her learn. One of these is the rooting reflex. Touch her cheek with your nipple and she will turn her head, rooting to get milk. Since her mouth is the source of much of her early pleasure, she will, as she grows, explore almost everything with it.

Satisfy her early physical needs with milk, preferably your milk. Keep her dry, clean, and comfortable. Satisfy her early social needs with your presence. Hold her, caress her, talk to her. In this way, you will keep her healthy and happy.

A baby changes your life-style, although you need not be "tied down." While tiny, she is portable—but you do have a human being, a helpless one, entrusted to your care, to love and to nourish.

You and your baby's father are individuals, too. Each of you has needs. Each of you must find ways to help meet the other's needs. Sharing chores may be helpful, but a good part of your lives will revolve around the baby.

If you work outside the home, you'll want to be sure your baby has loving care. You and your partner can stagger working hours to provide that care; or, you can find a mother substitute while you work. Make arrangements at work to have time off (an extended lunch hour perhaps) to nurse the baby. Or have your baby brought to you at work so that you may nurse her during your break.

Continue the balanced diet you started while you were pregnant. See to it that you all are getting the nutrients you need. Wait until your baby is old enough before you begin feeding her solid foods— five to six months at least. Then start her off wisely with your own nutritionally superior food or, at the least, the *plain* fruits, *plain* vegetables and the *plain* meats available from baby-food companies—not the high-meat dinners, custards, and desserts.

Follow a good guide to infant feeding such as that recommended by La Leche League in *The Womanly Art of Breast Feeding. The Natural Baby Food Cookbook* by Margaret Kenda and me will provide a guide with recipes and hints for family meals and for feeding your baby, whether by breast or bottle.

Go for your postpartum checkup at six weeks and again at six months. Take your baby for her physical exams and immunizations at six weeks and for monthly visits thereafter.

At birth, she has enough antibodies passed to her through the placenta to help protect her until her own defense system is functioning. If you breast-feed, you will continue to pass on antibody protection. The average breast-fed baby has less sickness than does the bottle-fed one. Even so, it is vital that she be immunized against diphtheria, pertussis (whooping cough), tetanus, polio, and measles—any one of which could be fatal. She also needs immunization against mumps, chicken pox, and rubella.

As your baby grows and matures, you will know her intimately. Her behavior, her moods, her changing attitudes, her contours will all become as familiar to you as your own body. Thus, you are the person to notice changes in her. A change of behavior may herald illness. Or it may be just a stage in her development.

We all go through cycles of development—changing month by month, year by year. The younger the child, the shorter the cycles. The infant in his first year changes rapidly, the toddler less rapidly, the school child more slowly. The stormy adolescent cycle is interminable; thence young adulthood, middle years, and maturity to senescence.

These behavioral stages tend to parallel physical stages—rapid change, disequilibrium, stability; rapid growth, awkwardness, plateaus, and leveling off. Normally, appetite follows these same cycles. Thus, the rapidly growing infant will eat increasingly large amounts with only short periods of leveling off of appetite. The preschool child's appetite will diminish, sometimes alarmingly, when he's at a leveling-off period of growth. Be prepared for these cycles and don't panic when they appear.

Fat is not synonymous with health, and stuffing a reluctant child will not keep him healthy. Just be sure what you feed him is nutritious and not empty calories.

Good nutrition will help to keep your family healthy. It will build resistance to disease. It will prevent the development of diseases of malnutrition. It will insure strong, healthy teeth; glowing complexion; bright, shining, lively hair; clear, sparkling eyes; mental alertness and the glow of health—in short, good physical and mental development. Good nutrition will help insure the heritage of your children's children.

KEEPING YOUR FAMILY WELL

Even in your healthy family, it is wise to be aware of warning signs of illness in your child. You, as her parents, know her better than any physician or nurse, neighbor or friend. You may not know as much about illness as they; but you are in a position to recognize the signs in your child—your usually healthy, well-nourished child.

Unusual fussiness for no apparent reason may be one of the first signs of illness, especially if it is accompanied by a drop in appetite and inability to sleep. Just as fussiness may indicate illness, so may unusual quietness and sleepiness. Don't be misled by a normal growth stage which may stimulate a complete change of schedule.

If your baby starts tugging or brushing at her ear or any other part of her body, along with a bit of crankiness, it's worth checking. Ear infections, especially, may come on rapidly without the warning of fever.

Vomiting and diarrhea are always serious in young infants. However, if your baby is breast-fed, vomiting of undigested milk shortly after feeding or large diarrhea-like stools may be an indication that she is taking in an excess of milk. This is more liable to happen following an increase in her appetite which causes her to suck more vigorously and frequently. The resulting increase in milk supply may, if she's a vigorous nurser, be a bit too much for her.

Fever is an obvious sign of illness. However, in a newborn a slight fever may be an indication that her environment is too hot. A very warm house and too many clothes and blankets may cause a small increase in temperature. A newborn's heat-regulating center has to learn to adjust to temperature change.

Babies can run much higher fevers than adults, so don't be shocked if your little one's fever suddenly spikes to 103 degrees. Do check in with her doctor though.

Fever has a purpose. It is one of the body's defenses against infection. It helps to fight invading organisms by making things too hot for them. Do not run for the aspirin at the first sign of a temperature. Not only will the aspirin lower the fever and allow the invader to get a better foothold, it will also mask symptoms.

A child with a fever will not want to be active. She will probably not want to eat much. Her body will usually feel very hot to touch; her face may be flushed and her eyes bright; or conversely, she may seem pale and listless.

Vomiting is often the first warning of fever and accompanying illness. There is one good rule to follow. If an illness is serious enough to *treat*, it's serious enough to see a doctor. With the exception of acute bacterial infections and certain other ailments, there are seldom specific medications for illnesses. Most medications help allay the symptoms—aspirin for fever and pain, cough syrup for cough, and so forth. The disease often will have to run its course.

It is not likely that your child, who is well nourished and well cared for, will be ill often. But young children occasionally come down with colds, flu, tonsillitis, allergies, and other problems in spite of our best efforts. Unfortunately, parents usually suffer more than the child does. I have had too many sleepless nights with my children, and they have been unusually healthy and accident-free.

A sick child always seems to be sickest at night. Invariably, the temperature peaks well after dark when doctors' offices are closed. And, of course, the lonely night hours always make things seem worse. Happily, children recover rapidly. The baby who was so sick yesterday acts today as if nothing had ever bothered her.

Knowledge of our world—nutrition, possible hazards, problems and successes—changes every day. New discoveries are made; new materials are synthesized; old materials are used in new ways. The only way any of us can begin to keep up with the world is to keep informed. *Read*—newspapers, magazine sections on new developments, labels, even to the minute print. *Question*—ask the doctor, the nurse, the nutritionist, the health educator. *Listen*—try to get reasonable, coherent answers to your questions. Get different points of view. You have a right to know, to weigh alternatives. In this manner, you can become aware of changes in the health field.

You can lessen trials of parenthood if you try to maintain a safe, secure, loving environment; if you provide your family with a varied diet containing all the nutrients; if you avoid as much as possible the hazards of contaminants and unsafe food additives; if you have adequate medical supervision; and if you respect the individuality of each child, allowing the opportunity for growth, adventure, exploration. In short, keep open the opportunity for self-realization.

IF THE UNEXPECTED HAPPENS

Your friend has done all she can to give her baby a good start in life. She has eaten a nutritious, balanced diet. She has had good prenatal care. She has avoided drugs, cigarettes, alcohol, and other hazards as much as possible. She has had little or no medication and anesthesia in childbirth, and yet . . .

Something is wrong. She cannot be sure exactly what the problem is. She's not really used to tiny babies, but she feels it. Her doctor reassures her. The baby is fine.

The baby *is* beautiful, with black hair and a turned-up nose. But he seems strangely limp, not as responsive as she expects him to be. His tongue seems to get in the way when she tries to feed him . . .

Or . . .

Something is wrong. They haven't shown her the baby yet. "The baby's all right, isn't he?" she asks, fearful, hoping, holding her breath.

"He has a problem, but it can be repaired. He has a cleft lip and palate. It can be fixed."

The doctor holds the baby out to her. The baby is bald. His eyes are huge and dark, his skin pink and healthy. His mother hesitates, hardly daring to look at his mouth. It's hard to take, but in spite of it he's beautiful. His mother loves him. . . .

In each case, the woman worries, wondering what she did wrong, what mistake she made, where she can find help. First, each needs to know that it is nothing she has done. It is not her fault. It may have been a genetic or chromosomal defect. It may have been a mutant gene. It may have been a developmental problem. Whatever the cause, she will need help.

In the first example, the baby was born with Down's Syndrome and the parents will need help getting a diagnosis, learning to cope with their concerns, their feelings. They will need help in finding out how to work best with their baby—and they will need to make their own decisions. In the second case, feeding the baby poses problems. How does the surgery work? Will it be successful?

For parents who face the problems of birth defects, diagnosed or undiagnosed, there are a number of sources for help. The department of health in the state where the family lives is one source. The health department of their city or the nearest large city is also qualified to provide them with information. A medical center or large general hospital, the public health nurse, or the visiting or district nurses association will be able to give them information. The National Foundation—March of Dimes is another source of help. In fact, any other unofficial agency concerned with a specific condition can help if a child is afflicted with that condition.

Birth defects can be as commonplace and readily treatable (if started early) as strabismus or as rare and tragic as the genetically induced Tay-Sachs disease.

There are a number of steps one can take in addition to eating a nutritionally adequate diet and avoiding the hazards listed in Chapter Three. Ideally, a woman should bear her children between the ages of twenty and thirty-five. A woman under twenty may not yet have completed her own growth, so pregnancy puts an additional strain on her resources. Even worse, however, is that teenage diets are traditionally among the worst of any group, other than those for the elderly. This creates an additional disadvantage to the teenage mother-to-be. Good nutrition and good prenatal care are mandatory to protect her health and that of her baby. And, according to Agnes Higgins of Montreal Diet Dispensary, with a good diet, high in protein and nutrients, the teen-age mother is no longer high risk.

Women beyond the age of thirty-five run a higher risk of having a baby with Down's Syndrome (mongolism) or with some other abnormality of the chromosomes. After forty, that risk is further increased. But most older women in good physical condition have beautifully healthy babies. Many doctors, however, believe amniocentesis should be performed to be on the safe side. For example, the chances of having a Down's Syndrome child after age forty are one in eighty, while before age thirty, they are only one in three thousand. Amniocentesis is a process whereby a little amniotic fluid is withdrawn from within the uterus and the cells checked for chromosome abnormalities. A number of disorders can be diagnosed in this manner.

A word of caution: Only a few disorders can be treated *in utero* with our present technology. If you opt to have amniocentesis and an untreatable disorder (Down's Syndrome, for example) is diagnosed, you will then be faced with the problem of either choosing a saline abortion or of continuing the pregnancy. You should also know that the procedure itself is not without risk.

If a couple knows a relative has been afflicted with what appears to be a birth defect or hereditary disorder, they may elect to seek genetic counseling, if only to set their minds at ease. This should be done before a woman who has had one baby with a birth defect has another pregnancy.

An Rh negative woman should be sure, if her husband is Rh positive, that her doctor checks her blood for antibodies during pregnancy and vaccinates her at delivery if her baby is positive. Now that the vaccine is available, erythroblastosis fetalis, the Rh disease, has become a rare occurrence.

Everyone needs opportunity—opportunity to succeed or fail. This is just as true for the child with a handicap as it is for the child without a handicap. He needs love, but a love which lets him try, a love which gives him the opportunity to develop his potentials to their fullest.

Provided with the stimulation, nourishment, love and opportunity, almost every child can, within his own limits, become a contributing member of society.

APPENDIX

SOURCES OF INFORMATION

American Academy of Pediatrics
1801 Hinman Avenue
Evanston, Illinois 60201

American Association for Maternal and Child Health
116 South Michigan Avenue
Chicago, Illinois 60603

American College of Nurse Midwives
100 Vermont Avenue, N.W.
Washington, D.C. 20005

American College of Obstetricians and Gynecologists
1 East Wacker Drive
Chicago, Illinois 60601

American Dietetic Association
430 North Michigan Avenue
Chicago, Illinois 60601

American Medical Association
535 North Dearborn Street
Chicago, Illinois 60610

American Nurses Association
2420 Pershing Road
Kansas City, Missouri 64108

American Society for Psychoprophylaxis in Obstetrics, Inc.
7 West 96th Street
New York, New York 10025

County Extension Service
County Court House
County Seat, Your County
Your State
> Information on food preparation, economics, food processing, farming, etc. Also free source of consumer-oriented U.S. government publications

International Childbirth Education Association
P.O. Box 40048
Minneapolis, Minnesota 55420

La Leche League International
9616 Minneapolis Avenue
Franklin Park, Illinois 60131
    Counseling telephone numbers:
            312-678-2822
            312-767-6015

Maternity Center Association
48 East 92nd Street
New York, New York 10028

National Childbirth Trust
9 Queensborough Terrace
London W.2, England

National Foundation—March of Dimes
P.O. Box 2000
White Plains, New York 10602

National Association for Retarded Children
420 Lexington Avenue
New York, New York 10017

National League for Nursing
10 Columbus Circle
New York, New York 10019

National Society for Crippled Children and Adults, Inc.
11 South LaSalle Street
Chicago, Illinois 60603

Planned Parenthood—World Population
810 7th Avenue
New York, New York 10019

Society for the Protection of the Unborn Through Nutrition (SPUN)
17 North Wabash, Suite 603
Chicago, Illinois 60602
    Nutrition Hotline:
        914-667-5199

Superintendent of Documents
U.S. Government Printing Office
Washington, D.C. 20402
        (Ask to be included on the mailing list for *Selected Government
        Publications;* also request listings for Consumer Service Publica-
        tions.)

United Cerebral Palsy Association
521 West 44th Street
New York, New York 10036

Zero Population Growth
367 State Street
Los Altos, California 94022

Another source of information and publications is your state university,
and your local public library.

BIBLIOGRAPHY

Apgar, Virginia, and Beck, Joan. *Is My Baby All Right?* New York: Trident Press, 1972.

A book for health service consumers which describes birth defects, their causes and prevention, what can be done for a child so afflicted. It includes a comprehensive listing of various agencies and organizations concerned with either prevention or help.

Bean, Constance A. *Methods of Childbirth; A Complete Guide to Childbirth Classes and Maternity Care.* Garden City, New York: Doubleday and Company, 1972.

This book does just what its title suggests. There is a wealth of material included; for example, lists of childbirth education classes by state, including affiliations, if any.

Bing, Elizabeth. *Six Practical Lessons for an Easier Childbirth.* New York: Grosset and Dunlap, 1967 (also Bantam Books, New York).

The Lamaze Method is covered.

Birch, Herbert G., M.D., Ph.D., and Gussow, Joan Dye. *Disadvantaged Children: Health, Nutrition, and School Failure.* New York: Harcourt, Brace and World; Grune and Stratton, 1970.

Excellent chapter on pregnancy and food, pp. 123-153. Points out consequences of poor nutrition on growth and development. An excellent bibliography is included.

Brewer, Gail Sforza. *What Every Pregnant Woman Should Know: The Truth About Diet and Drugs in Pregnancy.* New York: Random House, 1977.

The story and the research behind the need for good prenatal nutrition for every pregnant woman, with menus and recipes. Dr. Tom Brewer was the medical consultant for the book.

Brewer, Gail Sforza, Editor. *The Pregnancy Over Thirty Workbook.* Emmaus, Pa.: Rodale Press, 1978.

Just as useful for those under twenty.

Brewer, Thomas H., M.D. *Metabolic Toxemia of Late Pregnancy: A Disease of Malnutrition.* Springfield, Ill.: Charles C. Thomas, 1966.

Dr. Brewer points out that relationship between low protein intake and toxemia of pregnancy. He cites case histories and the failures of such treatments as diuresis.

Caliendo, Mary Alice. *Nutrition and Preventive Health Care*. New York: Macmillan, 1981.

Committee on Maternal Nutrition of the Food and Nutrition Board, National Research Council. *Annotated Bibliography on Maternal Nutrition*. Washington, D.C.: U.S. Department of Health, Education, and Welfare, Superintendent of Documents, 1970.

Committee on Maternal Nutrition of the Food and Nutrition Board, National Research Council. *Maternal Nutrition and the Course of Pregnancy*. Washington, D.C.: National Academy of Sciences, 1970.
The information on physiology of pregnancy and nutrition reinforces the fact that the classical low-calorie, low-salt regimen is out of date.

Day, Beth, and Liley, Margaret, M.D. *The Secret World of the Baby*. New York: Random House, 1968.
A beautifully and simply written and illustrated book. It covers fetology and early growth and development. It is written for young people but is appealing for adults also.

Dick-Read, Grantly. *Childbirth Without Fear*. New York: Harper and Brothers, 1944.
This is the classic.

Ewald, Eileen. *Recipes for a Small Planet*. New York: Ballantine Books, 1973.
This book is a must for vegetarians. It explains how to balance the incomplete proteins of vegetables. It also contains recipes which give the total grams of protein available per serving.

Ewey, Donna and Roger. *A Lamaze Guide, Preparation for Childbirth*. New York: Signet, New American Library, 1971.
A nicely written guide by a husband-and-wife team who have had the experience.

Friedmann, Theodore. "Prenatal Diagnosis of Genetic Disease." *Scientific American*, Vol. 225: No. 5, November 1971, pp. 34-42
Explains how amniocentesis can establish diagnosis of genetic defects and raises questions of legal, biological, and social implications.

Garden, Lytt I. "Deprivation Dwarfism." *Scientific American*, Vol. 227: No. 1, July 1972, pp. 76-84.
Children raised in an environment deprived of love and affection can be stunted in growth.

Gibbons, Euell. *Stalking the Wild Asparagus*. New York: David McKay Company, 1962.
Information on finding food in the wild. A large number of recipes are included also.

Higgins, Agnes C. "Nutritional Status and the Outcome of Pregnancy." *Journal of the Canadian Dietetic Association*. 37(1976):17.

Hunter, Beatrice Trum. *The Natural Foods Cookbook*. New York: Simon and Schuster, 1961.
This is probably the most natural of all natural food cookbooks. It doesn't even call for baking powder. Has a wealth of information and some rather fascinating recipes.

Jacobson, Michael F. *Eaters' Digest*. New York: Doubleday and Company, 1972.
This book is a must if you want to know what is going on in the food industry. The additives and their safety or lack of it are all discussed. There is also an introduction by Dr. Jean Mayer, the noted Harvard nutritionist.

Kenda, Margaret, and Williams, Phyllis. *The Natural Baby Food Cookbook*, Revised Edition. New York: Avon Books, 1982.
A guide to infant feeding that explains how to feed your baby home-cooked food. Recipes are included.

Klaus, Marshall and John H. Kennell. *Maternal-Infant Bonding*. St. Louis: C. V. Mosby, 1976.

Kretchmer, Norman. "Lactose and Lactase." *Scientific American*, Vol. 227: No. 4, October 1972, pp. 70-78.
Deals with the problem of lactose intolerance in populations lacking the enzyme lactase which converts lactose to galactose and glucose for absorption.

La Leche League. *The Womanly Art of Breast Feeding*. Franklin Park, Ill.: La Leche League International, 1963.
The whole story of how to breast-feed your baby.

Lappé, Frances Moore. *Diet for a Small Planet*. New York: A Friends of the Earth/Ballantine Book, 1971.
This book gives all the information you need to plan a vegetarian diet to provide for protein needs. It is also helpful for a meat eater to find out how to save money and food-growing land by adding more vegetable proteins

the diet. A needed book which everyone should read to provide a better understanding of the protein balancing for our diet.

Lawrence, Ruth A. *Breast-Feeding: A Guide for the Medical Professional.* St. Louis: C. V. Mosby, 1980.

Longacre, Doris Jansen. *More-With-Less Cookbook.* Scottdale, Pa.: Herald Press, 1976.

Mayer, Jean. "When You Think of Food, Think the 'Basic Seven,'" *Family Health.* Vol. 5: No. 12, December 1973, pp. 40-41.
A plea by the noted nutritionist for a return to the sensible "Basic 7" way of planning a balanced diet.

Moore, William M.; Silverberg, Margorie M., and Read, Merrill S., eds. *Nutrition, Growth and Development of North American Indian Children,* Washington, D.C.: Department of Health, Education and Welfare, Superintendent of Documents, 1972.
Information on malnutrition, infant sizes, growth and development among Indian children. There is some fascinating information on foods, prenatal diets, taboos, etc.

Newton, Niles. *The Family Book of Child Care.* New York: Harper and Row, 1957.
A really sensible guide.

Olsen, C. and M. Mapes. *Nutrition, Growth, and Reproduction: Reducing the Risks for Mothers and Infants.* Ithaca, N.Y.: Cornell University, May 1977.

Raphael, Dana. *The Tender Gift: Breastfeeding.* Englewood Cliffs, N.J.: Prentice-Hall, 1973.
A fascinating book, full of information, written by an anthropologist-mother. There is an introduction by Margaret Mead. Dr. Raphael gives a great deal of good advice which will be helpful to nursing mothers.

Raeder, Lois M., and Chow, Bacon. "Maternal Undernutrition and Its Long-Term Effects on the Offspring." *American Journal of Clinical Nutrition,* Vol. 25: No. 8, August 1972, pp. 812-821.

Salk, Lee. "The Role of the Heartbeat in the Relations Between Mother and Infant." *Scientific American,* Vol. 228: No. 5, May 1973, pp. 24-29.
Most mothers exhibit natural preference for holding baby on the left. If

deprived of infant in first twenty-four hours after childbirth, this preference disappears.

Scrimshaw, Neven S., and Gordon, John E. *Malnutrition, Learning, and Behavior.* Cambridge, Mass.: M.I.T. Press, 1968.
    Interrelationship of nutrition with ability and behavior.

Shanklin, Douglas R. and Jay Hodin. *Maternal Nutrition and Child Health.* Springfield, Ill.: Charles C. Thomas, 1979.

Shine, Ian, M.D. *Serendipity in St. Helena.* New York: Pergamon Press, 1970.
    A fascinating book tracing genetic defects among the people on a small island. Further notes high level of heart disease with low level of fat intake, along with ample exercise. It parallels increase in sugar consumption.

Shroeder, H.A. "Losses of Vitamins and Trace Minerals from Processing and Preservation of Foods." *American Journal of Clinical Nutrition,* Vol. 24: No. 5, May 1972.

Tanner, J.M. "Growing Up." *Scientific American,* Vol. 229: No. 3, September 1973, pp. 34-44.
    Interrelationships of heredity and environment on growth patterns.

Vellay, Pierre. *Childbirth Without Pain.* London: George Allen and Unwin, 1959.
    A classic book on the Lamaze Method of childbirth.

Williams, Dr. Roger J. *Nutrition Against Disease.* New York: Pitman Publishing Corporation, 1971 (also Bantam Books, New York).
    This book cites the research to back the claims. There is a chapter on prenatal nutrition. The book provides the rationale rather than a prescription. It is excellent reading for any thinking person.

Williams, Sue Rodwell. *Nutrition and Diet Therapy.* St. Louis: C. V. Mosby Company, 1982.
    This book is a text for nursing students and is the first to provide a complete new approach to prenatal nutrition along with citing the various research done in the field.

Winick, Myron, editor. *Nutrition and Fetal Development.* New York: John Wiley, 1974.

The Women and Their Pregnancies: The Collaborative Perinatal Study of the National Institute of Neurological Diseases and Stroke. Washington, D.C.: U.S. Department of Health, Education, and Welfare, Superintendent of Documents, 1972.

This is a statistical compilation of a study undertaken in some selected obstetric hospitals in the U.S. to try to determine the prenatal and birth influences which lead to the development of neurological disorders affecting babies. The tie-in between higher weight gain and lowered abnormality rate is shown statistically. It also quotes correlation between cigarette smoking and low-birth-weight babies.

Worthington, Bonnie S., Joyce Vermeersch, and Sue Rodwell Williams. *Nutrition in Pregnancy and Lactation.* St. Louis: C. V. Mosby, 1977.

Yudkin, John. *Sweet and Dangerous.* New York: Peter H. Wyden, 1972.
  Dr. Yudkin's indictment of sugar (sucrose).

INDEX

G

H

I

J

K

L

M

W

Y